W9-BGF-004

Daisy to the Rescue

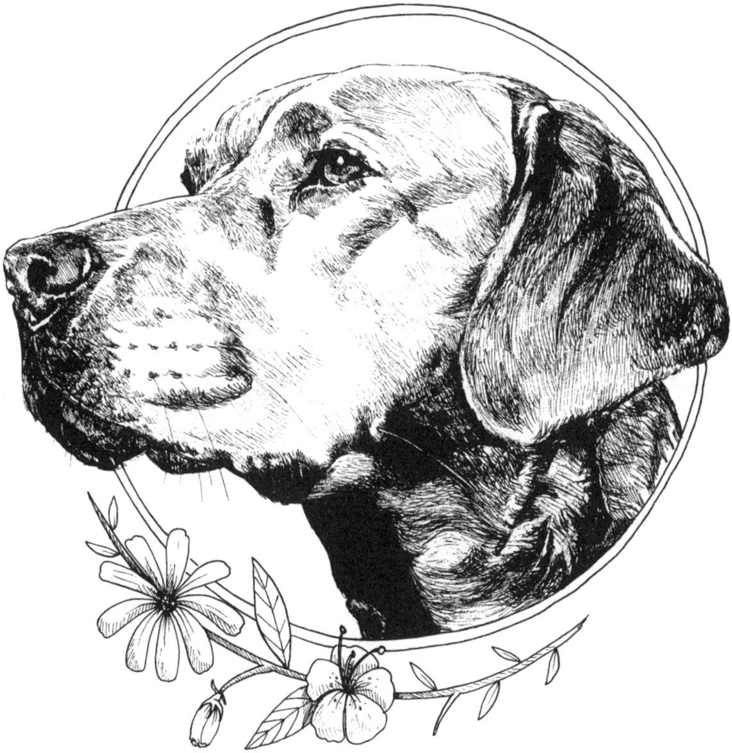

Daisy to the Rescue

TRUE STORIES OF DARING DOGS, PARAMEDIC PARROTS, AND OTHER ANIMAL HEROES

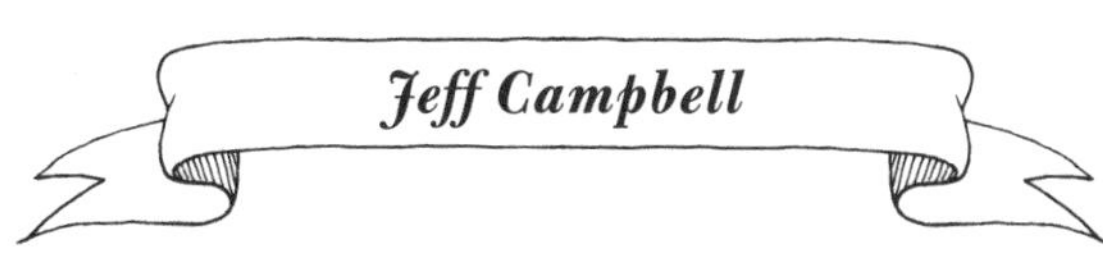

35 Stillman Street, Suite 121
San Francisco, CA 94107
www.zestbooks.net

We attempted to provide realistic and faithful portraits of all the animal heroes included in this book, but in cases where no visual references were available we relied instead on written or verbal descriptions of the animals involved, or, lacking that, on emblematic imagery of the given animal's species.

Front cover illustration:
• Derivative of a work provided courtesy of Maarten de Groot

Back cover illustrations:
• The illustrated portrait of Lulu is derivative of a work provided courtesy of the *Pittsburgh Post-Gazette*
• The illustrated portrait of Binti Jua is derivative of a work provided courtesy of the Tim Boyle/Getty Images

Young Adult Nonfiction / Animals / Pets
Library of Congress control number unavailable
ISBN: 978-1-936976-62-1
Cover design: Dagmar Trojanek
Interior design: Tanya Napier

Manufactured in the U.S.A.
DOC 10 9 8 7 6 5 4 3 2 1
4500485736

Connect with Zest!
zestbooks.net/blog
zestbooks.net/contests
twitter.com/ZestBooks
facebook.com/ZestBook
facebook.com/BookswithaTwist
pinterest.com/ZestBooks
instagram.com/ZestBooks

ACKNOWLEDGMENTS

First and foremost, I wish to thank Marc Bekoff for his help and contributions to this book. Quite simply, this book would not have been written without his inspiration, his guidance and generosity, and our previous work together. The world is a kinder place for all beings because of his example.

I am also deeply indebted to the entire team at Zest Books. Thank you to Dan Harmon for his faith in me and his editorial savvy; to Jan Hughes for her friendship and inspiration; to Jo Beaton, who goes back to the beginning; to Ramsey Beyer for her truly gorgeous illustrations (and to Pet Rescue in New York for their timely assistance with a certain cute puppy photo); and to Pam McElroy for her excellent copyediting.

I am also grateful to Doug Bohl at The Seeing Eye, for taking the time to talk and for his heart and wry humor. Laurie Albanese and my Writer's Circle writing group offered invaluable feedback. And for their longtime friendship and sage advice early in the process, I thank Jason Gardner, Georgia Hughes, Beth Weber, Lisa Bach, and Eric Ruhalter.

Finally, I owe an inexpressable debt of gratitude for the love and support of my family: to my beautiful wife, Deanna, who is twice the writer I will ever be, and to my son, Jackson, and my daughter, Miranda, who always wanted to hear more stories.

CONTENTS

PART ONE

DOMESTIC COMPANIONS

PART TWO

TRAINED TO SERVE, INSPIRED TO HEAL

PART THREE

WILD SAVIORS

PART FOUR

LEGENDS AND FOLKTALES

FOREWORD:

ANIMAL HEROES ABOUND

Daisy to the Rescue is an enlightening and incredibly inspirational book, and I can't imagine that readers won't be deeply moved and genuinely surprised by the fifty stories it contains. Altogether, this collection of life-saving animal rescues provides compelling evidence that a wide variety of animals—nonhuman and human alike—really can and do help each other in many different situations.

Jeff Campbell has carefully evaluated these dramatic stories and provided accurate accounts of what occurred. He pays close attention to what researchers have learned about animal emotions and intelligence, and he shows how these real-life experiences and current scientific data nicely fit together. These stories show that mutual caring exists between human and nonhuman animals, and solid science confirms that there is a biological basis for this mutual caring—for compassion and empathy, and the recognition that others need help—among numerous animals of different species.

Do we always know what is happening in the heads and hearts of other animals when they rescue those in need? No, we don't. In fact, this book helps illustrate why we need more research in this area. Both humans and nonhumans would greatly benefit if we understood more about the capabilities of other animals. Just what were Dory, Angel, Jambo, Ningnong, Chancer, Moustache, and all the other life-saving animals thinking and feeling as they helped others? I feel certain they were thinking and feeling something. Humans feel good when we help others, and there is no reason to doubt that nonhumans also feel good for being nice. It's well known that all mammals share the same parts of the brain that are important in processing emotions, and so it seems reasonable to hypothesize that nonhuman animals also feel good about themselves. The stories in this book show that we need to keep our heads and hearts open to the possibility that compassion exists in many other animals.

I've been studying the emotional and moral lives of nonhuman animals for decades. Over time, but especially within the past ten or so years, the database, including empirical data and solid stories, has greatly increased. Today, new studies about human-animal relationships appear regularly as part of the rapidly growing international and interdisciplinary field of study called anthrozoology. In a way, the stories in this book are the kinds of experiences that inspire scientists in the first place. All science is motivated by something a researcher saw or a story they heard—by observations and personal experiences. These events sometimes open the door to new areas of research so that we can learn more about the big hearts and complex brains of other animals. Citizen scientists, even if they are untrained observers, can provide important information to those of us who are lucky enough to make their livings studying other animals. What animals do in real life—what we observe in a wide variety of situations in which they help other individuals—counts as data. We are only just beginning to understand the strong emotional connection that can exist between animals.

I often like to say that "the plural of anecdote is data." When a good number of people send me the same story, I don't dismiss them. Rather, I recognize that these events contain something that needs to be given serious consideration. For example, after I reported on a magpie funeral ritual that my friend Rod and I once observed, I received numerous emails from people all over the world who had seen the same sort of event but never told anyone about it. At the time that I witnessed the magpies' behavior, in which they seemed to grieve for a dead companion, most scientists didn't think magpies were capable of this emotion, but now we do.

Likewise, I have often written about my companion dog Jethro, whom I adopted from the local humane society many years ago. I have often said that Jethro "rescued me"—that after Jethro became part of my life, we felt a deep need for one another. We recognized a mutual attraction that was central to our forming a deep relationship for twelve years. Indeed, when I originally visited the humane society to rescue a dog who needed a home, Jethro and I locked eyes across the span of the kennel, and I knew instantly that he was a special dog with whom I wanted to share my home and my life. Many others have since written to me about experiencing a similar deep connection with a companion animal, and this book is of course filled with people who describe being rescued this way—literally as well as figuratively.

Some skeptics ignore what we know from solid empirical research and dismissively say things like, "Oh, these are just stories with no scientific validity at all," or "People who believe that animals rescue other beings are being anthropomorphic." The animals, they claim, are merely acting *as if* they really care and know what they're doing. Simply put, these people are wrong, and when they say these things, they ignore our current knowledge about animal minds and what's in them. Often these people dismiss other animals because they feel that humans must be "superior" or "smarter" or "more caring" than other species, but they fail to realize that recognizing the amazing emotional and moral capacities of other animals does not diminish us. And it doesn't make other animals "better" than us. We don't have to embellish other animals to realize that they are amazing beings who truly care about what happens to them and to their family, friends, and other individuals, even those they don't know.

What I always find interesting is that some scientists speak about "research animals" such as dogs as if they're merely research tools. They use them in studies for our own benefits, and they are quick to belittle what the animals understand, know, and feel about what happens to them. At the same time, they don't hesitate to brag about how smart, emotional, and moral their companion dogs are—those animals they love and with whom they share their home. Something happens when scientists put on their white lab coats (and this also has been studied); for some, they don't even realize what they're doing. This lovely book should help to ground them, and us, and help us to realize when we are speaking out of both sides of our mouth. Our inconsistencies should lead us to question current scientific data, and to work to improve it, rather than using it to justify or rationalize attitudes that our own lived experience contradicts.

I hope that this compelling book stimulates more scientific research into the area of animal rescues. Just because we don't have data on a phenomenon doesn't mean it doesn't exist. The award-winning scientist Donald Griffin, "the father of cognitive ethology," or the study of animal minds, often stressed that the absence of evidence is not evidence of absence. What Dr. Griffin meant is that there are many phenomena about which we don't have scientific data, but this does not mean that the phenomena do not exist. We can't know for certain what the animals in these rescue stories were thinking and feeling, but one day perhaps we might, and perhaps what we learn will confirm that the animals are as aware and compassionate as the people in these stories frequently claim.

I would also like to hope that some readers, after reading these incredible stories, might be inspired to choose to pursue the study of animal behavior and the human-animal bond. This would be very helpful, as there are gaps in the database that need to be filled. As someone who has devoted his life to such study, I can confirm that it is some of the most gratifying and inspiring work you can imagine.

I can go on and on because I find this book to be so exciting and such a rich source of information, but suffice it to say, I'm sure that readers and the animals themselves will benefit from this forward-looking book.

Marc Bekoff

Boulder, Colorado

March 2014

INTRODUCTION

Would you believe that a pot-bellied pig could save a woman having a heart attack? How about dolphins fighting off a great white shark to save a surfer? Or wild African monkeys adopting a runaway boy? Or a golden retriever performing the Heimlich maneuver? Or how about a house cat doing anything at all—much less getting life-saving assistance—*on request*?

These scenarios may sound unlikely, yet every one of them happened. In fact, this book collects more than fifty real-life stories in which the actions of animals have meant the difference between life and death. By gathering these unexpected, sometimes heart-stopping tales of courage and compassion, this book celebrates the incredible animal heroes who help us exactly when we need it most—sometimes at risk to their own lives.

Some of these stories could be Hollywood movies. In fact, some already are (or soon will be). Dogs have braved blizzards, tackled a suicide bomber, and wrestled a cougar to save the people they love. Horses have faced off against a feral boar and a raging cow—and if you've ever met a mad cow, you know that's no joke.

However, saving a life means more than physical courage. Service animals devote their lives to improving ours, and occasionally they go so above and beyond the call of duty that they may as well be angels: a therapy dog taught herself how to predict heart attacks; a guide dog led her blind owner out of the chaos of the Twin Towers on 9/11; a dolphin was so devoted to one hopelessly paralyzed little boy that he inspired the boy's recovery as well as a new form of animal therapy.

When animals do these things, we are blown away. Despite what we see in the movies, we never expect animals to rescue us. When they do, we are humbled. We are so grateful, in fact, that we frequently hold up their noble actions as models for ourselves. We wish that we might all respond with such selfless bravery in times of dire need.

Usually, animals enrich our lives in ways we treasure but cannot measure. Then a life-saving moment comes along, and we realize just how priceless the animals in our lives really are.

Animal shelters like to ask, "Who rescued who?"

In these stories, there's no question. The animals save the day.

OKAY, MAYBE A FEW QUESTIONS

Then again, every time we hear about an animal saving someone's life, we can't help but wonder: Is it really true? Did everything happen the way the person said? And did the animal know what he or she was doing?

For that matter, is it *ever* possible to know what an animal is thinking?

These are excellent, important questions, and this book raises them throughout. Indeed, as heartwarming as rescue stories always are, they are even more fascinating for what they may reveal about the capabilities of animals and about the nature of the human-animal bond.

In other words, if we can't know what the animal understood, then it may be that there was no intentional life-saving rescue at all. Maybe the animal acted selfishly to save him- or herself, or maybe the animal acted out of blind instinct, or maybe the animal had no idea what was going on. A person may have escaped danger, but it was just dumb luck, a happy accident.

We know an animal did something, but establishing what is true—answering these simple, straightforward questions in a clear, definitive way—can be surprisingly difficult. In fact, it leads to a string of related questions:

- What about the rescue seems factual and beyond doubt and what's a matter of interpretation?

- Are there witnesses or other evidence?
- Could the person be deluding themselves?
- Can a person intuitively understand an animal's thoughts and behavior?
- What are the reasonable, accepted explanations for an animal's behavior?
- Is it credible that the animal did whatever the person claims?
- And if the animal did something that's never been seen before, can we verify it?

Most of all, by asking and trying to answer these questions, we are seeking to confirm what we most want to believe—or what life-saving rescue stories always seem to tell us: That animals can be compassionate, that sometimes they will fight for us, and that the loving relationships we experience with them are reciprocated.

To a degree, it is always an open question about what animals know and what motivates them. Yet when companion animals act to save their human family members, or when wild animals go out of their way to save a human stranger, it's hard not to see in these moments striking evidence of cross-species empathy, and even love, and perhaps a basic, shared understanding about life: That is, that living is hard, and all beings are in it together, and so we must care for and rescue each other.

Or is this just a feel-good story that humans make up?

So, let's begin by looking more closely at these questions. Using them, I'll explain why these particular stories were chosen and how this book is organized. I'll also summarize briefly what's generally accepted today about other animals and the human-animal bond. In this way, I'll provide the larger context for these incredible tales of animal heroism you're about to read.

Life-saving rescues frequently push the boundaries of what we think we know about animals. Yet when confirmed, they can change the way we see the world and the creatures we share it with.

ARE THE STORIES TRUE?

Often, the better question isn't "Is the story true?" but "What is true about the story?"

With a few acknowledged exceptions, all the stories in this book really happened; none are fictional and none are hoaxes. The exceptions are some of the legendary stories in part four, and in these, one goal is to distinguish what is real from what is folklore. In fact, there are so many verified stories of life-saving animals that you couldn't fit them all in one book. I squeezed in as many as I could, but some types of rescues are so common—such as dogs saving children from snakes—that they could almost be a book by themselves.

When choosing, I preferred stories with multiple witnesses that occurred within the last decade, and I included a few particularly famous stories from within the last twenty years. Simply put, these stories tend to be the most credible. They've received the most scrutiny and from more varied and reliable sources.

That said, there is no escaping the subjective nature of these tales. Sometimes the only real witness is the person who is rescued, and whether or not we believe their story often depends on how credible they seem and what sort of circumstantial evidence supports them. This is one reason why scientists often dismiss anecdotes like life-saving rescues. There is almost no way to examine the animal's behavior except within the context of someone's story or perspective, and untrained observers might miss important details or mistake what they are seeing.

That's okay. Thankfully, these aren't scientific studies. Instead, they are moving real-life events that raise intriguing scientific questions. In telling them, I have tried to be both honest and entertaining, while distinguishing between fact and speculation, between what the animal did and what the animal might have been thinking. See Sources & Further Reading for the sources I used and for more information on the stories and the science.

In addition, not all the stories are the same. Behavior that might seem unremarkable in, say, a German shepherd might be startling, or even unbelievable, in a kangaroo or a rabbit or a lion. Different species, and different types of behavior, raise different questions. To help clarify these distinctions, I've divided the stories into four parts:

Part one, "Domestic Companions," features those domestic animals who evolved to live with humans, particularly the companion animals who share our homes. Pet owners live and enjoy the human-animal bond every day, and what makes these life-saving rescues particularly notable is that they suggest just how valuable it may be to the animals themselves. Caring for animals can inspire them to care for us.

Then again, some animals are trained to help, assist, and heal humans. For them, saving lives is sometimes part of their job description. In part two, "Trained to Serve, Inspired to Heal," I look at those special individuals who went so far beyond their training that they helped rewrite the manual, redefining what service and therapy animals are capable of.

The stories in part three, "Wild Saviors," feature wild animals, including those kept in zoos and captivity. Most wild animals have no stake in whether humans live or die; they have few "selfish" reasons to help a person. Thus, when a wild animal rescues a human, it suggests that empathy and compassion may be widespread in the animal kingdom.

Finally, part four, "Legends and Folktales," examines life-saving animals in history. Stories of animals rescuing humans extend at least as far back as ancient Greece. Some are clearly myths, and some are real stories that, over time, have become so embellished they enter the realm of folklore. These stories, then, can be as much about our storytelling impulse as they are about the life-saving animal, and they raise two fascinating questions: Did the myths arise in part to explain real animal behavior? And are we predisposed to believe certain types of stories because they already exist in folklore?

CAN WE BELIEVE THE PERSON WHO TOLD THE STORY?

When someone is unexpectedly saved by an animal, the best the person can do is describe what happened as they understood and experienced it. However, the people in these stories are often self-aware that they may still be mistaken about an animal's behavior. After all, when your life is threatened, you aren't exactly in a normal frame of mind.

And there's the rub. Being truthful is not the same as being correct. A person might misinterpret what an animal is doing and attribute thoughts or intentions that don't exist.

In any situation, when people inappropriately attribute human-like emotions and intentions to animals, scientists call this anthropomorphism. In animal research, scientists go to great lengths to avoid anthropomorphizing. They design studies and learn to observe and describe animals in ways that try to "weed out" false assumptions and projections. For instance, facial expressions do not always mean the same thing across species; one oft-cited example is that a chimpanzee's grin is usually a sign of aggression, not friendliness. If researchers aren't careful, they will only see what they expect or want to see, not what the animal is actually doing.

With that in mind, what's amusing and perhaps telling is that, sometimes, even the rescued person doesn't believe what happened. They couldn't make the story up if they tried. In fact, afterward, they sometimes question what their intuitions told them about the animal in the moment. They feel they must have been mistaken.

As it turns out, they may not have been.

CAN SOMEONE INTUITIVELY UNDERSTAND AN ANIMAL?

In many rescue stories, the people involved describe having the intuitive sense that the animal understood the situation and meant to save them. Further, many stories contain moments of intuitive communication: Despite lacking a shared language, animals and people still make their intentions, meanings, or feelings clear in deadly circumstances when moments count. At times, heeding these intuitive understandings is what allows someone to survive when they otherwise might have died.

This is one of the most curious and compelling aspects of these stories. Even beyond what it apparently says about the awareness and intentions of animals, it suggests a remarkable intimacy and depth to the human-animal bond.

Can we intuitively understand animals, and they understand us?

In the last decade, a tremendous amount of research has focused on discovering what other animals feel and how they think. Being animals, this also pertains to us. In this research, scientists have themselves sometimes had to rely on their own intuitive hunches to understand animal behavior. As dolphin researcher Diana Reiss writes, "Oftentimes, working with an individual animal, one gains an intuition about the species' general behavior." In other words, at times, scientists find that our intuitions about other animals can be highly accurate.

Why is that? Here are three theories:

1 Evolution: Humans and domestic animals evolved together over millennia. It's now suggested that not only did humans evolve as they did in part to understand animals better, but caring for animals was integral to humans developing their best qualities, such as empathy and compassion (see page 244).

2 Mirror neurons: In humans and some other animals, certain brain cells called "mirror neurons" activate when watching someone else; these cells respond as if we are doing what we see the other doing. In this way, we mimic the other animal in our mind and intuit behavior simply by watching (see page 59).

3 The biochemistry of emotion: Contact with other animals feels good because it releases chemicals, like oxytocin, that are integral to creating social bonds. All animals have these biochemical responses, which indicate some equivalent emotional states (see page 159).

There is another more prosaic answer to this question. With our companion animals, we know each other extremely well. We know each other's moods and habits; we know how to get each other's attention and how to communicate our desires. That's how everyone works together to create a happy household.

Thus, when our companion animals act out of character, we notice. In a rescue, a pet's unusual behavior might be what alerts someone to danger, and it is often what suggests afterward that the animal understood the danger and intended to help. Could it be coincidence that an animal family member would just happen to act oddly at the very moment and in the very way necessary to save someone? For instance, consider Willie, the Quaker parrot (see page 64), and Toby, the golden retriever (see page 55).

Naturally, a person cannot prove an intuitive understanding. They know what they know, and that's all they can say.

Also, we probably intuit only a vague approximation of what another animal is actually feeling or thinking, and we certainly don't intuit everything about an animal. We aren't mind readers. Yet in these moments, we aren't anthropomorphizing either. We are correctly recognizing the animal's internal state. Sometimes the fact that people are saved is the best evidence that they understood correctly. Their intuition worked.

WHAT ARE THE ACCEPTED EXPLANATIONS FOR AN ANIMAL'S BEHAVIOR?

There are almost always several possible explanations, or interpretations, of an animal's behavior during a life-saving rescue. In fact, more than one explanation is probably correct, at least in part. Like us, animals are complex and may have many motivations, all of which may influence their actions.

The stories in this book often raise various interpretations of an animal's behavior, but they don't review every possibility every time. However, it's good to have the range of typical explanations in mind. Very briefly, here is a list of common explanations (besides self-aware compassion) that scientists and researchers often propose for animal behavior during a life-saving rescue:

> **Reciprocal altruism or mutualism:** These fancy terms describe doing something only to get something in return. Animals may know they depend on a person for food and shelter, and so they help the person, not out of caring, but because of what the person provides. This is sometimes called "pseudo-altruism" because an action may look like altruism when it's really a form of selfishness.

Self-protection: If a danger, such as a house fire, threatens both a person and an animal, the animal may act out of self-preservation. A dog might wake up an owner to be let out of a burning house, which saves the owner as an unintended consequence.

Biological mechanisms: Animals may act due to automatic biochemical or neurological responses, not intention or compassion. For instance, as mentioned above, mirror neurons or the release of oxytocin may inspire certain unthinking reactions that accidentally save someone.

Developed traits: This refers to how an individual animal was raised, nurtured, or trained; it's the influence of a particular upbringing. Trained animals may only be doing what they were taught. Even under new, unique circumstances, they might only be automatically applying their training without any emotion or intention.

Evolved traits: During a rescue, an animal may act only because its species evolved to act in that way. For instance, dogs (like wolves) are hierarchical social mammals who form bonded packs and instinctively "follow the leader." A dog might save a human "pack leader" because their genetic programming spurs them to.

Instinctual traits: All animals share a basic set of instinctual primal responses, particularly the well-known fight-or-flight impulse. When faced with a life-threatening danger, this instinct kicks in before the conscious mind is even fully aware of what's happening. Every life-saving rescue probably includes an element of this. The question is, is something else going on?

As a rule, scientists tend to be very cautious when theorizing about an animal's behavior. Most prefer to say that at times animals may act "as if" they exhibit certain thoughts or feelings—like empathy, compassion, self-awareness, and altruism—but we can't know.

In drawing conclusions, scientists often cite the principle of "Occam's razor," which says that observers should prefer the simplest explanation that adequately accounts for all details. If instinct or training are enough to explain an animal's actions, then more complex thoughts and emotions don't need to be considered. The animal *might* possess self-aware compassion, but unless some aspect of the story requires it, good luck getting a skeptical scientist to agree.

IS IT CREDIBLE THAT ANIMALS DO WHAT RESCUED PEOPLE CLAIM?
In other words, what do scientists already agree that animals can do?

It's a reasonable question. Too bad there isn't a straightforward answer. However, when it comes to animal minds and emotions, scientists don't agree about much, and when they disagree, they disagree strongly. Ethology, or the study of animal behavior, is often wracked by controversy and acrimony, skepticism and criticism, such that it's hard to make any definitive statement about what animals know and feel without qualifying it endlessly and finally acknowledging that, after much study and careful consideration, we still can't really *prove* what's going on inside the brains and hearts of other animals.

However, at the risk of oversimplifying, here is a summary of what most ethologists might agree to if you locked them in a conference room and withheld their coffee until they drafted a statement:

All Animals Feel and Think . . . Something

It wasn't always the case, but today it's hard to find a scientist who doesn't acknowledge that virtually all animals display emotions and sentience. All have some ability to feel and reason. The days of Descartes, when animals were assumed to be unthinking, instinct-driven automatons, are gone. In 2012, the "Cambridge Declaration on Consciousness" formally put this in writing, saying: "Convergent evidence indicates that non-human animals have the neuroanatomical, neurochemical, and neurophysiological substrates of conscious states along with the capacity to exhibit intentional behaviors."

Uh . . . *come again?*

The science-speak boils down to this: Animals don't act "as if" they have emotions and thoughts; they have them. The Cambridge scientists said this includes "all mammals and birds and many other creatures, including octopuses." So, still a little vague on the species, but it's a start.

What Animals Feel and Think Varies by Species

Naturally, the devil is in the details. Species differ in their capabilities, just like individuals differ, though it should be said that comparing the relative intelligence of species is a dubious exercise. Invariably, humans assume they are the "smartest" and focus mostly on arranging other species in a hierarchy of the "less smart." This "human exceptionalism" tends to downplay the unique abilities and attributes of other species and the ways that they are "smart" to suit their own needs.

For instance, humans are uniquely gifted toolmakers, but just because dogs can't build a motorcycle doesn't mean they aren't smart enough to knock one down to save your life (see page 85). Conversely, humans will never diagnose cancer by smelling it on someone's breath, as dogs can (see page 178).

In general, most animals are credited with possessing the "primary" emotions of fear, anger, joy, curiosity, pain, and grief. While the quality and expression of those emotions may be unique to each species, these are the basics that all seem to share. In fact, these emotions have been called the building blocks of reason and morality; they provide the critical information that tells us what to do and how to react.

Beyond that, the most significant question is, which species display self-awareness? That is, do animals know that they think and feel, do they have a sense of self and other, and do they understand that others have a different perspective and independent feelings?

To be possible, many "secondary" emotions require some level of self-awareness, and/or the awareness of other perspectives, such as guilt, shame, embarrassment, loyalty, deceit, pride, generosity, empathy, cruelty, sympathy, compassion, love, and certainly altruism.

Morality is also seen as requiring self-awareness. Moral reasoning—thinking in ethical terms like "right" and "wrong"—requires an understanding of social context, multiple perspectives, choice, and future consequences. However, researchers are also finding that a basic moral sense might be innate in humans and also present in several social mammals (see page 211).

Besides ourselves, only a few animals have exhibited some level of self-awareness to the satisfaction of most scientists. These include great apes, dolphins, elephants, and canines, including wolves and dogs (see page 59), though others are possible.

Not coincidentally, these also happen to be the species featured most often in this book.

CAN WE VERIFY WHAT LIFE-SAVING RESCUES TELL US?

Yes, verifying new information about animals is always possible, but it takes will and a lot of work.

Life-saving rescues often show animals acting in rare or unique ways. Since life-threatening situations are themselves rare, perhaps that isn't surprising. Imminent death provides a uniquely strong motivation. All involved may rise to the occasion, doing things they've never done before and wouldn't have done otherwise.

As a result, on occasion, life-saving rescues have been the catalyst that changed our ideas about animals. When, twice, gorillas comforted and rescued fallen children in zoos (see pages 195 and 206), these unprompted acts of kindness undermined the long-held belief that gorillas were "inherently violent."

When dolphins saved humans from sharks (see pages 221 and 232) and displayed empathy for disabled children (see page 109), it expanded our notions of how compassionate dolphins can be.

No one had any idea that dogs could predict heart attacks (see page 114) and signal cancer (see page 178), until one day they did. We didn't know dogs could find bombs (see page 166) until we asked them to try. In fact, scientists still don't fully understand how dogs smell or sense these radically different things, but we can still train dogs to use these abilities on our behalf.

Nevertheless, as scientist Marc Hauser writes, animal stories "are fascinating, but limited with respect to what we can learn from them. . . . We must not be satisfied with single observations, either from a casual observer or a rigorous experimentalist. Replication is at the core of all science."

Scientists and researchers never regard one incident, all by itself, as definitive proof of anything. And the problem with life-saving rescues is, you can't drop a rattlesnake next to a baby to see if a dog will intervene. Or toss a nonswimmer into a pool to confirm that dolphins will really help. It's illegal, not to mention unkind. A life-threatening scenario simply can't be replicated without changing the nature of the situation.

However, as primatologist Frans de Waal writes, "Single events can be incredibly meaningful. . . . If an experienced, reliable observer reports a remarkable incident, therefore, science better pay attention."

In other words, the burden shifts to scientists and researchers to design studies that focus on what these singular events show. If just one gorilla or parrot or seal or cat is observed displaying genuine compassion and altruism, then it becomes a potential for the entire species.

In itself, a single life-saving rescue may not "prove" anything, but it can open our eyes to what we don't know and still need to discover.

LIVES, TRANSFORMED

There is one final aspect to these stories that deserves mention: the effect of being rescued on the person saved.

We may not know what moves an animal, but invariably the animal's actions profoundly move the person. Sometimes a person's life is utterly transformed by their rescue. The animal indelibly marks the person's heart and inspires others far and wide. Sometimes, people devote the rest of their lives to animals, becoming advocates, founding organizations, and trying to share the love and healing they've received from animals.

It's hard to imagine that animals could inspire such love and compassion if they themselves lacked it. The evidence of these stories is that animals will often act in caring ways, perhaps because they have been cared for, and these events inspire people to create a virtuous circle of caring. Animals certainly don't intend this; they respond in the moment, and those actions create ripples of gratitude, love, and kindness.

Even if animals don't understand what they are doing, we aren't wrong to celebrate animals as heroes when they risk danger and save a life. Pure physical courage is always worth honoring. Whatever motivates the animal, we remain the recipients of an immense gift. Seen another way, what these rescues may show is that nature has programmed mutual caring into itself, so that all animals, whether they mean to or not, are capable of helping one another.

Mark Twain once quipped, "If you pick up a starving dog and make him prosperous, he will not bite you. This is the principal difference between a dog and a man."

Many of the stories in Part One involve rescued companion animals rescuing a family member in distress. Is this, as Twain implied, gratitude for being adopted, loved, and fed? Does the fact of being rescued and cared for make any difference to the animal?

As Twain so tartly noted, it doesn't always make a difference with people. We may never know what our companion animals understand about their circumstances nor if they remember when we first met. Yet, however it arises, the fact that a familial bond exists can seem to matter a great deal, and it often seems to inspire these jaw-dropping feats of courage.

A strong familial bond is evident with longtime pets, but sometimes the length of an acquaintance is strangely irrelevant. Owners sometimes describe connecting with animals instantly. Then, only days or even hours after meeting—with time for only a handful of meals—these new companions valiantly save their owners from death.

LULU THE POT-BELLIED PIG . . . STOPS TRAFFIC

NAME: *LuLu*

SPECIES: *Vietnamese pot-bellied pig*

DATE: *August 4, 1998*

LOCATION: *Presque Isle, Pennsylvania*

SITUATION: *Woman suffering a heart attack*

WHO WAS SAVED: *Fifty-seven-year-old Jo Ann Altsman*

LEGACY: *International media celebrity, exemplar of porcine compassion, won 1999 ASPCA award*

Quick: Which is smarter, a dog or a pig?

Bzzzzz. Time's up.

Your answer?

If you're Jo Ann Altsman, or George Clooney for that matter, it's obvious. Like, three hundred pounds of obvious. Pot-bellied pigs win, and you don't need a bunch of scientific studies to prove it. Just listen to this:

In August 1998, Jo Ann and Jack Altsman were summer vacationing on Presque Isle, Pennsylvania, a beautiful sandy peninsula that juts into Lake Erie. The couple had brought along their American Eskimo dog, Bear, and their pet Vietnamese pot-bellied pig, LuLu. A type of miniature pig, LuLu then weighed about 150 pounds, about the average for an adult in her species.

The Altsmans had originally purchased LuLu in 1997 as a fortieth birthday present for their daughter, Jackie. Whether by accident or design, Jackie never got around to taking LuLu home, and as the four-pound piglet grew, so did the Altsmans' love for her. They kept LuLu, and Jo Ann is eternally grateful they did.

PLAYING "DEAD PIGGIE"

On the morning of August 4, while her husband was out fishing on Lake Erie, Jo Ann suffered a heart attack in their vacation home. It was her second heart attack in eighteen months, and she fell to the floor, gasping, and couldn't get up. Jo Ann threw an alarm clock through a window and yelled for help, but no one heard her.

Meanwhile, her dog, Bear, started barking his head off, and LuLu "made sounds like she was crying," Jo Ann said. "You know, they cry big, fat tears."

Jo Ann was scared and crying, too, and "the more I cried, the more [LuLu] kept putting her head over me and making terrible sobbing sounds," Jo Ann said. "She kept trying to kiss me."

Then LuLu got an inspiration. She turned from Jo Ann and crashed headlong into the front door's doggie door—breaking it open just wide enough for her generous girth, but she cut her stomach squeezing through. LuLu then ran across the enclosed yard, knocked open the gate, and entered an adjacent road.

"I didn't know that she knew that I was in dire trouble," Jo Ann said. "I just kept telling her to go night-night."

Once in the street, as witnesses described later, LuLu decided to play "dead piggy." This was one of LuLu's favorite games, one in which "she knows she'll get attention," Jo Ann said. LuLu lay down in the middle of the road, forcing cars to drive around her.

But no one stopped.

So, for the next forty-five minutes, "LuLu kept coming back to check on me to see if I was better or if she could help me," Jo Ann said. Then LuLu would return to the road to play "dead piggy."

What about Bear? The dog just kept barking.

Finally, an anonymous man pulled over and got out of his car. Seeing the bloody injury on the animal's flank, and concerned for her safety (and perhaps her sanity), he followed LuLu as she led him back to her home—just like in the nursery rhyme, crying the whole way.

"I heard a man hollering through the door, 'Lady, your pig's in distress,'" Jo Ann recounted. "I said, 'I'm in distress, too. Please call an ambulance.'"

The man did, and Jo Ann was flown to a nearby medical center, where she had emergency open-heart surgery. Doctors told her that if another fifteen minutes had passed, she probably would have died.

How do you thank a pig who saves your life?

"She got a jelly doughnut," Jo Ann said.

Of course.

LULU IS LOVED TO DEATH

As author E. B. White understood, when you have a terrific, radiant, humble pig, the whole world wants to know. Afterward, back at their Beaver Falls,

Pennsylvania, home, LuLu and the Altsmans were overwhelmed with media attention. The *New York Times* ran a front-page story. LuLu was featured in *USA Today* and *People* magazine. TV programs from Germany, Australia, Italy, and Japan came calling. *National Geographic* did a TV segment, and LuLu appeared on the *Regis & Kathie Lee Show, The Late Show with David Letterman,* and *Oprah.*

It seemed like the story never got old. *Ripley's Believe It or Not* showed up, as did Animal Planet, the Discovery Channel, *Good Morning America*, and *20/20*.

People marveled at what LuLu's actions indicated about her intelligence and depth of feeling. Pigs have always been considered smart, but could a pig really understand what was at stake, respond creatively, and persist for nearly an hour?

"It would not be beyond the cognitive or intellectual power of a pig," scientist Marc Bekoff said. "There's really good evidence that pigs show empathy. Pigs are continually amazing." Yet he cautioned, "We don't know if pigs cry emotional tears. They seem to correlate with events where you would expect tears, but we don't know that yet."

However, with each passing year, LuLu kept getting bigger . . . and bigger and bigger. Four years later, by 2002, she had grown dangerously obese, ballooning to 335 pounds.

"We put her on diets constantly," Jo Ann said. But pigs like to eat, and as the world now understood, LuLu was no dummy. "She'd sit at the gate and cry for people to feed her. Everyone thought they were the only ones." Strangers fed her hamburgers, Pop-Tarts, ice cream, pizza, soda, candy—anything to thank this remarkable animal for what she'd done.

Tragically, on January 30, 2003, LuLu died at home after suffering a heart attack, one that was most likely brought on by her weight. She died prematurely at age five and a half. Pot-bellied pigs have a life expectancy of twelve to twenty years.

"She was the smartest, most special pig," Jo Ann said. "Whatever we do, we'll never have another LuLu."

"LOVE ME, LOVE MY PIG"

Pot-bellied pig owners are an exceedingly devoted group. By far the most famous has been actor George Clooney, who for eighteen years lived with his beloved Vietnamese pot-bellied pig, Max.

In fact, Clooney was himself a huge fan of LuLu. Clooney first met LuLu and Jo Ann on the David Letterman show, and later he phoned Oprah on-air when she was extolling the intelligence of dogs. "I know someone who's smarter," Clooner said, and Oprah flew LuLu out for a show.

In 1999, when LuLu received the "Trooper Award" from the American Society for the Prevention of Cruelty to Animals, Clooney was there with Max, who presented the award.

Clooney's infatuation with Max was legendary. Jo Ann said that the actor once confessed to her that "he's lost four girlfriends for sleeping with his pig. Can you believe that?"

Clooney once said, "You get a lot of grief from people when you sleep with a pig. I've had different reactions over the years. But I always say, 'Love me, love my pig.' What can I do?"

Max himself died in 2006, when he was nineteen years old and almost three hundred pounds. At the time, Clooney said he wouldn't get another pig, but the decision wasn't solely to honor Max's memory.

"He was funny, and he made me laugh," Clooney said. "But they're work, because they'll destroy everything if you let them."

DORY THE RABBIT ... LEAPS INTO ACTION

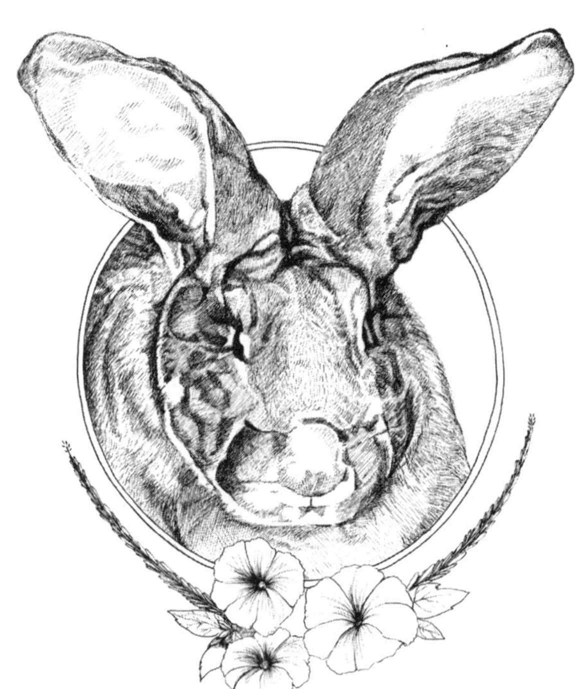

NAME: *Dory*

SPECIES: *Rabbit*

DATE: *January 2004*

LOCATION: *Cambridgeshire, England*

SITUATION: *Diabetic owner slips into a coma*

WHO WAS SAVED: *Forty-two-year-old Simon Steggall*

LEGACY: *First known rabbit to scent diabetes, honorary member of Britain's Rabbit Welfare Association*

This life-saving rescue almost sounds like the opening scene from a BBC sitcom: As the lights fade up, a man enters the front door, exclaiming, "Blimey, what a day!" He kisses his wife, turns on the telly, clicks to his favorite show, and instantly falls asleep in a plaid armchair, snoring and oblivious—even as an enormous, mischievous twenty-pound rabbit jumps onto the chair, hops on his chest and bats him around.

Cue canned laughter, and cut to a shot of the wife rolling her eyes: *Oh, that Dory!*

Except in this case, the breadwinner wasn't snoring, and the rabbit, Dory, wasn't playing. Forty-two-year-old Simon Steggall of Cambridgeshire, England, had come home and slipped into a diabetic coma, and though he couldn't speak or move, he could still feel and hear. A diabetic since childhood, Simon required insulin shots four times a day. However, if diabetics miscalculate either their shots or their food intake, their blood sugar levels can drop to dangerously low levels without warning.

"It's like a flick of a switch," Simon said.

Victoria Steggall, not realizing that her husband was in distress, scolded the misbehaving rabbit. The Steggalls had adopted Dory three months before as a house pet, and they were training the three-foot bunny to stay on the floor. Who wants a couch covered in rabbit fur?

However, Dory didn't take heed of Victoria's commands. "The rabbit came up on my lap and started tapping and digging at my chest and licking at my face," Simon said. "That caught Victoria's attention, and she realized something was wrong."

The Steggalls once owned a black labrador retriever who would cower in a corner whenever Simon's blood-sugar levels fell too low. Victoria wondered: *Was Dory indicating her husband's diabetic condition?* Victoria tried to rouse Simon, and when he didn't wake up, she rushed to get his glucose gel. When rubbed on Simon's gums, the gel usually spiked his blood-sugar levels back to normal, but it didn't work this time.

Immediately, Victoria called the paramedics. When they arrived, they injected Simon with a medicine that forced his liver to dump its stored glucose, and Victoria's husband came around.

WHAT THE RABBIT KNEW

"I work for the ambulance service," Victoria said, "and I'm embarrassed that the rabbit spotted it before I did."

Simon said, "My specialist said he had heard of cats and dogs acting this way, but never a rabbit."

Indeed, dogs can be trained to respond to someone's glucose levels. As a person's metabolism changes, they sweat and smell differently, and someone who becomes hypoglycemic (a condition when someone's blood sugar level drops too low) gives off a particular odor that dogs can recognize. As the story of Pudding shows (see page 91), cats can smell this imbalance as well. Now that rabbits have joined this club, we have to wonder how many other animals might have this ability. Further, if many (if not all) domestic dogs, cats, and rabbits can detect hypoglycemia, then what prompts certain animals to react in a seemingly "care-giving" fashion while others don't?

The short answer is, we don't know. Studies are still needed to determine the exact chemical signal animals sense, and also to determine whether untrained animals respond solely to biological cues or if, in certain circumstances, they are choosing to signal a problem with their behavior.

Whether or not Dory knew what she was doing or meant to wake Simon up, "Dory saved my life," Simon said. For that, Dory was the first animal elected as an honorary member of Britain's Rabbit Welfare Association.

An association member, Ingrid Tarrant, said, "Rabbits are the most misunderstood of animals. People just don't realize how intelligent and sociable they are."

"It's a great honor," Victoria Steggall agreed. "I'm very impressed and so is Dory, though I had to help her fill in the application form."

Oh, that Dory!

RABBITS TO THE RESCUE, AGAIN

Dory's not the only rabbit known to alert owners about someone's diabetic condition. In 2006, a bunny named Robin did the same thing—and saved two lives at once.

The Murphy family, from Port Byron, Illinois, had bought Robin in a garage sale. Ten days later, in the middle of the night, the rabbit started going crazy in her cage. Robin's commotion woke up Ed Murphy, whose wife, Darcy, was still snoring. Ed shook his head over the rabbit's odd behavior and tried to get back to sleep.

Robin wouldn't quit, however, and "it wasn't like her at all," Ed said.

Ed checked on his wife again. Darcy wasn't only snoring: Her skin was bright red and her breathing was raspy and shallow. Darcy was pregnant and had recently been diagnosed with gestational diabetes. Ed suddenly realized that Darcy had gone into insulin shock. Immediately, Ed called 911, and paramedics revived her.

A month later, Darcy gave birth to a healthy girl, but that happy outcome almost didn't happen. "If Robin hadn't made all that noise," Darcy said, "the baby and I would have died."

MKOMBOZI THE DOG . . . RESCUES AN ABANDONED BABY

NAME: *Mkombozi*

SPECIES: *Mixed-breed dog*

DATE: *May 2005*

LOCATION: *Near Nairobi, Kenya*

SITUATION: *Abandoned newborn*

WHO WAS SAVED: *"Angel," a two-week-old girl*

LEGACY: *World-famous icon of motherly love, won 2005 North Shore Animal League America Award*

Abandoning an infant goes against every maternal instinct nature has devised. Yet it may be this same maternal instinct that inspires animals to occasionally rescue and protect abandoned human babies. This is one explanation given whenever animals are found caring for feral children (see page 200), and it almost certainly plays a role in the stories of dogs rescuing abandoned infants. Sadly, there is more than one such story.

FINDING AN ANGEL

The most famous incident occurred near the Ngong Forest outside Nairobi, Kenya, in May 2005. A stray female dog who had recently given birth to a litter of puppies was scavenging for food in a rubbish heap. There, she found a newborn baby wrapped in some tattered clothing.

The dog grabbed the rags in her mouth and carried the baby across a busy road and under a barbed-wire fence, eventually placing the infant with her own remaining puppy in a shed where she lived. The dog's puppies had not been healthy, and all but one had already died. Witnesses said they saw the dog carrying the bundle but didn't know what it contained. Not long after, two children from the family that owned the shed heard the baby crying. They went to investigate and immediately told their mother, Mary Adhiambo.

Mary said she found the dog "lying protectively with her puppy beside the soiled baby lying in a torn black cloth. I held the baby in my arms and carried it into the house."

Mary took the seven-pound, four-ounce girl to the hospital. The baby had a badly infected umbilical cord and was suffering from exposure. Authorities estimated she was about two weeks old and must have been abandoned for two days.

Hospital staff named the child "Angel," and the heart-warming rescue attracted international attention. Donations and offers of adoption poured in from around the world. When no one came to claim the baby, and her mother was never found, Angel was eventually placed with a new family.

ADOPTING A SAVIOR

Meanwhile, the dog was dubbed "Mkombozi," which is Swahili for "savior." Jean Gilchrist, executive director of the Kenya SPCA, speculated that Mkombozi was perhaps driven by the deaths of her own puppies to care for the human infant. "Other dogs might have just left [the baby] there to die," Gilchrist said. "She's obviously a very special dog."

Mkombozi was also street-wise and wary of people, and she "wasn't happy when we all poured into the compound," Gilchrist said. At first, Mkombozi ran away, but neighborhood kids found her and brought her to the SPCA, which bathed, fed, and dewormed her. In the middle of these events, Mkombozi's last puppy died, and the SPCA formally adopted Mkombozi, where she became, Gilchrist said, "a member of our office staff and an ambassador for the canine population."

However, as events unfolded, some people voiced frustration and even skepticism about the story. First, some doctors at the hospital said Angel didn't show the scratches they would expect if she had been dragged through a barbed-wire fence. Others complained about the unfairness of the sympathy being heaped on Angel, when hundreds of abandoned Kenyan babies languished, wanting for adoption.

Finally, others doubted that any dog would ever be motivated to rescue an abandoned child. While a variety of motivations are possible, it may also be that events ended exactly the way Mkombozi intended.

Mkombozi, Gilchrist said, "is a very intelligent dog. It's very easy to put human emotions and thoughts to animals, but I don't think we give them enough credit sometimes. I think she knew that this baby should go back to where the other children were, to be looked after."

In other words, Mkombozi was just being who she was, a nursing mother caring for a helpless baby—any baby.

CANINE RESCUERS

If this were the only story of a dog rescuing an abandoned infant, we might be tempted to dismiss it as a fabrication or exaggeration. Yet here are four very similar stories that are even more recent.

MATERNAL INSTINCTS

Scientists have long puzzled what makes up our so-called "maternal instinct." Caring for children is certainly critical. Fail in that, and no species will last long. But how does nature keep exhausted parents on task?

First, and perhaps most important, are hormones, and the main culprit is oxytocin. Meaning "quick birth" in Greek, oxytocin is produced in the hypothalamus, the part of the brain that regulates our organs and bodily functions, and it assists with a pregnant woman's labor contractions, stimulates the release of breast milk, lowers blood pressure, slows the heart rate, and inhibits the production of stress hormones.

For a mother who has just given birth, this feel-good hormone floods her system at "the sight, sound, smell, and even thought of her baby," writes Meg Daley Olmert in her book *Made for Each Other*.

Men experience this rush of oxytocin as well, and this hormone is considered essential for the parental bonding that takes place after birth.

Studies have also shown that infantile facial features can elicit paternal feelings in anyone, not just doting parents. This is why the big head, big eyes, tiny nose, and fat squishy cheeks of a baby are so irresistible. Further, this caring response kicks in when we encounter the juvenile members of any species. That's why we go "aawwww!" at the sight of kittens, puppies, and wild animal babies, even those babies who will one day grow into ferocious, deadly predators.

Since oxytocin is also implicated in what creates the human-animal bond (see page 244), it would seem that all animals are programmed to care for babies, perhaps no matter what species.

In August 2008, in a shantytown on the outskirts of Buenos Aires, a dog named La China found an abandoned newborn infant in a field. Without leaving any bite marks, La China carried the hours-old baby about 150 feet to her own litter of puppies, where the infant's cries were heard by

La China's owners. The baby's mother, a fourteen-year-old girl, was later found and admitted to abandoning her child.

In June 2012, in Winkongo, Ghana, the search for a lost farm dog led to an unexpected discovery: The dog had spent the night under a bridge nestled with an abandoned two-week-old baby girl. The baby was rescued, and the press dubbed the dog "Hairy Poppins."

In June 2013, in Bangkok, Thailand, a dog named Pui found a premature baby infant in a plastic bag in a garbage dump. The dog carried the bag home and barked till his owners appeared, thus saving the child. Pui won an award from the local Red Cross, but his owner, Poomrat Thongmak, said, "It was a surprise to us, since Little Pui never brought anything home, only barking at strangers when he's out and about."

Finally, in December 2013, in Birmingham, England, a German shepherd named Jade noticed an abandoned baby hidden in a carrier bag while taking a walk in the park with his owner, Roger Wilday. The baby was less than twenty-four-hours old and had probably been in the park under an hour. Jade ran off, sat by the bag, and wouldn't move until a confused Wilday came over. Wilday called the police, and the baby made a full recovery.

FRISKY THE DOG . . . KISSES HIS OWNER

NAME: *Frisky*

SPECIES: *Schnauzer-poodle mix*

DATE: *August 28, 2005*

LOCATION: *Biloxi, Mississippi*

SITUATION: *Man trapped in a flooded house during Hurricane Katrina*

WHO WAS SAVED: *Eighty-year-old George Mitchell*

LEGACY: *New Orleans hero for loving perseverance in the eye of the storm*

In late August 2005, Hurricane Katrina dropped its shoulder like a linebacker and prepared to pummel coastal Louisiana and Mississippi. However, despite federal evacuation orders, some Gulf Coast residents refused to get out of the hurricane's way. George Mitchell of Biloxi was one of them.

As he figured it, August 28 was his eightieth birthday, he was a widower, and he'd already survived three hurricanes. "Camille was as bad as it gets," Mitchell rationalized, referring to the epic hurricane that flattened Mississippi in 1969.

George's only concession was to move to a neighbor's house on higher ground. In addition, George took along his dog, Frisky, who, at nineteen years old, was also a senior citizen. The scruffy schnauzer-poodle mix had been George's devoted companion for seventeen years.

As it turned out, Hurricane Katrina wasn't stronger than Camille, but she was much, much bigger.

By 11 pm on Sunday night, as the storm neared land, the wind ripped off the back door of the boarded-up house, revealing surging tides and trees bent double. George hunkered down in the master bedroom and put Frisky on top of an inflatable mattress, but soon the dark waters entered the house. Everything started rising.

"I felt like I was standing in a giant washing machine," George said. "I could see fish swimming around my legs."

Two venomous water moccasins swam nearby as well. George flung one snake away and held on to the mattress to keep Frisky from tipping off. Then, as the waters rose to within a foot of the ceiling, George himself had to start swimming, and he grasped the mattress to help keep his own head above water. With the power out, the only light came from a flashlight.

After about four hours of treading water constantly, George revised his appraisal of Katrina. "This thing was the monster of them all," he said. "It had to have come straight from hell."

George had adopted Frisky in 1987. The stray, ash-gray, scraggly-haired mutt had wandered onto his porch, and his wife had hectored him into giving the sad-looking dog "a proper home." Now it looked like they were reaching the end together.

FACING THE RIVER JORDAN

Minutes stretched like hours as Katrina raged on and continued to grow in intensity. The storm wouldn't officially make landfall till around 6 am Monday morning, when, most infamously, numerous levees protecting New Orleans gave way, causing catastrophic flooding. When it was over, Hurricane Katrina would be responsible for over 1,800 deaths and over $80 billion in property damage, making it the costliest, and one of the deadliest, natural disasters in US history.

And yet, strangely enough, in the tiny, battered house, a sense of peace slowly settled inside George. He knew he couldn't keep swimming all night, and eventually he thought, *This is it.*

"I really was at peace," he said. "It was a quietness I never heard before in my life, even during the war. I was thinking, you know, of what type of life I'd led and how great my wife had been. You know, pretty pleasant things, really. That's when I knew I was ready to let go."

As George later described it, the time had come for him to cross the River Jordan.

"And all of a sudden," George said, Frisky "leaned over the edge of that mattress and he laid the kisses to me. He got right as close as he could, looking in my eyes."

Frisky "kissed me and kissed me and kissed me," George said. "He would not stop licking until I snapped out of it."

George said he felt like Frisky was saying, "Come on, let's get this show on the road. We're going to get through this."

SWIMMING TILL MORNING

What prompted Frisky's sudden outburst of affection? Was the timing coincidental, or did the dog read George's thoughts on his face? Somehow, at the moment George was accepting death, Frisky kissed him back into the present moment and reminded him that he was loved and that he wasn't alone.

After all, without George, Frisky had little hope of surviving the storm.

"That's what worried me," George said. "What would happen to him?"

Concerned for Frisky, George pushed aside thoughts of death and hung on. After that moment, every time exhaustion overwhelmed him and he stopped treading water or he released his hold on the mattress, Frisky came up and licked his face, over and over again, keeping him conscious, keeping him determined.

Finally, as if pushed back by the somber gray light of dawn, the water slowly receded. George's feet touched the ground, and by noon, it was low enough to walk. George grabbed Frisky and awkwardly waded out of the house.

With the help of nearby rescue workers, George and Frisky were taken to a hospital, where they recuperated together for nearly two weeks. Afterward, they moved to a retirement home together. Frisky died in 2007.

At the time, George said, "I couldn't ever express the closeness between he and I. He took care of me, he sure did. When it counted most, this dog lived up."

HONEY THE COCKER SPANIEL . . . MEETS THE NEIGHBORS

NAME: *Honey*

SPECIES: *Cocker spaniel*

DATE: *October 31, 2005*

LOCATION: *Nicasio, California*

SITUATION: *Man trapped in an overturned vehicle*

WHO WAS SAVED: *Sixty-three-year-old Michael Bosch*

LEGACY: *Won 2006 North Shore Animal League America Award and Rescue Dog of the Year*

In October 2005, sixty-three-year-old Michael Bosch decided he needed a dog. His wife often traveled for work, and he'd recently had heart surgery, and he figured a new canine pet would keep him company and keep him fit at the same time.

Michael visited the local animal shelter and was moved by a quivering and scared five-month-old cocker spaniel, Honey. In that mysterious, intuitive way that people and pets often connect, they bonded instantly.

"She followed me like a shadow from the very first day," Michael said. "She loved to snuggle on my lap."

After two weeks, Michael and Honey were "nearly inseparable," and on Halloween morning, without a second thought, Michael took Honey with him to go run some errands.

TROUBLE BACKING OUT

At the time, Michael lived in Nicasio, California, among the remote, redwood-covered hills of Marin County. Beautiful, but like most area homes, his was accessed by a steep, narrow driveway. Backing out was tricky, and that morning a flash of sunlight blinded him at a critical moment. He reversed too far and his SUV tumbled over the edge, somersaulting four or five times till a tree limb punctured the roof and the car came to a halt, upside-down, at the bottom of a fifty-foot ravine.

Michael's left leg was pinned by the branch, which had embedded in the dash. In addition to various cuts and contusions, he had five broken ribs, or so doctors counted later. Thankfully, Honey appeared unhurt.

Unable to get free, Michael tried to call 911 on his cellphone, but of course, he couldn't get a signal at the bottom of the ravine. He couldn't turn around to sound the car horn, either. In excruciating pain and starting to panic, Michael took a nitroglycerin pill to forestall having another heart attack.

A hole in a rear window offered a glimmer of hope. Gently picking up his silky-haired, flop-eared, fifteen-pound puppy, Michael eased Honey out of the car, patted her bottom, and said, "Go home, Honey."

Michael's wife was away, so as Honey took off at a run up the wooded slope, Michael had no expectation that the dog, even if she went home, would bring help. *Stuff like that only happened in the movies,* he thought.

Seven hours later, Michael was still trapped and alone. As the light faded, the cold increased, and his pulse weakened, Michael began to make a reluctant if grateful appraisal of what had been a good life.

A DISOBEDIENT POOCH

What Michael couldn't know was that Honey didn't go home. She ran about a half mile to neighbor Robin Allen's house, a place the dog had never been before. It's possible that Honey went other places as well, or got lost for a time. This is what Michael half-expected, given that his home was still brand-new to her.

However, when Robin arrived home from work, there was Honey, "waiting for me," Robin said. "She got all agitated and ran in circles. She was frantic. She was obviously trying to tell me something, because she wouldn't let me catch her."

When Robin did eventually catch her, she read the address on Honey's tag and drove her home. Once out of the car, Robin didn't need Honey's guidance; she could hear faint shouts for help coming from the ravine.

Trained service dogs, of course, can learn many commands and specific words, and they can be taught how to get human assistance in an emergency (see page 120). But Honey was an untrained puppy and a virtual stranger to her surroundings. She probably didn't even understand what she'd been told, but she knew what was needed.

She also expressed her meaning to a stranger using the only communication tools she had, body language and vocal tone. It could be that Honey was simply afraid for herself; she was upset about being abandoned and lost. But Robin, the focus of Honey's communication, didn't think so.

"She was bringing me here," Robin said. "She was directing me."

Robin found Michael and called 911. Within minutes, a helicopter arrived, and within an hour, emergency workers had cut Michael free of the SUV. He was flown to a hospital for immediate care. Doctors felt he wouldn't have survived much longer.

A few days later, Honey was allowed to join Michael as he recuperated in the hospital, and it was as if "all my pain went away," he said. Honey took up a permanent spot by his feet in bed, becoming yet another blessing Michael was grateful for. As he said, "I probably wouldn't be alive today if it weren't for Honey."

"BUDDY, WE NEED TO GET HELP!"

In April 2010 in rural Alaska, a real-life Lassie was caught on film. One night, a fire broke out in a workshop on a remote property. After escaping the blaze himself and then rescuing his five-year-old German shepherd, Ben Heinrichs turned to the dog and said, "Buddy, we need to get help!"

Shy and untrained, the dog instantly ran into the woods. *Going off to hide*, Ben figured.

Nope. Buddy was doing what he'd been told.

Coincidentally, Trooper Terrance Shanigan was just then trying to find the reported fire. He'd become disoriented on the pitch-black, rural dirt roads and was about to make a wrong turn. At that very moment, a German shepherd appeared in his headlights.

On a hunch, Trooper Shanigan followed the dog. "It was body language," he said later. "I felt like the dog was telling me to follow. He gave me a look, and started to lead me down another road, and that's when I just committed to the dog."

For the next minute or so, Trooper Shanigan's dashboard camera filmed Buddy as he guided the police car through three turns to the house and regularly looked over his shoulder as if encouraging the trooper (for video, see the Source Notes). Because of Buddy's help, the Heinrich's home was saved from the blaze.

"He wasn't running from me, but was leading me," Trooper Shanigan said. "It's just one of those things, that we're thinking on the same page for that brief moment."

An interesting turn of phrase. How remarkable that Buddy could nonverbally communicate so clearly that the trooper felt they were sharing the same thoughts.

SHANA THE HALF-BREED WOLF ... DIGS A TUNNEL OF LOVE

NAME: *Shana*

SPECIES: *Half-breed wolf and German shepherd mix*

DATE: *October 12, 2006*

LOCATION: *Enchanted Forest Wildlife Sanctuary, near Alden, New York*

SITUATION: *Elderly couple trapped outside in a snowstorm*

WHO WAS SAVED: *Eighty-one-year-old Eve and Norman Fertig*

LEGACY: *Local hero, saved elderly, devoted animal rescuers*

Does gratitude for being rescued ever directly inspire animals to play the rescuer? If so, few deserve this karmic blessing more than Eve and Norman Fertig.

Eve has helped rescue and rehabilitate animals her entire life. When Eve was a child during the Depression, her father turned their Bronx tenement apartment into a de facto SPCA, rescuing abandoned dogs, cats, and pigeons and finding them homes. Later, as a wife and mother, Eve rescued waterbirds, and when it came time to retire, her devoted husband, Norman, agreed to fulfill her lifelong dream.

"I always wanted to live in the woods and take care of animals," she said.

Around 1976, the Fertigs founded the Enchanted Forest Wildlife Sanctuary near Alden in upstate New York, and Eve began teaching courses in wildlife rehabilitation at local community colleges. At first the sanctuary was inside their home, and they took in injured birds—hawks, owls, kestrels, crows, parrots—but eventually they expanded with an aviary and various outbuildings.

They rehabilitated other animals as well, and around 1999 they saved a two-week-old half-wolf, half-German shepherd pup from nefarious breeders who intended to use the pup for dog fights. Wolves are one of Eve's favorite animals—she considers the wolf the "the guardian of the forest"—and Shana became the couple's devoted companion. As a burly, tawny-and-black adult, Shana grew to an intimidating 160 pounds, but she trailed Eve on her rounds like "a little lamb."

AN UNEXPECTED SNOWFALL

On October 12, 2006, the Fertigs were ministering to their injured charges, feeding and exercising them, as they did every evening. However, while inside, they didn't realize that an unseasonal, violent snowstorm was blowing in. Around 7 pm the lights went out, and as Eve put it, "We go outside to see what's happening and down comes one massive tree."

Trees were falling all over the property, and the couple was quickly trapped in the narrow alley between two buildings. Both now eighty-one years old, and without winter coats or gloves, Eve and Norman were unable to climb over or under the trees. For the next two and half hours, all they could do was huddle for warmth as the temperature dropped and the snow piled higher.

"We were in big trouble," Eve said. "I said, 'Norman, we can't stay here. We'll die.'"

Around 9:30 pm, Shana located them and immediately started digging through the deep snow. It took the dog nearly two hours, but eventually she reached them, creating a narrow tunnel the width of herself and about twenty feet long. The tunnel extended from the tree almost to their home's back porch.

Afterward, it would be more than five months before Shana's feet healed from the injuries she received while digging.

When Shana finally broke through the snow and emerged from the tunnel in the narrow alley between the buildings, the half-wolf barked at the Fertigs, her message clear: Follow me.

THE SCANDAL OF DIVORCE

Norman looked at the tunnel and refused. He said he'd spent too much time in foxholes in Okinawa during World War II.

In her no-nonsense Bronx accent, Eve let him have it: "Norman, if you do not follow me, I will get a divorce."

"That did it," Eve said. "He said, 'A divorce? That would scandal our family.' I said, 'All of our family is dead, Norman!'"

Shana grabbed Eve's jacket and pulled the eighty-six-pound woman onto her back. Norman took hold of Eve's ankles, and for the next two hours Shana pulled the couple through the tunnel.

"It was the most heroic thing I've ever seen in my life," Eve said.

Nevertheless, the whole way, Eve had to keep encouraging Norman to persevere. "Oh, he thought we would never get out."

Around 2 am, the Fertigs finally reached their back door and fell inside the house. There was no electricity or heat, but Shana lay with them and kept them warm all night. "She kept us alive," Eve said. "She really did."

Firefighters arrived the next morning and urged the Fertigs to take shelter at the firehouse. The only trouble was, animals weren't allowed, so Eve and

Norman decided to stay in their powerless home with Shana. For several days, firefighters brought them food and water.

Eve said, "They kept looking at that tunnel, and said, 'We've never seen anything like it.'"

Afterward, Shana won several awards for bravery, including a hero's plaque from the local firefighters.

As for Eve, despite threats to retire, she finds it hard to quit teaching or to let go of the "wild innocents" in her care. She said, "My dream is, when I do retire, like Johnny Appleseed, to leave seedling wildlife rehabilitators all over New York State."

TOBY THE GOLDEN RETRIEVER . . . PERFORMS THE HEIMLICH MANEUVER

NAME: *Toby*

SPECIES: *Golden retriever*

DATE: *May 25, 2007*

LOCATION: *Calvert, Maryland*

SITUATION: *Woman choking on an apple*

WHO WAS SAVED: *Forty-five-year-old Debbie Parkhurst*

LEGACY: *First dog to perform the Heimlich maneuver, 2007 Dog of the Year*

Okay, dogs have done some pretty amazing things to save people. But a dog who performed the Heimlich maneuver to save his choking owner?

That seems, well . . . *unlikely* is one word that comes to mind.

Yet Debbie Parkhurst claims that her tawny, two-year-old golden retriever, Toby, mimicked the technique when she couldn't breathe and was moments from blacking out.

Toby's veterinarian, Doug Foreman, used a different word to describe Toby's feat, calling it "some kind of miracle."

"He wasn't making a joke," Debbie replied. "He's very spiritual, and now I have to agree with him."

A BITE OF APPLE

Here's what happened: On Friday, May 25, 2007, in her Calvert, Maryland, home, Debbie took a break from her jewelry-making business and went to the kitchen to get a snack. Mistakenly indulging a virtuous urge, she chose an unpeeled apple.

"Normally I peel them, but I read in *Good Housekeeping* magazine that the skin has all the nutrients, so I ate the skin," she said.

The bite of apple got lodged in her throat, and she began to choke. Unable to breathe, "I tried to do the thing where you lean over a chair and give yourself the Heimlich," Debbie said. "But it didn't work."

Increasingly panicked, Debbie beat on her chest with her fist, and this behavior attracted the attention of Toby.

"The next think I know, Toby's up on his hind feet, and he's got his front paws on my shoulders," she recalled. "He pushed me to the ground, and once I was on my back, he began jumping up and down on my chest."

Due to Toby's efforts, the food became dislodged from Debbie's windpipe. Then, she said, "As soon as I started breathing, he stopped and began licking my face, as if to keep me from passing out."

PAW PRINT ON THE HEART

Normally, Debbie considers Toby "goofy," and Foreman said, "Toby isn't what you would call the most-trained of dogs. In fact, he's about the last dog I would expect to do something like this."

Golden retrievers are notoriously excitable, and so we might wonder if perhaps Toby mistook Debbie's behavior as an invitation to play a new game called "beat on my chest really hard." However, this explanation also seems unlikely.

To begin with, Debbie was clearly in trouble. She was scared and suffocating. Dogs are particularly attuned to human emotions, especially with their owners (which is what makes them such good service animals; see Part Two). So to believe Toby was playing, we have to believe Toby was either ignoring or ignorant of Debbie's emotions.

Further, Toby jumped on Debbie with such force that "I literally have paw print-shaped bruises on my chest," Debbie said. Thus, if Toby wasn't trying to help, his actions were being hurtful. In addition, Toby stopped his "game" and started comforting Debbie the moment she could breathe again.

Perhaps most of all, Debbie knows when Toby is fooling around. "I know it sounds a little weird," she said, "but I think he had a sense of what was happening."

So, if Toby was trying to help—where did he get his textbook technique? It's not like humans instinctively know to perform a series of abdominal thrusts when someone is choking. The technique was invented by Dr. Henry Heimlich in 1974. Before then, it was a few hard slaps to the back (and good luck, chap).

While Dr. Foreman suggested divine intervention, there is another possibility. In social animals like dogs, researchers describe something called "program-level imitation." This refers to how animals imitate by creatively adapting actions to their own bodies. For instance, this is how dolphins learn to throw a Frisbee and how dogs learn to turn doorknobs: Lacking hands, they figure out how to use their mouths to accomplish the same thing. In addition, "mirror neurons" in the brain allow dogs (and other social animals) to automatically intuit the feelings of another (see page 59).

It might be that simple: Toby observed Debbie, saw that her actions meant to relieve her distress, and then imitated her in order to help. Toby may have understood Debbie's purpose—that she needed a sharp burst of air from her lungs to clear food stuck in her throat—but he didn't need to know that.

"I have no idea where he learned it from," Debbie said. "But I can tell you that I'm going to peel and mash my apples from now on."

That Debbie is alive to snack again is all because of the alert, compassionate actions of Toby. "They say dogs leave a paw print on your heart," she said. "He left a paw print on my heart, that's for sure."

WILL PEOPLE EVER LEARN TO CHEW?

As it happens, Toby isn't the only dog to have performed the Heimlich maneuver. On New Year's Eve 2014, a black mixed-breed German shepherd and golden retriever, Nell, used the "canine Heimlich" to rescue Leslie Hailwood of Liverpool, England.

The story, as Leslie tells it, is that sometime before midnight she popped a chocolate into her mouth, which lodged at the back of her throat. She tried to get it back out, but it wouldn't budge. Just when Leslie started to panic that she might choke to death, Nell jumped onto the sofa in front her.

Nell "looked straight at me," Leslie said, "got up onto her back legs . . . and with her two front paws she just lurched at me and hit me in the chest." That did the trick.

"There's no doubt in my eyes that Nell saved my life," Leslie said. "She's never jumped up on me like that before. She knew I was in trouble and knew exactly how to wind me."

Nell was then seventeen months old and in training to be a guide dog for the blind. Leslie was only boarding Nell till the dog completed training and was assigned. Suffice it to say, the Heimlich maneuver was not part of her training.

"This is just another example of how talented guide dogs can be," said a spokesperson for Nell's guide dog association. "In many cases, they instinctively know how to help."

MIRRORS INSIDE, MIRRORS OUTSIDE

Leaving other animals aside, how is it that *people* can intuitively sense what another is feeling? How is it that we "just know" when a person's grimace reflects rage, regret, pain, or asphyxiation?

The answer, apparently, is that we are hardwired to know, using special cells called "mirror neurons." Mirror neurons activate automatically whenever we observe another person or animal, which, as researcher Meg Daley Olmert writes, "causes our brain cells to fire as if we are actually making the movements ourselves." This mimicking helps us understand what the other is doing and feeling because we ourselves, in our minds, are now doing it and feeling it.

Mirror neurons were first discovered in monkeys in 1996. Dr. Giacomo Rizzolatti, one of the researchers of this groundbreaking discovery, said, "Mirror neurons allow us to grasp the minds of others not through conceptual reasoning but through direct simulation. By feeling, not by thinking."

Mirror neurons are the culprit behind the "monkey see, monkey do" impulse. If someone yawns or laughs, we feel the involuntary urge to do the same. In fact, studies have shown that we are able to copy facial expressions after only milliseconds.

Currently, mirror neurons appear to be present in humans, monkeys, apes, elephants, dolphins, and dogs. Mirror neurons may actually be a necessity for social animals, since they allow us to understand the internal state of others at a glance, even across species.

Nevertheless, this automatic mental process does not require or imply self-awareness. To establish self-awareness in other animals, "mirror recognition" is the gold standard. That is, if animals appear to recognize their own image in an actual mirror, this seems to confirm that they are self-aware. So far, only apes, elephants, dolphins, and possibly magpies have clearly passed this test. Yet it may also be that some species use sound or smell as their primary method of self-recognition, as with birds and dogs, respectively.

Why is this distinction important? Because, as odd as it sounds, it explains how animals can reflect others—and know accurately what others are feeling—while not necessarily being self-reflective and self-aware about their own experience.

KHAN THE DOBERMAN PINSCHER . . . TOSSES THE TODDLER

NAME: *Khan*

SPECIES: *Doberman pinscher*

DATE: *October 2007*

LOCATION: *Cairns, Australia*

SITUATION: *Toddler threatened by a venomous snake*

WHO WAS SAVED: *Seventeen-month-old Charlotte Svilicic*

LEGACY: *Australian "wonder dog" famous for risking his life for newly adopted family*

When Khan, a Doberman pinscher, was first rescued by a kennel in Cairns, Australia, he was so severely malnourished and abused—with several broken ribs from the beatings he'd received—that he was almost put down. However, the kennel's owner had originally bred Khan, and she couldn't bring herself to end his life.

Then, in October 2007, the Svilicic family adopted Khan, and only four days later, the dog repaid their kindness forever.

SNAKE IN THE GRASS

The family's seventeen-month-old daughter, Charlotte, was playing in the backyard garden, and Charlotte's mother, Catherine, was watching from the kitchen window. Catherine grew concerned as she saw their newly adopted pet begin to act aggressively toward her daughter. Khan was insistently nudging and pushing at Charlotte, clearly trying to move the toddler, but she wouldn't budge.

Suddenly, Khan bit the back of Charlotte's diaper and flung her more than three feet through the air, so that she landed behind him.

"Charlotte looked pretty shocked," Catherine said, "and then Khan screamed."

Immediately, Catherine realized a snake was attacking Khan, and that Khan's intervention had saved her daughter from being bitten instead.

"If I hadn't seen it with my own eyes, I would never have believed it," Catherine said.

Khan was bitten in the right front paw by a king brown snake, the most widespread and largest venomous snake in Australia. Brown snakes are notorious for their savage attacks, but Khan was lucky: He pulled away and ran inside, where he collapsed. After gathering her daughter, Catherine rushed Khan to the hospital, where he was given an antivenin and quickly recovered.

Brown snakes account for about half of Australia's snake-related deaths, and apparently local hospitals keep plenty of antivenin on hand. (So, no worries, mate!)

Afterward, the Australian media, including the morning talk shows, inundated the Svilicic household with calls, wanting to hear the story firsthand.

It was overwhelming, but Catherine understood why.

"He saved [Charlotte's] life by risking his own," she said. Plus, not every altruistic hero is a formerly abused dog. "From now on, he's Khan the Wonder Dog. Khan's a star."

The kicker? The kennel owner, Khan's breeder, said that Khan's grandfather once did the same thing.

ALL INDIANA JONES NEEDS IS A DOG

Indiana Jones is one tough archeologist. Nazis? Poison darts? Burning zeppelins? No problem. But snakes? They are the one thing this notorious ophidiophobic can't stand.

If only Indy would bring along a dog. Stories of dogs protecting people, especially children, from snakes are so common that they might be the most prevalent type of life-saving animal rescue. Perhaps it's a matter of circumstance, since snakes often live near humans, or perhaps dogs just share Dr. Jones's feelings on the matter.

In any case, snake stories illustrate, time and again, that dogs will deliberately put themselves in harm's way to save a person, since when it comes to snakes, dogs often pay a price for their heroism.

Consider this small sampling (in which, by the way, all the dogs survived):

- In 2003, in Hudson, Florida, Fran Oreto's seven-year-old golden retriever Brutis saved her two young grandchildren, age two and four, by grabbing a writhing, biting sixteen-inch coral snake in its mouth as the snake slithered in the backyard grass near the kids.

- In 2007, in Masonville, Colorado, one-year-old Booker West was saved when the family's ten-month-old Chihuahua, Zoey, raced around a birdbath and in front of the toddler just as a three-foot rattlesnake struck—biting Zoey in the head instead of Booker.

- In January 2012, near Ipswich, Australia, two young girls went out their front door to play. One girl saw a brown snake coiled beneath the swingset and yelled, "Snake!" Immediately, their Australian cattle dog, River, emerged from the house, attacking and killing the snake despite the bites she received.

- In June 2013, a husband and wife were hiking in Marin, California, when their thirteen-month-old Anatolian shepherd, Shakira, jumped back and refused to let the wife past. An unseen rattlesnake sat right where the wife was about to step. Wisely, Shakira neither barked nor attacked, allowing the snake to slither away.

- In August 2013, in Hueco Tanks, Texas, two young sisters were playing in the mud when a hiss and rattle announced an unseen rattlesnake coiling to strike. At that moment, the family's ten-pound Chihuahua-poodle mix, Psycho, ran in between and took the strike in the face.

WILLIE THE QUAKER PARROT . . . LEARNS A NEW WORD

NAME: *Willie*

SPECIES: *Quaker parrot*

DATE: *November 2008*

LOCATION: *Denver, Colorado*

SITUATION: *Toddler choking on food*

WHO WAS SAVED: *Two-year-old Hannah Kuusk*

LEGACY: *Perhaps the only parrot known to use human language to save a life*

Meagan Howard just needed to go to the bathroom.

It was November 2008, and the nineteen-year-old was babysitting her roommate's two-year-old daughter, Hannah, while Hannah's mom attended a class. Little Hannah was in the living room of their Denver apartment watching television and eating a Pop-Tart. Meagan's bird, Willie—a small, lime-green Quaker parrot with a white face—was chattering amiably in his cage. Meagan would only be away for a minute—what could go wrong?

As it turned out, plenty.

SOUNDING AN ALARM

Seconds after Meagan left the room, "Willie started screaming and flapping his wings, and I have never heard so much panic in his voice," she said. "I thought maybe the cat was getting after him. But then he started saying 'Mama baby' over and over and over again."

Panicked, Meagan rushed back out as Willie kept screeching "Mama baby!"

"I . . . looked at Hannah," she said, "and Hannah's face was turning blue because she was choking on her Pop-Tart."

Meagan hurried over to the girl and performed the Heimlich maneuver, dislodging the obstruction. Once Hannah could breathe, her color returned to normal. Oddly enough, Willie calmed down as well.

"The minute I took charge," Meagan said, "Willie quit squawking, as if he knew things were under control."

Meagan was stunned. A life-threatening crisis had arisen and been averted in the blink of an eye. But, she said, "if [Willie hadn't] warned me, I probably wouldn't have come out of the bathroom in time."

When Hannah's mom, Samantha, came home, she was shaken, too.

"The part where [Hannah] turned blue is always when my heart drops, no matter how many times I've heard it," Samantha said. "I'm very grateful for the both of them because they both saved her."

Meagan was quick to credit Willie, calling him "the real hero."

THE MEANING OF WORDS

Naturally, the first thing we wonder is: Did Willie actually know what he was saying?

"He calls me Mama," Meagan said, "so he was clearly trying to get my attention. He's loud and talkative, but what really amazes me is that he added the word 'baby' on his own."

Willie also says "I love you," "step up," and, Meagan admitted, "some other words that aren't so nice." However, she claims the parrot added this new word to his repertoire himself—and not only that, but he used it for the first time appropriately and in context to signal an emergency.

Parrots are legendary vocal mimics, and Willie certainly must have heard the word "baby" many times before. But mimicry does not necessarily indicate understanding. To use words like this, in a way that echoes human grammar, implies a level of awareness and smarts that most birds are not credited with.

However, when animals are sufficiently motivated, they often reveal abilities we didn't realize they possessed. This applies to many rescue stories in this book, and it was often the case with science's most famous parrot, Alex (see page 67).

Putting aside issues of language comprehension, Willie acted with clear intention—sounding an alarm that was directed at Meagan because Hannah was choking. The timing of the squawking, and its intensity, are more than mere coincidence.

What would be fascinating to know is whether Willie was merely upset because Hannah was upset, or if Willie reacted the way he did because he truly cared about Hannah and meant to help her.

We can't know, but Hannah's mother, Samantha Kuusk, said, "Don't ever underestimate animals because he's living proof that they're absolutely remarkable and way more intelligent than people give them credit for."

BIRD BRAINS

In 2007, a year before Hannah Kuusk choked on a Pop-Tart, perhaps the most famous talking parrot in the world died, the African grey Alex.

Dr. Irene Pepperberg's experiments with Alex revolutionized the way we regard "bird brains." By the end of his life, Alex had learned over a hundred words; he could identify objects by color, shape, material, and number; he displayed a concept for zero; and he used equivalency to link the written numeral 6, say, with six objects.

Alex was considered at least as smart as a five-year-old child, and twice as pugnacious. He could act proud, jealous, and vain. If fellow parrots got answers wrong, he admonished and corrected them. Most of all, he couldn't stand boredom, and he frequently disrupted experiments he grew tired of.

In one famous example, Dr. Pepperberg was trying to get Alex to identify different colored blocks, but Alex wouldn't cooperate. Each time, he responded by asking for a nut. Finally, exasperated, Alex said slowly, "Want a nut. Nnn . . . uh . . . tuh."

In her book *Alex & Me*, Dr. Pepperberg wrote, "I was stunned. It was as if he were saying, *Hey, stupid, do I have to spell it out for you?*" Alex had sounded out a complete word without having ever been trained to do so.

Indeed, breakthroughs with Alex often occurred when the bird was apparently communicating his frustrations by causing trouble. In these tricksterish moments, he demonstrated that, yes, he was thinking for himself.

As Dr. Pepperberg wrote, "Alex taught me to believe that his little bird brain was conscious in some manner, that is, capable of intention."

Alex also demonstrated that he was capable of affection. The emotional rapport between scientist and bird was most poignantly captured by their exchange on the night before Alex died. As Dr. Pepperberg put him in his cage to sleep, unaware that there was a problem, Alex said, "You be good. I love you."

"I love you, too," Dr. Pepperberg replied.

INKY THE CAT . . . KNOCKS ON THE DOOR

NAME: *Inky*

SPECIES: *Domestic cat*

DATE: *January 23, 2009*

LOCATION: *Wellsville, New York*

SITUATION: *Man crushed by a falling attic door*

WHO WAS SAVED: *Sixty-one-year-old Glen Kruger*

LEGACY: *Local hero who proved that even felines can channel their "inner Lassie"*

As the saying goes, you can't tell a cat to do anything. We give cats the run of our homes, we feed them, we love them, and yet, if we need them to do something—well, good luck with that. Cats don't have owners, only servants. But just because cats don't usually cooperate doesn't mean they can't, nor does it mean they don't know perfectly well what we want of them. For instance, take Inky.

CAT PEOPLE

Glen and Brenda Kruger adopted the black-and-white, tuxedo-patterned Inky when she was just three months old. The abused, malnourished kitten was left in a box on an acquaintance's porch.

"She was beat up, bruised, and bloodied," Glen said. The Krugers first took the kitten to the SPCA, but the next day they returned to adopt her. As he said, "We bonded immediately."

In fact, Glen had always had an affinity for felines. His "playmates" growing up were the cats on his family's dairy farm. "My hearing was damaged by chainsaws and the noise of farm equipment," Glen said, "so I learned to connect with animals. They respond to what they see and what you do."

Over the years, Inky grew into a typical indoor-outdoor cat. During the day, she preferred to be outside, roaming the woods of upstate New York. At night, she would come inside, along with the Krugers' five other cats. This was in part a wise precaution to avoid predatory foxes and coyotes, but Inky also developed a fondness for Glen's lap on cold winter evenings.

Flash forward to January 23, 2009. It was almost midnight, and Glen descended into the cellar to shut down the wood stove before going to bed. Returning to the top of the stairs, Glen reached to turn off the light, and instead dislodged a board that propped up a broken, spring-loaded, drop-down attic door above his head.

The falling door slammed into Glen like a battering ram and sent him tumbling head first to the bottom of the cellar stairs. He was badly hurt and couldn't move; later, he was diagnosed with a fractured vertebrae, a broken arm, a dislocated shoulder, and deep cuts to his head.

Glen yelled for help, but to no avail. His wife was asleep at the other end of the house and didn't hear him.

A SIMPLE REQUEST

"The open attic hatchway was dumping about five-degree air down on top of me," Glen said, "and I was starting to go into shock. I happened to notice Inky staring at me at the top of the stairway with huge eyes. Something moved me to tell her to get Brenda."

That's all Glen said, "Go get Brenda," and Inky ran away. Glen's first thought was, *I'm sunk.* Like most cats, Inky only came when called if there was food involved.

However, "Inky went to my wife's bedroom and jumped against the door and caterwauled loud enough to wake her up," Glen said.

Brenda thought that all the scratching and yowling meant the cat wanted to go outside, so she got up to let Inky out. When Inky led her to the open cellar door, Brenda found her injured husband and quickly called 911.

Glen's recovery lasted six months, and due to spinal compression, he lost several inches in height and still suffers limited neck mobility. He had to quit his job and go on permanent disability. Nevertheless, Glen feels only gratitude and amazement.

"There is a very good chance I would be buried by now, if it wasn't for Inky," he said. "I was blessed."

CATS RAISE A RUCKUS

Stories of cats alerting people to household dangers—such as fires or gas leaks—are fairly common. With their excellent sense of smell, cats can detect a problem before we do—and often before a smoke detector does. These timely warnings save lives, and for this we are immensely grateful.

Yet a cat's warning may indicate nothing more than self-preservation. Cats know we control the doors and windows. For all we know, when there is a problem and our cat wakes us up, it may mean only: letmeouttahere!

For this reason, scientists tend to dismiss these events. Motivations are extremely hard to distinguish when everyone is equally threatened. Part of what makes Inky's actions so compelling is that she herself was free from danger.

That said, consider these stories:

- In March 2007, in Indiana, a leaking gas pump filled the home of Eric and Cathy Keesling with carbon monoxide. In the night, their cat, Winnie, jumped on Cathy, clawed her hair, and mewed angrily. Cathy woke briefly but passed out again. Winnie kept pawing her and crying till Cathy overcame her dizziness, realized the problem, and called 911. Apparently, the only open window in the house was the one where Winnie usually slept.

- In October 2007, in Minnesota, a ruptured gas pipe filled the basement of Trudy Guy's home with gas. Around 2 am, her cat, Schnautzie, jumped on her chest and batted her nose. Trudy ignored the cat and went back to sleep. But Schnautzie woke Trudy again, and this time "sniffed the air like a dog," Trudy said. Alerted by this odd behavior, Trudy discovered the leak, and she and her husband escaped the house.

- In October 2008 in Michigan, the seven-member Busscher family was wakened around 5 am by the unearthly screeching of their black-and-white cat, Oreo. Upon investigation, they discovered a fire inside their attached garage. Only after everyone had fled outside did the house's smoke detectors go off.

ANGEL THE GOLDEN RETRIEVER . . . WRESTLES A COUGAR

NAME: *Angel*

SPECIES: *Golden retriever*

DATE: *January 2010*

LOCATION: *Bar Boston, British Columbia*

SITUATION: *Boy attacked by a cougar*

WHO WAS SAVED: *Eleven-year-old Austin Forman*

LEGACY: *Canadian canine hero for saving boy despite near-fatal mismatch with cougar*

Golden retrievers are known for their excitability. Indeed, the Forman family liked to call Angel, their eighteen-month-old golden, "the kangaroo," since she seemed to have springs for legs.

You might say, when retrievers *aren't* tearing around causing trouble, that's when you should worry. At least, that's one lesson of this particular January evening in 2010.

Eleven-year-old Austin Forman was collecting firewood in the backyard of his home in Bar Boston, British Columbia. Yet Angel, instead of bounding all over the place like an Australian marsupial, was sticking to him like glue. Austin thought this was so "cute" he interrupted his work to go inside and tell his mom, Sherri.

When Austin returned to his wheelbarrow, he discovered why.

SHADOW CAT

In the shadow of the woodshed, about ten feet away, Austin saw what he thought was a strange dog. It was about 5:30 pm and almost dark. Then the animal crept forward, and "as it went underneath the light," Austin said, "I saw that it was a cougar."

In that instant, the cougar pounced, and as it did, Angel leaped, too, jumping over a lawn mower and intercepting the big cat.

"The dog knew something was up because she ran toward me just at the right time," Austin said, "and the cougar ended up getting her instead. It happened so fast I wouldn't have known what hit me."

"Shocked and scared," Austin ran inside. At first, Sherri couldn't make out what her son was saying. Unable to calm down, Austin screamed, "A cougar is eating Angel!"

By now, the cougar had dragged Angel, her head in its mouth, out of sight under the porch, but the dog was "whining and making noises like we've never heard before," Sherri said. "We knew that cougar was killing our dog."

RESCUING AN ANGEL

Sherri called 911, and as luck would have it, Constable Chad Gravelle was less than a minute away. Gravelle knew the Formans, and when the dispatcher sent him the call, his heart sank: He mistakenly thought the cougar had gotten Austin.

Thus, when Gravelle arrived, "I was a little bit more relieved that Austin was okay," he said.

But rescuing Angel was problematic, if not impossible. Gravelle said the dog and the cougar were "all kind of tangled up" in the tight, dark space under the porch. With a flashlight in one hand and a pistol in the other, Gravelle knelt down, scooted as close as he dared, and from about six feet away, fired.

"I could just see about two or three inches of the cougar's head sticking out from behind Angel," Gravelle said. "Luckily, I was able to get a good shot off."

Gravelle killed the cougar, but too late. Angel was no longer moving. Austin's cousin climbed under the porch to pry Angel's snout from the dead cougar's jaws, "and out of nowhere," the cousin said, "the dog breathed a gasp of air, just like it comes back from being dead."

Bloodied and dazed, Angel got up, "walked to Austin, sniffed him to make sure he was alright," Sherri said, and "sat down."

A BOY'S BEST FRIEND

Angel was taken to a local animal hospital, where she was treated for a skull fracture along with severe cuts and bite wounds to her head, neck, and hind leg. Within a week she was on the mend, both physically and emotionally.

"She's a golden retriever," her veterinarian said. "They're always happy."

The Formans said they had never seen a cougar near their yard before, and across British Columbia, there have been only about thirty cougar attacks (five fatal) over the last century. Despite the rarity of even seeing a cougar under normal circumstances, the Formans believe Angel knew all along that a predator was stalking Austin.

“She has a spirit unlike any animal I have seen,” Sherri said. Chad Gravelle called her the “bravest dog” he’s ever known. Gravelle was so moved that, a month later, he decided to name his newborn son after Austin.

It can be hard for an eleven-year-old boy to know how to say thanks for his life. Afterward, Austin bought Angel a steak and helped build her a plush new doghouse.

“I feel very, very lucky,” Austin said. “If it wasn’t for my dog, I don’t think I would be here. She was my best friend, but now she’s more than a best friend—she’s like my guardian now.”

"FREE-OF-CHARGE MUTTS"... FEND OFF A SUICIDE BOMBER

NAME: *Rufus, Target, and Sasha*

SPECIES: *Mixed-breed dogs*

DATE: *February 11, 2010*

LOCATION: *Paktia Province, Afghanistan*

SITUATION: *Suicide bomber entering army barracks*

WHO WAS SAVED: *Fifty US military personnel in the 48th Infantry Brigade*

LEGACY: *National media stars for unexpected defense of US troops in a war zone*

It's a truism of war that the shared peril of battle can inspire tight, lasting bonds of trust and friendship among virtual strangers. This story is about how the same thing occurred between soldiers and three stray dogs in the desolate, war-wracked hills of Afghanistan.

FRIENDSHIP IN A FOREIGN LAND

In late 2009, not far from the Pakistan border, a pack of feral dogs roamed in and around the military base of the 48th Infantry Brigade. According to Sergeant Terry Young, one dog in particular liked to join their football games. "She would come running out onto the field, wiggling her backside—it was the cutest little thing."

The soldiers named the dog "Target" because the Afghan border police—who shared the base and had no love for dogs generally—sometimes aimed at her during rifle practice.

Another dog they named Sasha. "She was a sweetheart," said Young.

Meanwhile, Sergeant Chris Duke made a point of feeding scraps to a third dog, whom he named Rufus. "When you'd come back from a mission," Duke said, "you just wanted something familiar to get your mind off what you'd seen. I'd go play with Rufus."

The three dogs lifted everyone's spirits, so the soldiers let them stay, even though the military frowned on keeping dogs at the base. Worries about disease were one issue, but food was another. "We didn't have any dog food," Duke said. "We were just getting the rations as they came in, and we were in short supply at times."

In a way, you might say the dogs really adopted the soldiers, who were the source of two scarce commodities, affection and food. As proof, in only a few short months, the strays bonded so tightly with the men that they willingly risked their lives to defend them.

AN UNWELCOME VISITOR

On the night of February 11, 2010, most of the brigade was in the main barracks enjoying a normal evening playing cards, unwinding, sleeping, and using the Internet.

Outside, a man in an Afghan border police uniform approached the barracks. Sensing something wrong, the three dogs ran to the doorway and started barking and snapping at him.

Duke said the dogs were "going crazy, barking and growling, which was abnormal." Several soldiers tried to shout down the dogs, yelling, "Be quiet! Stop barking!"

"Target and Rufus latched onto him," Young said. "He was able to get the door open, but that was as far as he got."

The man was a disguised Taliban intruder. Unable to get inside and not wanting to be discovered carrying twenty-four pounds of C4 explosives, he detonated himself.

In the blast, Sasha was killed and five soldiers were wounded, including Duke. Yet none of the approximately fifty soldiers in the barracks were killed. Rufus and Target were also severely injured, with shrapnel wounds and most of their hair singed off.

"There isn't a doubt in my mind [that the dogs] saved my life," Duke said.

"If the dogs wouldn't have been there that night," Young said, "to be honest with you, I really don't even want to think what would have transpired. [The bomber] would have killed a lot of my friends."

In the aftermath of the explosion, the soldiers quickly tended to the wounded, including Target and Rufus, and secured the area from further attack. While quick to praise the heroism of his fellow soldiers, Duke also pointed out the irony of the incident.

"The U.S. Army spends unlimited amounts of money to make sure we have the best equipment, the best weapons, the best armored vehicles," he said. "And the one thing that saves your life is a free-of-charge mutt that you really don't do much but pay him attention and give him a piece of jerky every now and then. It's kind of strange. It was surreal."

BRINGING THE HEROES HOME

Today, we can only speculate about how the dogs sensed that the disguised man was dangerous. Duke said the dogs didn't normally confront newcomers—like trained guard dogs might—so it seems they responded to something specific about this person.

Scientist Marc Bekoff said the animals were probably alerted by "composite signals" from the man. "Dogs sense a fluidity of movement or gate, postures, gestures, and facial expressions. Definitely odor comes in. This man was probably exuding the fear odor. They may have been reading the man's discomfort, not his intent."

We don't yet know where this ability in dogs to read emotions comes from, though many feel it is one result of domestication. Whatever the reason, Bekoff said, "Dogs just have a keen ability to read us. They just know. Some scientists don't like saying that because we don't have the data. But I don't know anybody who would deny it."

In any case, despite being feral animals in a war zone who had themselves been shot at, the dogs demonstrated the ultimate loyalty to the soldiers. The soldiers, in turn, felt extremely loyal to them.

Over the following months, Sergeant Young and Sergeant Duke nursed their injured dogs back to health. Then, when the soldiers finished their tours of duty, they wanted to bring Target and Rufus, respectively, back to live with them in the United States. This proved so difficult that, initially, they had to leave the dogs behind in Afghanistan.

Even putting aside the significant expense involved, flying unlicensed animals from a foreign country is a bureaucratic nightmare. But the soldiers were on a mission. They partnered with several veterans' charities, who helped them raise funds and promote their cause. In particular, Hope for the Warriors helped raise the money necessary to fly the dogs to the United States. Said Robin Kelleher, a charity spokeswoman, "This is the most unique wish we've ever granted."

CELEBRATION AND MOURNING

Rufus came to live with Duke—along with his wife, infant son, and three other dogs—in a small Georgia town, where Duke joined the county fire department. Duke said, "To think that I'm going to have [Rufus] for the rest of my life —it's exciting."

Tragically, Target's return did not end so happily. In November 2010, a few months after arriving in Arizona to live with Young, Target escaped from Young's backyard. It was assumed that Target, unused to confinement, had jumped the fence in order to roam. Young hadn't gotten an identification tag for Target yet, so when the dog was captured a few days later, she was taken to the pound.

Frantic to find her, Young eventually located Target and made an appointment to pick her up. But the night before Young was scheduled to come, a shelter worker confused Target with another dog and mistakenly euthanized her.

Young and his family were heartbroken. When Rufus and Target first arrived in the states, they had received a hero's welcome. The national media had broadcast their amazing story, and just a month before, Young and Target had appeared on the *Oprah Winfrey Show.* Now, condolences poured in from around the country.

Young had told Oprah that Rufus and Target had "earned the right to be treated like soldiers, so that's exactly how we treated them."

In the end, Young grieved for Target as if he were a soldier, too.

STORMY THE QUARTER HORSE ... DROPS-KICKS A FERAL BOAR

NAME: *Stormy*

SPECIES: *Quarter horse*

DATE: *September 13, 2010*

LOCATION: *Sulphur, Louisiana*

SITUATION: *Children threatened by a feral boar*

WHO WAS SAVED: *Siblings nine-year-old Emma and seven-year-old Liam Leonard*

LEGACY: *Local hero for equine valor and stouthearted devotion in the face of an attack*

Stormy was acting skittish. The brown quarter horse was dancing and snorting and almost too antsy to control. Her bareback rider, nine-year-old Emma Leonard, didn't know why.

It was the afternoon of September 13, 2010. Emma and Stormy were exploring an unknown trail not far from their home. Emma's brother, seven-year-old Liam, was walking in front.

"Liam likes to be the point man, the scout," their father, Kevin Leonard, said, "so he's always leading." Rather than ride on Stormy, Liam preferred to be on the ground, pretending to be a foot soldier. With a rubberband gun in hand, Liam scanned the woods for imagined enemies.

Then, all of a sudden, a very real danger crashed through the undergrowth: A huge wild pig, with brown bristles and sharp tusks, burst in front of them and stopped not six feet from Liam. The feral boar radiated menace, making an aggressive clicking noise and almost daring the boy to take another step. Emma knew that boars fiercely protect their territory, and this one's behavior didn't need translation.

"Run, Liam!" Emma shouted.

But Liam was frozen in fear.

Stormy—who had been unaccountably nervous just moments before—quickly took charge. She trotted between Liam and the pig, drawing the animal's attention. As she did this, Stormy also gently nudged Liam with her nose, pushing him away, in the direction of the house.

With Emma clinging to her neck, Stormy strategically positioned herself with her rear facing the pig. In the next moment, as the boar tensed to attack, Stormy kicked out with her back hooves and struck the boar square in the snout.

The dangerous beast squealed in pain and ran away, and the children raced home in a panic. "They were white with fright and crying so much that I could barely understand them," said their mother, Kathy.

FIGHT OR FLIGHT

All animals experience a primal fight-or-flight urge in the face of a life-threatening danger. This is pure survival instinct, and no one is immune to it. One definition of heroism, or courage, is the ability to overcome this instinct in order to help save someone else.

When animals do this on our behalf, we are doubly amazed, for we know all too well that it takes a powerful motivation to override the wild urge to do whatever is necessary to save oneself.

Of Stormy, Kevin Leonard said, "She could have saved herself easily but left the kids in real danger. But she didn't do that. I feel that she was motivated out of love to protect the children."

If so, Stormy had good reason to love the Leonards of Sulphur, Louisiana. She had been rescued a few years before as a thirty-year-old mare who was so starved and emaciated that she was eating the bark off trees. A local nonprofit rescue center, Steeds of Acceptance & Renewal (SOAR), took her in.

"In spite of her age, she recovered remarkably well from the abuse," said Heather Dionne, the head riding instructor. "She could still collect herself, bridle up and jog, and with wonderful cadence and style." It was obvious that "someone had spent a lot of time training her."

At first, SOAR enlisted Stormy as a therapy animal for kids with disabilities, but they wanted to find her a permanent home. "When we discovered a family in search of a horse for their young daughter to love and learn from, we felt a prayer had been answered," Dionne said.

Emma, in turn, doted on Stormy. She would rush home every day after school, eagerly finishing her homework and chores, so she could spend time with her horse. As girls will, she gave Stormy hoof pedicures using hot pink paint.

Whatever Stormy felt that day, "she took care of those kids," Kathy said, "and we will forever be grateful."

Indeed, Stormy took care of the kids as fiercely as any mother protecting her own children.

As Emma simply put it, Stormy "was very brave, and she loves me."

EQUINE GUARDIANS

Jonathan Swift imagined an entire society run by intelligent horses (the Houyhnhnm) in *Gulliver's Travels*, and his satire wasn't so far off the mark. Horses are among the few social mammals that scientists believe clearly display self-awareness, empathy, and compassion. Horses show a remarkable sensitivity to human emotions, and an incredible gift for reading people, which was long ago demonstrated by the infamous Clever Hans (see page 295). But horses also show a proclivity to help people, such as in the stories of Molly (see page 154) and Betsy (see page 147).

Just to confirm how brave and protective horses can be, here are two more life-saving rescues:

- In August 2007, Scottish farmer Fiona Boyd went to lead a scared calf to a shed, only to have the calf's overprotective mother attack her. Perhaps misinterpreting Boyd's intentions, the cow charged, knocking Boyd to the ground, butted her again as she got up, and then fell on the farmer as if to crush her. Boyd curled into a ball and thought, "This is it. I'm going to die." Then her fifteen-year-old chestnut mare, Kerry, intervened. Kerry kicked at the cow and drove her away, giving the injured Boyd time to crawl under a fence to safety. "I am in no doubt Kerry saved me," Boyd said. "If she hadn't been in the same pasture, I really believe I would have been killed."

- During a town parade in Vivian, Louisiana, in March 2008, a pit bull broke loose and attacked a group of riders, who frantically dismounted to avoid being thrown by their rearing horses. As Chloe-Jeane Wendell jumped to the ground, the pit bull snarled and turned on the teenager. Chloe-Jeane's horse, Sunny Boy, started as if to run away, but then abruptly jumped in front of Chloe-Jeane, squared up, and kicked the dog with his hind hooves. Soon after, the dog was subdued. "I was shocked," said Chloe-Jeane about Sunny Boy. "Usually he avoids other animals."

KABANG THE ASPIN . . . STOPS A MOTORCYCLE

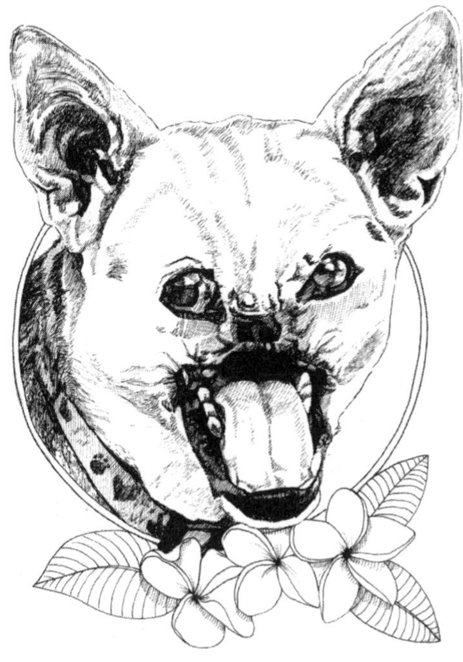

NAME: *Kabang*

SPECIES: *Aspin, mixed-breed Philippine street dog*

DATE: *December 14, 2011*

LOCATION: *Zamboanga City, Philippines*

SITUATION: *Two girls in the path of a motorcycle*

WHO WAS SAVED: *eleven-year-old Dina Bunggal and three-year-old Princess Diansing*

LEGACY: *The Philippines' most famous street dog, universally adored for unthinkable bravery*

This life-saving rescue provides a stunning example of selfless courage. And yet, what makes it a truly unique, awe-inspiring tale of cross-species compassion are the circumstances that made the rescue possible and the reaction that followed in its wake.

Let's start with the rescue itself, which occurred on December 14, 2011, in Zamboanga City in the Philippines.

LOOK BOTH WAYS BEFORE CROSSING THE STREET

Two girl cousins—eleven-year-old Dina Bunggal and three-year-old Princess Diansing—were walking on their own close to home. As the pair went to cross the busy Nuñez Extension, a divided four-lane city artery, they did not see a motorcycle bearing down on them. Just as the motorcycle was about to hit them, the Bunggal family dog, Kabang, emerged out of nowhere and jumped at the motorcycle, knocking it over just in time to keep it from slamming into the girls.

Dina and Princess both fell; they were bruised but unhurt. Likewise, the fallen motorcycle rider emerged unscathed. Kabang, however, struck the motorcycle's front wheel head-on, and as the bike rolled, the dog's snout and upper jaw got caught in the spokes and, to put it bluntly, were completely torn off.

Jovito Urpiano, a worker eating lunch nearby, witnessed the incident and said that Kabang jumped with such force that "I thought somebody threw the dog on the motorcycle." No one had, and Jovito felt certain that the dog acted intentionally to save the girls.

In his nearby workshop, Rudy Bunggal, Dina's father, also saw what happened and rushed to the scene. "The bones holding [Kabang's] upper snout were crushed," Rudy said, "and we could not do anything to save it. We just pulled her off the wheel."

Once freed, Kabang ran away and disappeared.

That Kabang was even around to save the girls was a puzzle. Rudy said Kabang didn't normally wander away from their home, and "we could not believe she went out when she sensed that the girls were in danger."

Afterward, no one could find Kabang. As the days turned into weeks, the Bunggals assumed that Kabang must have died. The top half of her face was gone. Surely, the blood loss alone would have been enough to kill her; no dog could survive such catastrophic injuries.

But after two weeks, Kabang unexpectedly reappeared. Her destroyed face was shocking. She had only a bottom jaw, and her wounds were infected and improperly healed. The Bunggals took Kabang to veterinarian Anton Lim, who treated her with antibiotics, but he couldn't close the surreal, gaping wound. City animal control officials suggested that Kabang be euthanized.

The Bunggals refused. "It does not matter if she's ugly now," Rudy said. "What is important to us is she saved our children, and we cannot thank her enough for that."

"Without her," Dina said, "maybe I will not be alive today." Her mother, Christina, simply called Kabang "a hero."

THE PLIGHT OF PHILIPPINE STREET DOGS

By all rights and Philippine custom, Kabang shouldn't have been alive to rescue anyone.

Rudy found her in a swamp when he was harvesting *kangkong*, or swamp cabbage. The weeks-old puppy—a black, tan, and white shepherd mix—had been abandoned and left to die. She was the type of mongrel that is scorned in the Philippines and disparagingly called an "askal," which is short for *asong kalye*, or "street dog," in Tagalog. Today, the more politically correct term is "aspin" (which is short for *asong pinoy* or "native dog"), and Rudy brought the puppy home to raise her for meat.

Eating *azucena*, or dog meat, is not unusual in impoverished Philippine communities, and the Bunggals were certainly poor. They lived in a shanty, where Rudy worked as a "vulcanizer" repairing punctured tires, and Christina sold candy. Together, their daily income was about $3.50.

"The dogs we raised did not last longer than three months," Rudy said. "It's our only way of eating meat. Life is difficult, and I have to feed my family."

The Bunggals named the dog Kabang (which means "spotted" in Visayan), fed her coffee creamer, and let her sleep with Dina and Princess, something none of their other dogs had been allowed to do. Kabang guarded their home; she would sit on Rudy's vulcanizing tools to prevent thefts. She only left the shanty to play with the children.

When three months came and went and Rudy still hadn't slaughtered the dog, Christina and even the neighbors were puzzled. Typically, everyone shared, and looked forward to, a little *azucena*. Instead, for reasons Rudy could not explain, Kabang's cheerful, devoted personality had softened his heart, and he lost the urge to kill the dog for meat.

One neighbor said, "Rudy became a different person when Kabang came. He became humane to animals."

As the aspin's status shifted from future meal to household companion, the Bunggals started feeding Kabang their own food, even precious milk. "We did not mind if she was an addition to our expenses," Christina said. "We regarded her as part of the family."

After Kabang saved Dina and Princess, the family absolutely venerated the one-year-old dog.

"I believe she was God's gift to us," Rudy said.

A "SUPERSTAR" WITH HALF A FACE

After Kabang's incredible rescue, word of her heroics spread across the Philippines, and people came to visit and have photos taken with her. Some people brought food, medicines, and vitamins for Kabang; others donated money and clothing to the family.

"She has become a superstar," Rudy said. "We are so thankful. We did not ask for those things, but still we are thankful."

The Bunggals would soon discover the true meaning of "superstar." In February 2012, a nurse in upstate New York, Karen Kenngott, was moved by Kabang's story and launched Care for Kabang, a social-media-fueled fundraising effort. Kabang herself was, as always, in good spirits—calm, happy, and despite the still-gaping wound, healthy enough to become pregnant—but she was unlikely to survive long without extremely expensive and perhaps unique surgeries.

Care for Kabang went viral, and by September 2012, it had met its goals, raising over $20,000 from over forty countries. Then, on October 8, accompanied by Philippine veterinarian Anton Lim, Kabang was flown to the state-of-the-art Davis William R. Pritchard Veterinary Medical Teaching Hospital at the University of California at Davis.

Complications arose immediately. US doctors discovered that Kabang had a golf ball-size tumor, which first needed to be treated with months of chemotherapy. Thus, amazingly, if not for her grisly condition, Kabang's cancer never would have been discovered, and she would have died anyway.

As Kabang regained her strength from the chemotherapy, doctors strategized what to do with her face. Some felt her condition was "beyond repair," and euthanasia remained the most humane option, but the Bunggals would not hear of it. So, to avoid long-term aftercare, the US vets decided against a face transplant or reconstruction. Instead, they would repair the wound using skin from the side and top of her head, remove two infected molars, reconstruct her left eyelid, and use stents to re-create two nostrils. Most of this was accomplished in one successful five-hour surgery in March 2013.

Afterward, one of the chief surgeons said, "She's not a pretty dog, but she is a happy dog."

Indeed, Kabang recovered successfully and was as joyful as ever. She could eat by grabbing food with her tongue, and she could even catch a ball using her lower jaw and her two remaining upper molars.

"I don't think it's an accident that she is alive," Dr. Lim said. "It all happened for a reason, and this opportunity is not being lost on us."

In other words, Kabang had more lives to save, and in June 2013, she was flown home to the Philippines.

THE "PRIDE OF ZAMBOANGA" RETURNS

The "Pride of Zamboanga," as the city's mayor called Kabang, received an official hero's welcome upon returning home. She rode in a pickup truck festooned with balloons as a motorcade threaded through the city. At the town hall, Kabang received an honorary ambassadorship to promote animal welfare and responsible pet ownership, and afterward, she joined other dogs and their owners for a big party in the park.

Ultimately, city officials hoped Kabang would help transform the reputation of aspins , encouraging their adoption and saving fellow Philippine street dogs from a long history of mistreatment and from occasionally becoming meals.

Yet Kabang's homecoming was also bittersweet. During Kabang's time in the United States, Christina and Rudy Bunggal separated; they cited their financial problems and Rudy's ongoing drinking. But now the world was watching, and everyone wanted to know: Who would care for Kabang, and under what conditions?

Rudy Bunggal still owned her. He said many people had offered to adopt Kabang, "but I said no. I told them Kabang will stay with us."

No one wanted Kabang returned to her previous shanty life. For city officials, this was one problem they could solve: They gave Rudy Bunggal a house—under one condition, the mayor said, "That he will take good care of Kabang."

Rudy felt as if he'd won the lottery, and Christina agreed to visit regularly with Dina and Princess.

Like a fairytale, Kabang transformed the life of the man who saved her and whose own unexpected act of altruism set off a chain of events too unlikely to pass as fiction. Afterward, the circle of compassion Kabang engendered encompassed much more than one heartrending moment of bravery. She moved people around the world and from all walks of life with her rare, indomitable spirit, just as she continues to challenge our assumptions of what courage, joy, and beauty look like.

PUDDING THE MAINE COON . . . PLAYS DOCTOR

NAME: *Pudding*

SPECIES: *Mixed-breed Maine coon cat*

DATE: *February 8, 2012*

LOCATION: *Sturgeon Bay, Wisconsin*

SITUATION: *Woman having a diabetic seizure*

WHO WAS SAVED: *Thirty-six-year-old Amy Jung*

LEGACY: *Rare cat to scent diabetes and become therapy animal, lauded for instant devotion*

On the afternoon of February 8, 2012, the aptly named Pudding—an impressive twenty-one pound, orange-and-white Maine coon mix—was lounging on the counter of the Door County Humane Society in Sturgeon Bay, Wisconsin. Amy Jung and her son, Ethan, walked in, hoping to visit and play with the cats, since the felines were allowed to roam free in the no-kill shelter.

What did Pudding see in the mother and son? Who knows, but the fat orange cat "owned me the minute our eyes met," Amy said.

Eight-year-old Pudding had been at the shelter about a month. He and Wimsy, his three-year-old feline buddy, were brought in after their previous owner died. Carrie Counihan, the shelter's executive director, knew Pudding well and said she noticed when the normally laidback feline connected so strongly with Amy, a stranger.

"He just gravitated to her," Counihan said.

Amy hadn't intended on taking home an animal, but she couldn't deny kismet. On the spot, Amy adopted Pudding, and what the heck—she adopted Wimsy, too, just so they wouldn't be separated.

Once at the Jung's home, Pudding surveyed the joint like he'd built it. "He just really took right over," Amy said. "Really second nature."

So far, so good. Just another feline Henry VIII.

THE DOCTOR IS IN

That night, around 9:30 pm, Amy put Ethan to bed and went to sleep herself. About an hour and a half later, she was dragged from unconsciousness. Pudding was camped on her chest, meowing, swatting her face, and even biting her nose.

Disoriented, Amy suddenly realized she was in the grip of a diabetic seizure, which caused her body to tremor and convulse. Amy had been diagnosed with diabetes as a child and recognized the symptoms.

Unable to get up, she cried out, "Ethan!" But her voice was too weak and Ethan remained asleep. As if recognizing what Amy wanted, Pudding ran to Ethan's room and jumped on his bed, waking him. Once Ethan realized his mother was in trouble, he phoned his father, who was out of town on a business trip, and his father guided him in injecting his mother's medication.

Ethan later said he wouldn't have woken up if it wasn't for the cat, and Amy is convinced she'd be dead without Pudding's intervention. Her doctor agreed.

"If something or someone hadn't pulled me out of that," Amy said, "I wouldn't be here."

Counihan said, "The fact that Pudding did what he did without knowing [Amy] that well is just amazing to me."

A REGULARLY SCHEDULED CHECK-UP

Pudding's behavior was remarkable on several levels.

As with the rabbit Dory (see page 34), Pudding reacted to the drop in Amy's glucose levels, which emits a specific odor cats can detect. In this case, the real question is, was Pudding's behavior also a deliberate attempt to help? Was he trying to wake Amy up because he recognized the change in her metabolism as a life-threatening problem?

"I don't think we can know that he meant to save her life," scientist Marc Bekoff said. As with dogs who detect diabetes, "the odor makes them uneasy and inspires some kind of soliciting behavior or care-giving response, but is it running through their head that there's a medical problem? I don't think so."

Bekoff compares the situation to the "alarm pheromones" that are released when some animals and insects are attacked; this pheromone elicits specific fight-or-flight behavior in others of the same species. Nevertheless, we don't know for sure what is triggering or motivating the animal's behavior. "I don't know if anybody has ever done these studies," Bekoff said. "It would be lovely to know."

On the other hand, bolstering the impression that in some way Pudding meant to help is the fact that in the middle of the episode he left Amy to wake up Ethan. Amy said she was amazed that "somehow Pudding learned Ethan's name within hours of coming home." Of course, Pudding may not have learned Ethan's name, but as with Inky (see page 68), he may still have understood Amy's meaning: I need the other human in the house.

Even more amazing, in the weeks that followed, Pudding continued to alert Amy about her diabetes. Whenever her blood sugar level dropped, he would meow and plant his great royal self at her feet until she remedied the imbalance.

Eventually, Amy's doctor told her, "Realistically, you can't be without him." Not long after, Amy registered Pudding as a therapy animal so the cat could legally accompany her.

By all accounts, Pudding reverts to his lord-of-the-castle ways when he isn't playing doctor. But with his alert and seemingly caring devotion, he's in danger of ruining the haughty reputation of felines everywhere.

LILLY THE PIT BULL . . . CONFRONTS A FREIGHT TRAIN

NAME: *Lilly*

SPECIES: *Pit bull*

DATE: *May 3, 2012*

LOCATION: *Shirley, Massachusetts*

SITUATION: *Unconscious woman in the path of an oncoming train*

WHO WAS SAVED: *Fifty-six-year-old Christine Spain*

LEGACY: *Paragon of the pit bull breed, ambassador for canine altruism and devotion*

In 2009, Boston police officer David Lanteigne adopted Lilly, a mahogany-brown pit bull with marigold-colored eyes, and gave her to his mother, Christine Spain. All her adult life, Christine had struggled with alcoholism, and David thought that the pit bull might act as a therapy dog. Caring for an animal might help Christine overcome her depression and anxiety, which was critical to helping her stay sober.

David could never have imagined how important this canine gift would be.

From day one, Christine embraced Lilly and smothered her with love and attention. "For the past three and a half years," David said, "it's her entire life. She's been eating, sleeping, and breathing this dog. The dog is everything to her. She brings her on five or six long walks a day."

Lilly "keeps her thinking well," David said, and so "Lilly has played a crucial role in helping my mom drastically reduce her drinking."

OFF THE RAILS

Unfortunately, May 2, 2012, was not one of Christine's good days. She drank heavily that evening, and just after midnight on May 3, while walking home from her boyfriend's house with Lilly, Christine passed out and fell across the railroad tracks that run through Shirley, Massachusetts.

How long she lay like this, we don't know. Yet the rumble of an oncoming freight train surely must have spurred Lilly to action. In the locomotive's headlight, the train's engineer saw the pit bull struggling to pull the unconscious woman off the tracks. He threw the emergency brake and, to his amazement, watched as the dog ran around to the front as if positioning herself to protect Christine from the impact.

Unable to stop in time, the train struck the animal, while Christine, pulled clear and perhaps shielded by her dog, was unharmed.

Unsure exactly who had been hit or how badly, the engineer immediately called emergency services. Within minutes, in a cacophony of sirens, pulsating lights, and frantic shouts, emergency personnel ran up to find Lilly stoically resting her head on the chest of the still-unconscious Christine. The pit bull was bleeding profusely from catastrophic injuries, including a fractured pelvis and a horrifically crushed right front paw.

"She saved my mom's life," David said. "We rescued her, and she made almost the ultimate sacrifice returning the favor."

Lilly was rushed to the MSPCA Angell Animal Medical Center in Boston, where a veterinary team evaluated her condition. In the days that followed, Lilly had several surgeries. Her right front leg was too damaged to repair, so the entire limb was amputated, and steel plates were inserted to support her pelvis.

Slowly, as Lilly recovered, the next chapter of her life began.

INTO THE FIRE

As many stories in Part One show, when humans and their companion animals face a mortal danger together, the animal will sometimes risk his or her own safety to save the human. In these situations, despite the animal's primal urge to flee, love and loyalty are stronger.

House fires are another common situation, and stories of dogs who brave flames to save family members appear regularly. Here is one about a brave pit bull like Lilly:

In February 2013, in Wellston, Oklahoma, a fire broke out at night in the home of sisters Rhonda and Evelyn Westenberger. The women were asleep, and their ten-year-old pit bull terrier, Baby, barked and jumped on them to wake them up. As flames filled the hallway, the sisters and Baby escaped.

However, their five other dogs remained inside, trapped and too scared to come out. So Baby went back inside and drove them out, all except one, whom Baby grabbed by the neck and dragged to safety.

The Westenberger's home was destroyed, but everyone escaped, and the family felt only gratitude. Of Baby, Rhonda said, "I'm so proud of her. She's my hero. She's the hero for all of us."

REHABILITATING THE REPUTATION OF PIT BULLS

To help fund Lilly's costly medical treatments and her long-term physical rehabilitation, David started a charitable fundraising effort. News accounts spread the word of Lilly's courageous actions—for which she received the MSPCA's 2012 Animal Hero Award—and donations and good wishes poured in from around the world. Lilly's medical bills quickly topped $15,000, but generous public donations reached $76,000. David donated the extra money to the MSPCA's pet assistance fund.

Then, David decided that Lilly's story—not just her selfless bravery but her work as a therapy animal—might help transform the public's perception of pit bulls as inherently dangerous, violent, and unsafe.

"They are the most affectionate, loving, caring dogs that you'll ever meet," David said.

Jean Weber, the MSPCA's director of animal protection, said, "I hope her actions will underscore the truth about pit bulls—that they are amazing animals and are as devoted to their family as any other dog."

Since then, Lilly has become a three-legged ambassador for her breed, appearing at fundraisers and charity events, and Lilly's Fund, the organization David started, works to promote the adoption of pit bulls who still remain in shelters.

Meanwhile, Lilly remains loyally devoted to Christine—two wounded souls for whom the welfare of the other is the priority of their existence.

CZARUE THE STRAY . . . KEEPS A LOST GIRL WARM

NAME: *Czarue*

SPECIES: *Mixed-breed dog*

DATE: *March 1, 2013*

LOCATION: *Pierzwin, Poland*

SITUATION: *Lost toddler in a freezing marsh*

WHO WAS SAVED: *Three-year-old Julia*

LEGACY: *Local hero for the life-saving companionship dogs display every day*

The devoted companionship of dogs is often described as "life-saving" in itself. That may be an exaggeration, but it emphasizes how important we find their mere presence. Our canine companions seek us out for physical affection—for tummy rubs, scratches behind the ear, and warm laps to sleep in. In turn, we treasure their warm bodies next to ours, the licks to our hands and faces, the foreheads boring into our calves and cheeks.

For social animals, companionship is a necessity. We wither without it. As recent scientific research has made clear, all animals benefit from the biology of touch (see page 159). These good feelings give us the strength to keep going in rough times, and occasionally, a dog's body heat provides a live-giving fire on nights too cold to survive on our own.

This rescue story is no more complicated than that.

LOST IN THE WOODS

In Pierzwin, a small town in western Poland, three-year-old Julia's best friend was Czarue, a muscular, coal-black village mongrel. No one owned Czarue, but Julia always sought him out and spent all her time with him. Danuta Balak, Julia's grandmother, said the girl would beg, "Granny, the dog needs to come in the house." Then Julia would feed Czarue the bread that her grandmother had cut for her.

One Friday afternoon, on March 1, 2013, Julia went outside to play with Czarue, a sight so common no one remarked on it. This time, however, she and the dog wandered too far into the surrounding marshes and forest, and Julia became lost. She kept walking and walking, with Czarue by her side, till night fell and she couldn't see where she was going.

About four miles from home, Julia stopped, too tired to continue and too far away for anyone to hear her call out. Julia had no food or water; she was without a coat and wet from the damp earth. As the temperature dropped to around 23 degrees Fahrenheit, she hugged Czarue for warmth and comfort. All she had was the dog. Exhausted, frightened, and freezing, Julia fell asleep with Czarue in her arms.

Meanwhile, Julia's parents had raised the alarm, and a two-hundred-person search party was organized, including search dogs and a police helicopter.

All night they scoured the damp, dark woods near town without success. Then, several hours after dawn, just before 8 am, firefighters heard a dog barking, and soon after, a girl's voice crying for her mother.

"We went in the direction and saw the child lying in the shrubs," said firefighter Grzegorz Szymonowski. "She was wet because there was water in the forest."

Szymonowski added, "For the whole night the animal was with the girl. It never left her. It is thanks to this dog that the girl survived the night."

At the hospital, Julia was treated for shock, swollen hands and feet, and light symptoms of frostbite. But without the companionship of a stray mutt too devoted to leave her side, it could have been much worse.

A DOGGIE BLANKET

Perhaps the only rescue story more common than dogs fighting off snakes (see page 60) is dogs keeping lost or injured people warm (and alive) when they are trapped outdoors on freezing nights. This act doesn't reveal anything new that we don't already know about dogs, who frequently display their willingness to comfort humans in distress.

It bears noting, though, that in most situations dogs don't need any help surviving a winter night outdoors. With their sometimes thick fur and normal body temperature of around 101 degrees Fahrenheit, they usually do fine on their own. It's *we* who need *them*, and dogs frequently huddle next to us even when they could easily leave and roam free.

Here are a few more stories:

- ☆ In October 2002, in the countryside outside Melbourne, Australia, seventy-eight-year-old dairy farmer Noel Osborne was knocked down by a cow in the farmyard and broke his hip. Unable to move, he survived the cold and storms over five nights because of two animals, both named Mandy: His border collie, who slept with him each night and brought gifts of old bones, and his goat, who apparently let the farmer milk her for three days.
- ☆ In February 2007, on Oregon's Mount Hood, three mountain climbers and a mixed-breed black labrador named Velvet fell into an un-

seen canyon during an unexpected blizzard. One person was seriously injured, and their gear was scattered, so they created a makeshift shelter out of two sleeping bags and a tarp. All night, as they huddled under the intense storm, Velvet moved from person to person, keeping each climber warm in turn. After they were rescued the next day, Matt Bryant said, "Thanks to Velvet, none of us was suffering from hypothermia or frostbite."

- In February 2010, outside Prescott, Arizona, three-year-old Victoria Bensch was saved by the family's Queensland heeler, Blue, who stayed with the girl during a freezing night after she became lost in the rocky, brush-covered countryside outside their home. When rescue teams arrived the next morning, Blue first moved to protect Victoria; then, when Blue realized the rescuers meant to help, he excitedly jumped into the helicopter with her.

- In April 2013, on his property outside Rylstone, Australia, seventy-six-year-old Herbert Schutz crashed his car, which rolled and trapped him beneath it. Despite a skull fracture and two broken hips, he remained conscious and alive because of the steadfast companionship of his loyal kelpie, Boydy, who stayed glued to his owner over three frigid nights.

LASSIE, GET HELP! LIFE-SAVING ANIMALS IN POP CULTURE

Grab a bag of popcorn, and snuggle in a cozy chair. Here is a short list of famous books, movies, TV shows, and characters that define our pop culture image of life-saving animals.

ST. BERNARD WITH A BARREL

In the 1810s, the public was gripped by the tale of a red-haired St. Bernard named Barry who single-handedly saved a boy buried in an avalanche in the Swiss Alps. Gauzy, romanticized depictions of the rescue, in which the boy clings to the back of the burly dog, soon adorned postcards and products of all kinds. Perhaps because they thought it looked dramatic, one artist added a barrel of liquor beneath the dog's chin—though the last thing someone with hypothermia needs is alcohol!

Barry was real (see page 262), but this particular life-saving rescue was a writer's fantasy. Nothing can stop a good story, though, and the world's first canine superhero was born.

In modern times, the iconic St. Bernard has undergone a few makeovers. Looney-Tunes cartoons in the 1960s had a field day mocking the inherent ridiculousness of a St. Bernard lugging a keg to a rescue: In "Pike's Peak," a St. Bernard saves Yosemite Sam and then mixes *himself* a martini. In 1981, Stephen King transformed the life-saving St. Bernard into a rabid killing machine in *Cujo*, perhaps the scariest fictional dog ever. Then the pop culture pendulum over swung in the opposite direction: In the 1992 movie *Beethoven,* the titular hero is a slobbering dopus in constant need of rescue himself. Poor Barry!

MOWGLI & *THE JUNGLE BOOK*

In 1894, Rudyard Kipling published a collection of "Just So" stories called *The Jungle Book*. By far the most famous tales involved a feral Indian boy who gets adopted by wolves and learns the ways of the jungle. Raksha is the she-wolf who first saves the child, protects him from the evil tiger Shere Khan, and gives him his name, Mowgli, which means "frog" in wolf. Mowgli then becomes a pupil of Baloo the bear and a friend to the black panther Bagheera.

Kipling was inspired by a long Indian tradition of wolf-child legends in which stolen or abandoned children were supposedly saved by merciful wolf packs (see page 277). But what really cemented the legend of Mowgli and his jungle friends was the 1967 animated Disney movie, which taught a generation of kids about the "bare necessities of life"—aka, jungle hijinks and parentless adventures while dressed in a loincloth. Of the many modern adaptions, one of the best is the 1989 Japanese anime *Jungle Book Shonen Mowgli*.

RIKKI-TIKKI-TAVI

Rikki-Tikki-Tavi is another famous life-saving animal first brought to life in Rudyard Kipling's 1894 story collection *The Jungle Book*. Rikki-Tikki-Tavi is a mongoose who gets adopted by a British family in India; they hope Rikki will protect them from venomous snakes. Sure enough, two black cobras, Nag and Nagaina, resent the British family and try to do them in, but the mongoose thwarts the snakes and, in epic one-on-one battles, kills them both.

Here again, Kipling reimagined a well-known bit of folklore: the "faithful hound" story, whose most famous version is Gelert the wolfhound (see page 254). In these, a faithful animal saves a child from being killed, but is mistaken as the killer and is tragically put to death. Thankfully, Rikki doesn't suffer this fate and lives. In 1975, the animated movie *Rikki-Tikki-Tavi* by Chuck Jones made us all believers in the essential goodness of the mongoose.

TARZAN, LORD OF THE JUNGLE

In 1912, Edgar Rice Burroughs published the first serialized stories about Tarzan, and in 1914 he published the first book. Then Burroughs went on to write twenty-five novelized sequels, and over the next century, Tarzan was featured in about a hundred films, along with countless radio shows, comic books, TV programs, and even a stage musical.

A better epithet would be Tarzan, Lord of Pop Culture!

Ah-aaaaaa-ahahahaahh!

Tarzan's real name is John Clayton. His parents, a British lord and lady, were killed, orphaning young John in the jungle, where he was adopted by a tribe of great apes. The she-ape Kala first protects John from the brutal ape leader, Kerchak, and even from her own mate, Tublat, and she gives him his ape name, Tarzan. Sound a little familiar? Kipling readers thought so, too, and all his life Burroughs refuted charges that he'd stolen his premise from the Mowgli stories.

After being raised by apes, Tarzan's signature move, beyond becoming super strong, is to reject civilization, choosing to spend his adult life with his ape buddies—because, of course, nature is much more noble and pure than those overeducated Europeans. Eventually, Tarzan meets Jane, they have kids, and the whole thing becomes very *Father Knows Best*, only with more vine-swinging and furry fisticuffs.

RIN TIN TIN

Rin Tin Tin was a real dog who was rescued by an American soldier on a WWI battlefield in 1918. After the war, Rin Tin Tin came to America, moved to Hollywood, and got bit by the acting bug. Soon, he became the world's most famous German shepherd: not because he was a life-saving dog, but because he played one in the movies.

Rin Tin Tin's first movie was *Where the North Begins* in 1923. With that film, Rin Tin Tin saved not a person but a movie studio: Warner Bros. was on the verge of collapse, but Rin Tin Tin's movies became so popular that the studio grew into a powerhouse. Rin Tin Tin appeared in twenty-seven films all told, and he was such a beloved star that, as legend has it, he actually received the most votes for Best Actor in the 1929 Academy Awards. Academy officials, however, forced a recount so a human would win.

Rin Tin Tin died in 1932, but his name lives on. Today, Rin Tin Tin XII stands alert on his marks and ready for . . . "Action!"

LASSIE

Lassie is a fictional collie whose life-saving adventures were featured in seven films from 1943 to 1951. However, the character is defined by the American TV show that ran from 1954 to 1973, the fourth longest-running TV series in US history.

Week after week, this boy-and-his-dog adventure followed the same formula: A young boy (often seven-year-old Timmy Martin) does something he shouldn't and falls into some kind of trouble—like, into an abandoned mine, quicksand, swift rivers, deep lakes, and over cliffs. Only Lassie can save him, and she does, barking to get help as necessary. Timmy, meanwhile, learns a darn good lesson about following the rules.

Lassie got a star on the Hollywood Walk of Fame in 1960. She's also immortalized in the classic joke: "Hey, there's Lassie!" *Bark bark bark bark bark.* "What!? Timmy fell into the well! Let's go!"

The irony? A well is the only place Timmy never actually fell.

OLD YELLER

Old Yeller is a Baby Boomer touchstone, a defining moment of many a 1960s childhood. A 1956 novel by Fred Gipson that became a 1957 Disney movie, *Old Yeller* is about a mongrel dog who is adopted by a young boy, Travis, in the 1860s. Old Yeller saves his adopted family from a bear, feral boars, and eventually a rabid wolf, who infects the beloved dog with the disease. Soon, Old Yeller gets sick, and dangerous, and a grieving Travis has no choice but to put down his very best friend . . . Anybody got a tissue?

FLIPPER

You can hear the TV writer's pitch already: What if we remade *Lassie* . . . with a dolphin? Brilliant, right?

Yes, yes it is. From 1964 to 1967, *Flipper* was an American TV show about a fictional bottlenose dolphin who befriends a marine preserve warden and his two sons in Florida. Flipper helps rescue other animals, capture criminals, and save the two boys whenever they get into inevitable tight spots: "What, Flipper? Poachers are killing crocs in the lagoon! Let's go!"

SKIPPY

Skippy the Bush Kangaroo was an Australian TV show from 1966 to 1968, and it's basically just *Lassie* and *Flipper* with an Australian accent. This time, the fictional hero is a bouncing, kicking, crime-fighting, piano-playing, life-saving marsupial.

Skippy was made into a 1969 movie and revived with a new cast in 1992. The show follows the remarkable adventures of a wild, female, eastern grey kangaroo, who befriends Sonny Hammond, the son of a national park ranger. Does Skippy always arrive just in the nick of time to king hit the blokes stealing all the joeys and keep Sonny out of danger? What do you think, mate?

PART TWO

TRAINED TO SERVE, INSPIRED TO HEAL

Many animals, especially dogs, are trained to serve in ways that improve our quality of life. In some capacities, saving lives is part of the job description, such as with police K-9s, bomb-detection dogs, and medical detection dogs. Animals used in therapy also save lives, even if the impact may be less direct. They may provide someone with a reason for living and inspire the person to heal themselves. It would be reasonable to ask, Why do animals do this?

"The skeptic would argue that the animals used in therapy have been trained through reinforcement and rewards for their roles," writes journalist and science writer Eugene Linden. "But . . . there is a world of difference between the rote performance of a task and cooperation energized by an emotional involvement."

Service animals are highly trained, but the emotional involvement of the animals in these stories is evident. Some seem almost "called" to service and are inspired to heal and to help in ways that go far beyond their training. In fact, they display such remarkable generosity and compassion that we might suspect that the real reward is the human-animal bond their devotion inspires.

FONZIE THE DOLPHIN . . . MAKES A BOY LAUGH

NAME: *Fonzie*

SPECIES: *Atlantic bottlenose dolphin*

DATE: *1990 to 2004*

LOCATION: *Key Largo, Florida*

SITUATION: *Child partially paralyzed and disabled by a stroke*

WHO WAS SAVED: *Three-year-old Joe Hoagland*

LEGACY: *First cetacean to demonstrate life-changing benefits of dolphin-assisted therapy*

Joe Hoagland was born in 1986 with a rare congenital heart defect that required two open-heart surgeries by the time he was eleven months old. Despite this rocky start, he was a "delightful, normal two-year-old boy," said Deena Hoagland, Joe's mother. But when Joe was three, he required a third open-heart surgery, during which he suffered a stroke.

Joe was in a coma for eight days, and afterward, when he awoke, the right half of his brain was severely damaged and his left side was paralyzed. "He was less than a newborn," said Deena. "He didn't have a swallow response. He couldn't talk. He couldn't cry."

Nor could Joe stand, hold up his head, move his left arm, or see out of his left eye. Doctors were doubtful that Joe would ever recover. They said he'd likely remain in a wheelchair and need constant assistance his entire life.

"This was the worst possible thing, next to death, that could have possibly happened," said Peter Hoagland, Joe's father.

A SPLASH IN THE FACE

The Hoaglands had recently moved to Key Largo, Florida, and during the six weeks after Joe's stroke, Deena searched for a public pool where they could swim. Despondent and traumatized, Joe was not responding to traditional speech and physical therapy. Deena thought that being in the water, which Joe loved, might lift his spirits.

Yet she couldn't find any local public pools, and area hotel pools didn't want them. Increasingly desperate, Deena contacted Dolphins Plus, a dolphin research center that had a program of public dolphin swims in their own protected lagoon. Initially, Dolphins Plus also turned Deena away, but she persisted, and when owner Lloyd Borguss finally said okay, she hung up and went over that moment.

When Deena and Joe arrived, it was time for the afternoon feeding, so they joined the staff on the low dock to watch. The dozen or so dolphins were excitement personified; they leapt and chattered and caught fish in midair. Then one eighteen-year-old—a 600-pound male—buzzed through the party and stopped at the edge of the dock, eyeballing Joe in his mother's lap.

"That's Fonzie," said Borguss. "He likes to make trouble."

Fonzie made a lap of the lagoon and came back to stare fixedly at Joe, as if curious. Fonzie did this again, and again, and then with a playful flick of his powerful tale, Fonzie splashed Joe.

As Deena wiped seawater from her son's eyes, Joe smiled and giggled.

"I was beside myself with joy," said Deena. "I cried. I was overwhelmed at that moment because I had not heard that giggle for a long time. And this dolphin, it appeared to me that he pushed all the others away as if to say, this kid is mine. It was just a magical moment."

After that, Deena and Joe returned every day. Though it defied explanation, the dolphin and the boy shared some kind of instant, unspoken bond. Each day the scene repeated; as one resident marine biologist said, "Fonzie would rush to the dock as soon as Joe came down, and he'd push the other dolphins out of the way."

After a few weeks, the Dolphins Plus trainers urged Joe to get into the water with Fonzie. Joe was eager, but Deena was too nervous. Finally, in mid-September 1990, Deena agreed so long as Joe wore a life jacket, and the experience transformed not only Joe's life but that of his parents and of many children like him.

FONZIE THE LEFT-HANDED DOLPHIN

For a few years prior to this, Dolphins Plus had been experimenting with the idea of dolphin-assisted therapy (DAT). They had no formal program, just some intriguing observations.

Betsy Smith, a Dolphins Plus researcher, said at the time, "As soon as I put a handicapped child in the water, the dolphin relaxes, becomes very different, very quiet and calm, and will stay with and work with that child for as long as it takes."

This is what happened with Joe Hoagland. Lloyd Borguss said, "Joe was really our first full-time case. He was literally an experiment in progress."

In the water, Fonzie sensed that Joe's left side was immobile, useless. Fonzie nuzzled Joe's left leg gently, as if moving it for him, and the dolphin also liked to approach Joe from below and rub against his whole body, which made Joe laugh. Always, Fonzie modulated his tremendous strength to the limits of a partially paralyzed, forty-pound boy.

"Then Fonzie would present his dorsal fin for Joe to hold on to and he'd pull him around the pen," Deena said. "Joe would bob along in his little life vest, grinning from ear to ear."

Most of all, the joyful, trusting relationship they developed gave Joe the motivation to do the physical therapy necessary to rehabilitate himself. Joe would "do anything" to play with the dolphin, Deena said, "so I created left-hand Fonzie. I told Joe that Fonzie was a left-handed dolphin, so if he tried to feed him with his right hand or tried to throw a ball with his right hand, then Fonzie wouldn't play with him."

After that, Joe worked at his left hand night and day, all so he could hold a fish for Fonzie. He worked so hard that his parents once found him trying to clench his limp hand in his sleep as he talked to himself: "Open, shut them. Just keep trying, and you'll get it."

"His doctors had given us a long list of 'nevers,'" Deena said, but over the following months, Joe overcame almost every one. Sometimes with help and always with difficulty, Joe learned to move his left leg enough to swim independently, to throw a ball overhead with both hands, to hold a hoop for Fonzie to jump through, and to hold a fish—always using his left hand. With each breakthrough, Joe's confidence and determination soared.

At the end of a year, Joe's recovery had reached the point where he could walk down to the dock by himself carrying a bucketful of fish for Fonzie. Though his full recovery would take years, Joe's dramatic transformation stunned everyone.

"I like to say what happened to my son may not be a miracle," Deena said, "but it certainly seems miraculous."

FUN WITH DOLPHINS, GUARANTEED

Joe continued to work with Fonzie for the rest of the dolphin's life. When he was fourteen, Joe said, "Fonzie and I are so close, we are like brothers. Fonzie understands things about me that other kids can't. He knows that I'm different and he doesn't care—he really likes me the way I am. Whenever he sees me, he gets excited because he recognizes me."

What is it that happened between Joe and Fonzie? Marine biologist Chris Blankenship called it "emotional therapy." Still, Blankenship admitted that "there's an aspect to dolphins that no one yet understands."

Beyond the motivation to heal himself, Joe said, "What the dolphins have given me is just more faith in myself and a sense of belonging. I know I can just jump in the water, and they'll accept me."

It's hard to say what the dolphins know and intend, but they are active, not passive, participants. Like Fonzie, certain exceptional dolphins will sometimes seek out and focus on disabled, autistic, or injured swimmers. This may begin as simple curiosity, but if it's allowed to, this fascination can develop into a deeper, more profound relationship, one characterized by mutual caring, trust, and devotion. As with therapy dogs, the loving attention people experience in this human-animal relationship is healing in itself. Joy inspires breakthroughs and provides a focus and purpose for getting better. In fact, as Joe alluded, the nonverbal communication people experience with dolphins may be what allows it to strike the heart so directly.

Whatever the case, as dolphin-assisted therapy worked near-miracles for her son, Deena Hoagland became determined to share it with others. In 1997, she and her husband, Peter, founded Island Dolphin Care at the Dolphins Plus center. Deena was a trained therapist herself, and the Hoaglands developed multiday dolphin programs for kids with a variety of special needs, including autism, cancer, cerebral palsy, cystic fibrosis, depression, developmental delays, heart disease, and others.

Island Dolphin Care continues its work today, and the only thing the program guarantees is fun, since there is a mystery at work that can't be quantified in specific criteria. Yet participants regularly report children achieving many "milestones" as a result: the first word spoken, the first sentence, new motor skills, the first laugh.

Naturally, as Joe grew up, he also came to work for Island Dolphin Care. Fonzie died in 2004, but other dolphins like Squirt, Sarah, Bella, and Fiji continue to do for others what Fonzie did for Joe.

"When you come close to these animals," Deena said, "you know you are close to something amazing. Something extraordinary. When they come up close to you, and look at you, it takes my breath away."

DAKOTA THE GOLDEN RETRIEVER ... PREDICTS HEART ATTACKS

NAME: *Dakota*

SPECIES: *Golden retriever*

DATE: *1995 to 2001*

LOCATION: *Texas*

SITUATION: *Man suffering unstable angina and depression*

WHO WAS SAVED: *Fifty-four-year-old Mike Lingenfelter*

LEGACY: *First dog to detect heart attacks, internationally renowned, won numerous awards*

The last thing Mike Lingenfelter wanted was a therapy dog.

He said that when doctors first suggested he get one, "I laughed, 'You gotta be kidding,' I told them. 'There's no way.'"

In 1992, Mike had had two heart attacks only a week apart, which required open-heart surgery. Afterward, the heart damage this caused led him to suffer unstable angina—extremely painful, unpredictable episodes when the blood to the heart is temporarily restricted. The angina attacks "felt as if my chest was being squeezed in a vise," he said.

Mike had to quit his job as a public transit engineer, and over the next two years, he became depressed and suicidal. He knew he was making life miserable for his wife, Nancy, but that only increased his desire to be gone.

"I was fifty-four years old," Mike said, "and I felt like my life was over. I was sitting around waiting to die."

BAD HEARTS AND SECOND CHANCES

His doctors kept insisting: A therapy dog would provide comfort and give him something to focus on besides himself. After all, caring for another is excellent medicine.

Angry at the world, Mike stubbornly refused.

Then, in 1994, his doctors threatened to hospitalize Mike if he didn't get a therapy dog, so he relented. Local connections hooked Mike up with a rescued golden retriever named Dakota, who had only failed service dog training because of heartworm disease and an old hip injury.

Dakota didn't make a good first impression. On the first night, "he'd pick things up, haul them around," Mike said. "You know, all retriever. The next morning I was ready to take him back."

Dakota had a favorite toy, a stuffed green frog, which he kept offering to Mike over and over, insisting that he take it. Mike told Nancy, "This is the most obnoxious animal I've ever been around."

Nancy wasn't having it. "He's just like you," she retorted. Both of them had bad hearts and were getting second chances.

That got to Mike. When he took Dakota for a morning walk, he saw the animal with new eyes. Dakota had an intelligent, inviting face; there was, Mike had to admit, something special about him. By walk's end, Mike's resistance had melted, and he agreed to keep Dakota.

ONE ALERT CANINE

As it turned out, the doctors were right. Within weeks, Mike was, in his own words, "too busy tending to Dakota to spend any time feeling sorry for myself or thinking about suicide."

Within six months, he no longer needed his anxiety medication, and he'd become a true believer in animal-assisted therapy—so much so that in spring 1995, Mike decided to share Dakota. They visited hospitals and care centers, where Dakota would interact with sick kids and the elderly.

A little more than a year later, in fall 1996, Mike was giving a school presentation on therapy dogs, when Dakota began acting funny. He pawed and nosed at Mike as if he wanted something. Mike took Dakota into the hallway and was immediately laid low by an angina attack.

Mike had at least one to two attacks a week, and by then Dakota had seen hundreds of episodes. Mike wondered, had Dakota's odd behavior signaled this one? He didn't believe it. But sure enough, the next time one occurred, Dakota did the same thing, performing the classic signaling of a seizure-alert dog.

From that moment on, Dakota alerted Mike every single time an angina attack was imminent, usually two to five minutes ahead. This allowed Mike to find a safe place to lie down and take preventive medication that eased the symptoms. Further, Dakota soon joined Mike during the episodes, providing him physical comfort.

"I just plain hold on to him until the pain passes," Mike said. "He has taught me to pick up his breathing rate to prevent me from hyperventilating when the pain is beyond my ability to tolerate."

Dakota was the first dog to demonstrate the ability to recognize heart problems.

"No one taught Dakota this behavior—he learned it himself," Mike said. "And I, of course, had no idea that he could ever do such a thing."

Mike registered Dakota as an official service dog, allowing Dakota to accompany Mike everywhere he went.

SAVING MORE LIVES

No one knows exactly what a dog senses prior to a seizure or heart attack. The animal may smell a chemical change or enzyme or notice a subtle physical tremor. Yet dogs who have this ability can now be trained to signal or "alert" when an attack is coming.

It was Dakota who eventually put two and two together and decided to intervene with Mike. Once, the furry, auburn-haired guardian even woke up Mike and Nancy when Mike was having a full-blown heart attack in his sleep. If Dakota hadn't, Mike surely would have died.

With Dakota next to him, Mike was able to return to work. He became an engineer for DART, the Dallas Area Rapid Transit, and Dakota soon expanded his life-saving efforts. In 1999, on three separate occasions, Dakota signaled on three of Mike's coworkers. Though none had had previous heart issues, all three knew and trusted Dakota, and they immediately contacted their doctors. Each found they had unknown but critical heart problems, two of which required immediate surgery.

In his book *The Angel by My Side,* Mike also tells the story of a very different type of intervention. That year, when Mike was on a business trip, Dakota also alerted on a stranger, a young man who casually dismissed the dog's legendary nose. However, Mike learned afterward that only days later the young man committed suicide.

"Maybe it wasn't physical," Mike said, "but his heart was definitely in some serious trouble."

FAME, ADVOCACY, AND ILLNESS

In 1999, Dakota won the Delta Society's Service Dog of the Year award, and as the media learned of Dakota's remarkable ability to predict heart attacks, his story and fame spread across the country. People were amazed and disbelieving in equal measure.

In the meantime, Mike was also becoming an advocate for service dogs. In the late 1990s, restaurants and stores were often still unaware of the 1990 Americans with Disabilities Act, which enshrined access for service animals as a legal right. They were also sometimes skeptical of Mike's "invisible disability," and they refused to let him enter with Dakota. Rather than suffer quietly, Mike educated those he met, gladly letting them call the police if necessary, since the police knew the law. Dakota's service vest was his uniform, and it alone was all the proof Mike needed to show that Dakota was a medically necessary companion.

Then, in 2000, at the height of his celebrity, Dakota was diagnosed with lymphoma. In most cases, this would have been a death sentence, but Dakota was a rare individual. After getting state-of-the-art treatment, he miraculously recovered, becoming cancer-free.

Mike's joy, however, was short-lived. In 2001, Dakota developed a debilitating lung illness that he could not overcome, and he died that summer. But Dakota lived long enough to help train his successor, another golden retriever named Ogilvie—who with no other teacher but Dakota learned to signal Mike's impending angina attacks as well, but with far less accuracy and consistency.

Mike still has a hard time believing what Dakota was capable of and the love he displayed. He once said, "I never thought angels came with brown eyes and a furry tail, but this one did."

ARE ANIMALS PSYCHIC?

Companion animals sometimes display an uncanny sixth sense, as if they know things they shouldn't know. The cat mysteriously hides when it's time for the vet. A lost pet returns home across a thousand unfamiliar miles. A dog, like Dakota or Cheyenne (see pages 114 and 141), senses someone's intention to commit suicide and intervenes. A sense of smell doesn't explain everything, so what's going on?

Researcher and biologist Rupert Sheldrake wrote about this issue in *Dogs That Know When Their Owners Are Coming Home*. In it, he examines "three major categories of unexplained perceptiveness in animals: telepathy, the sense of direction, and premonitions." Sometimes lumped together as "extrasensory perception," or ESP, Sheldrake proposes these abilities are possible because of "morphic fields," which are like invisible connections that social animals use to bond to their primary group. Because of these connections, a dog might know at a distance—without any sensory information or clues from routine—that their owner is coming home.

Traditional, mainstream scientists typically say that a "psychic" or supernatural explanation is no explanation at all. Sheldrake's ideas are controversial. But even if his theories are wrong, he identifies animal behaviors that continue to defy conventional explanation.

For some, the explanation isn't psychic but spiritual. They feel that companion animals, particularly dogs, have divine gifts to heal us. The Illinois-based Lutheran Church Charities believes that dogs intuitively express God's love, and so they created their famous Comfort Dog Ministry, which brings trained therapy dogs to visit the bereaved after major tragedies, like the 2013 Boston Marathon bombing.

Mike Lingenfelter called Dakota an angel, and he didn't mean metaphorically. Before Dakota, Mike would never have accepted that idea, but after his experiences he wrote: "There are powers at work here in our universe that we can never comprehend. I don't understand, but I believe . . . because I've seen it all."

ENDAL THE LABRADOR RETRIEVER . . . BECOMES ENDAL, THE WONDER DOG!

NAME: *Endal*

SPECIES: *Labrador retriever*

DATE: *1998 to 2009*

LOCATION: *Clanfield, England*

SITUATION: *Disabled, wheelchair-bound vet with speech and memory problems*

WHO WAS SAVED: *Allen Parton, a former Royal Navy Chief Petty Officer*

LEGACY: *Hall-of-fame-worthy service animal called "the most decorated dog in the world"*

Few service dogs exemplify what it means to go "above and beyond the call of duty" as much as Endal. For twelve years Endal partnered with British war veteran Allen Parton to become one of the most skilled, intelligent, and honored service dogs in modern history.

Allen Parton's life changed when he was in a near-fatal car accident during the Gulf War in 1991. A Royal Navy Chief Petty Officer, Parton awoke from a coma unable to recognize his wife and teenage children. He had severe memory loss and trouble making new memories; he lost his ability to speak; he had visual perception problems; and his debilitating physical paralysis would confine him to a wheelchair for the rest of his life.

"The fear and shock of what had happened to me made me furious," Allen said. "I refused to accept I was disabled, and I'm ashamed to say that I was horrible and rude to everyone."

If anything, as the years passed at home in Clanfield, England, Allen's life only grew worse. "I was like a blob in a wheelchair," Allen said. "I didn't have any emotions. I had no contact with people." Feeling isolated and useless, Allen twice attempted suicide.

Then one day in 1998, a missed bus forced Allen to accompany his wife, Sharon, to her work at a dog-training center, the Canine Partners for Independence. As Allen later told the story, it was the tawny, one-year-old labrador retriever who chose him, not the other way around.

"Endal was on one side of the room, and I was on the other," Parton said. "He decided he liked me and he managed to get a reaction out of me."

What did Endal do? He climbed onto Allen's lap, licked his face, and wouldn't go away. "It was a cathartic experience," Allen said. "Until I met him, I was in the depths of despair. But when he refused to leave my side at the training center, I suddenly saw a chink of light."

HEY MISTER, WHAT ELSE CAN YOUR DOG DO?

When Endal started, Allen couldn't talk, so one of the first things Endal had to master was Allen's own personal sign language. He did, and as with many of Endal's skills, it was self-taught.

"If I touched my head, I wanted my hat," Allen said. "If I touched my face, it was for the razor. He learned hundreds of commands in signing. Eventually one day, in this very silent world we lived in, I grunted. That was like an electric shock going through him, he was so excited. They said I'd never speak again, but Endal just dragged the speech out of me."

Just like in the movies, Endal readily fetched the newspaper and the mail, but there seemed no end to the chores he could handle. Endal did the laundry: opening the washer door, putting in the dirty clothes, then taking out the wet clothes. He did the shopping: grabbing items from the shelves, putting them in the cart, and handling the cash and change when it was time to pay.

If there was a button, switch, lever, or knob, Endal used his nose or paw to work it. Endal punched the sidewalk crossing buttons and made sure Allen didn't roll into the street. He bought bus tickets, opened train doors, and helped pull Allen onto public transport.

Maybe Endal's favorite chore was getting his own food and bowl at meal time.

"I don't think there's any period in a 24-hour day that I don't put my hand down somewhere and he isn't there," said Allen. "I didn't make him do these things. He just decided that alongside my chair was where he wanted to be."

Endal never did only what he was taught. He actively looked for other ways to help.

One day, Allen was struggling at an ATM machine, so Endal jumped up and grabbed the cash, card, and receipt for him. Afterward, Endal learned to insert the card and even once punched in the PIN number using a stylus.

"It was amazing," Allen said. As far as anyone knew, Endal was the first dog ever to use an ATM, and "he had never been taught."

Ultimately, Endal learned over two hundred commands, among which were a number of "firsts" like the ATM.

SAVING A LIFE AND A FAMILY

Endal's true worth wasn't measured in tricks and chores, however. One day, Allen fell asleep in the bathtub, and Endal pulled the plug to save his companion from drowning.

In May 2001, a car accidentally backed into Allen, toppling his wheelchair and knocking him unconscious, and then drove away. Putting together both instincts and training, Endal pulled Allen into a recovery position, placed a blanket over him, pushed his cell phone near his face, hit the emergency button on the phone, and ran to a nearby hotel, urgently barking until people emerged to help.

Further, Allen said, "He fills in my memory problems—he has saved me physically and psychologically."

Perhaps most important, Endal's relentlessly optimistic personality seeped into Allen and changed his attitude about life.

Endal's tail never stopped wagging. "Endal was very gentle, nurturing me every day, and encouraging me to do things," said Allen. "He was a good therapist."

This, in turn, helped save Allen's marriage and his relationship with his family.

Before Endal, Allen's depression and his dependency on Sandra was causing serious strain. In any marriage, Allen said, "You need space, and Endal gave us that—in real terms, saved our marriage."

Though Sandra once joked that she was "second best" next to Endal, the couple renewed their vows in 2002. It was as if life for Allen Parton could start all over again.

THE WORLD'S MOST FAMOUS SERVICE DOG

"I got Endal as a one-year-old who had been taught social skills," Allen said. The eager Lab hadn't had any formal advanced training before he donned his red service vest, so how did he come to resemble a canine superhero?

Some of his skills reflected training Endal received after he started working with Allen, but that doesn't account for Endal's relentless motivation. Allen said, "Endal just looks at me, sees my weakness, and becomes my strength."

Over the years, accolades and awards have been showered on Endal, almost beyond count. Endal won numerous "Dog of the Year" awards, several "Lifetime Achievement" awards, was named "Dog of the Millennium," and had a street in his hometown named for him. Perhaps his most prestigious award was the 2002 Gold Medal from the People's Dispensary for Sick Animals (PDSA), which is the animal equivalent of England's George Cross for exceptional bravery and devotion to duty during peacetime.

Endal has been the subject of a book and a British TV documentary, and a Hollywood version of his life is in development. By Allen's count, Endal made over four thousand public appearances and patiently played along with 342 film crews.

In 2008, anticipating Endal's impending retirement, Allen adopted another service dog he named EJ, for Endal Junior. Proving his worth one last time, Endal not only accepted EJ at Allen's side, but also actively taught him up to 90 percent of the tasks that he had learned.

Then, in March 2009, Endal's declining health and old age caught up to him. Numerous issues, such as arthritis and seizures, had severely deteriorated his quality of life, and Endal was put down, Allen said, while lying "peacefully in my lap surrounded by those that loved him most."

Afterward, Allen wrote: "I still can't pick a point in my life when I can say that I did something in life that deserved Endal's unconditional love and devotion. . . . I have been truly blessed, but now I realize that Endal was never only my dog, he was everyone's, and the world truly is a sadder place today for his passing."

IN AN EMERGENCY, DIAL 911

One of the more unusual tasks that service dogs are trained for today is dialing 911 in an emergency. You might think operating a phone would require fingers, if not an opposable thumb, but you'd be wrong.

Dogs have no problem learning how to knock a phone off the hook—many do that already!—and then stabbing with a paw or biting down on a single button. You just need to program 911 into your speed-dial first.

Of course, dogs also need to be trained to recognize a true emergency, such as seizures or diabetic shock.

Plus, it doesn't hurt to let the police know that a 911 call from your house might be the dog. It would explain the barking and save time.

Sound far-fetched? Here are a few incidents that have made the news:

- Lyric, an Irish setter, dialed 911 twice in 1996 to save Judy Bayly when she stopped breathing from severe asthma attacks.
- Belle, a beagle, dialed 911 in 2006 when Kevin Weaver passed out from a diabetic seizure.
- Buddy, a German shepherd, saved Joe Stalnaker three times by dialing 911, most recently in 2008, when Joe passed out from head-injury-related seizures.

And if you're thinking, *Great, another dog trick*, consider that in 2006 a cat dialed 911, too. In 2003, Gary Rosheisen tried to teach Tommy, his orange-and-tan tabby, to dial 911 if he ever fell out of his wheelchair from a ministroke. As anyone might, Gary finally gave up. After all, who can train a cat to do anything?

But three years later, the anticipated emergency happened. The police received a silent 911 call, decided to check it out, and found Tommy sitting by the unhooked living room phone.

ROSELLE THE GUIDE DOG . . . LEADS THE WAY OUT

NAME: *Roselle*

SPECIES: *Labrador retriever*

DATE: *September 11, 2001*

LOCATION: *New York City*

SITUATION: *Terrorist attack on the World Trade Center*

WHO WAS SAVED: *Fifty-one-year-old Michael Hingson*

LEGACY: *World famous for unstinting devotion during 9/11, model for guide-dog relationship*

On the morning of September 11, 2001, Michael Hingson went to work early to prepare for a sales training he was leading that day. Michael loved his job and his office on the 78th floor of the North Tower of New York City's World Trade Center—even though, being blind since birth, he had never enjoyed the view. As he worked, Michael's guide dog, Roselle, snoozed by his feet under his desk.

At 8:46 am, a tremendous boom from somewhere above rocked the building, which shuddered and groaned and then, as if in slow motion, steadily tilted over perhaps twenty feet. Visitors for the sales training screamed, and Michael and his coworker David said good-bye, certain that they were about to plunge to their deaths.

Then Tower 1 slowly righted itself, and as it did, Michael's wheat-colored labrador retriever woke lazily from her nap, yawning.

Later, in his book *Thunder Dog*, Michael described his experience. He wrote that David looked out the window and reported seeing "smoke and fire and millions of pieces of burning paper."

David screamed, "We have to get out of here now!"

"I agree," said Michael, "but let's slow down and do it the right way."

No one had any idea what had caused the explosion. Yet Michael knew two things: They had to leave by the stairs, not the elevators, and they couldn't panic.

Because of Roselle, Michael didn't.

"If she had sensed danger, she would have acted differently," Michael wrote. But Roselle sat next to him, calmly waiting for his command. In the moment, he thought, "I choose to trust Roselle's judgment and so I will not panic. Roselle and I are a team."

SEVENTY-EIGHT FLOORS, ONE STEP AT A TIME

What Michael and everyone else who escaped the World Trade Center that day learned only afterward was that the Middle East terrorist group, Al-Qaeda, led by Osama bin Laden, had hijacked four passenger airplanes and were using them to attack the United States. Two planes were flown into the World Trade Center, one hitting each tower; one was flown into the Pentagon; and one crashed in rural Pennsylvania after its passengers fought the hijackers for control of the plane.

The events of 9/11 have become an indelible before-and-after moment in American history; afterward, everyday life was irrevocably changed. But in the moment, within the chaos and confusion of the towers, people understood very little of what was happening while forced to make snap, life-or-death decisions.

Michael Hingson and Roselle were experts at proceeding blindly, which made them almost uniquely qualified to help others that day.

First, Michael ensured that all of the guests for the sales training left safely. Then, after partially shutting down the office, he and David left as well. In the tower lobby, they chose Stairwell B.

At the top, Michael instructed Roselle, "Forward," and the trio descended the first of the 1,463 stairs that led the way out.

They descended the first ten floors in about nine minutes. As they did, the stairwell grew more crowded, sweaty, and hot, and the smell of jet fuel sometimes made it hard to breathe. People were largely silent and orderly, but panic bubbled beneath the surface.

At one point, a woman grew hysterical, yelling that they wouldn't make it. People stopped to encourage her, and Roselle nudged her till she petted him, which helped her relax. Soon, she kept going. "Roselle has worked her magic," Michael wrote.

As the heat and claustrophobia increased, David also panicked, but Michael reassured him, "If Roselle and I can go down the stairs, then so can you."

Then Michael suddenly thought, what if the lights went out? Darkness wouldn't hinder him or Roselle—she navigated by smell and feel as much as sight—but it could trigger pandemonium.

Of course, Michael thought, *Roselle and I will lead the way*. Out loud, Michael shouted: "Don't anybody worry. Roselle and I are giving a half-price special to get you out of here if the lights go out."

People laughed, the mood lifted, and the steady pace down continued.

Around the thirtieth floor, firefighters going up started passing them on the stairs. Each one stopped to see if Michael needed assistance, but Michael didn't need help. Instead, Roselle offered herself to be petted, providing many of the firefighters with what would be their last experience of unconditional love.

At the twentieth floor, water from the sprinklers made the stairs wet, and the stairwell became even more packed. Progress slowed to a crawl, but finally, after about forty-five minutes total, Michael, Roselle, and David reached the lobby of Tower 1.

Everyone was instructed to exit through the shopping concourse, and now people hurried. In another fifteen minutes, they emerged outside.

ESCAPING THE FALLING TOWERS

Michael and David paused on the street; David described the chaotic, surreal scene and Michael tried unsuccessfully to call his wife. Suddenly, the police yelled for everyone to run: The South Tower was collapsing. All 110 stories were coming down.

People fled heedlessly, as did Michael, who kept a "death grip" on Roselle's harness. The streets bounced like a trampoline, the sky rained debris, and "a deafening roar" like a hellish freight train filled the air.

By some miracle, Michael and Roselle survived and found themselves still with David. They were then immediately enveloped in the horrific, toxic dust cloud that followed, which they couldn't help but inhale. "I am drowning," Michael wrote, "trying to breathe through dirt."

The trio was overwhelmed and terrified, each of them choking, blinded, dehydrated, and dazed. Nothing could have prepared any of them for this; as Roselle's trainer later said, "Most dogs in that situation would have flipped, and that's the truth." Yet as they stumbled on, Roselle bravely kept working, steadily guiding Michael and David as they sought shelter to escape this unrelenting nightmare.

Feeling an opening on their right, Michael anxiously instructed Roselle to enter, but she stopped him: He was about to fall down a subway stairwell. Proceeding cautiously, they descended the stairs and got off the street.

At the bottom of the stairwell, in the station's arcade, a woman blinded by the dust was calling out wildly for help, hysterically afraid of falling on the tracks. Michael took her elbow and explained about Roselle.

"This time the blind really is leading the blind," Michael wrote, and together they found an employee locker room where others had gathered. There, they could breathe freely again, drink water from a fountain, clean up, and strategize how to get home.

A NEW PURPOSE

Michael Hingson never let his blindness define him. As a child, he learned to use echolocation to ride a bicycle, and he even once flew a plane. "Blind people face unnecessary barriers, and we can do far more than people think," he wrote.

On 9/11, Michael and Roselle survived because they were a team. They knew how to rely on and read each other. If Roselle was unafraid, then Michael felt safe; if Michael stayed calm and focused, then Roselle did the same. Neither was alone, and their bond allowed them to be brave for others.

Michael and Roselle made it home safely, and in the months that followed, Michael decided that the reason he'd lived was so that he might share "some of the things I learned growing up blind that went a long way toward helping me survive that day."

Michael became a public speaker and a spokesperson for Guide Dogs for the Blind, the organization that had trained Roselle. Together, they spread their message about trust and teamwork.

Sadly, in 2004, Roselle developed a blood disorder that was likely related to her exposure to environmental toxins on 9/11. Because of this, she retired in 2007. She successfully battled the disease for several years, but eventually Roselle died due to failing health in 2011.

Michael cannot explain why Roselle was so dedicated and brave on 9/11. Her actions went far beyond her training. Simply put, they reflected the exceptional qualities of herself.

"I've had many other dogs," Michael wrote, "but there is only one Roselle."

BLIND LOVE: OMAR & SALTY

Incredibly, Michael Hingson and Roselle weren't the only guide-dog team to escape the World Trade Center on 9/11. Omar Rivera and Salty did, too.

In 1987 at age twenty-eight, Omar lost his sight due to glaucoma, and in 1998 he teamed with Salty, a broad-shouldered, cream-colored labrador retriever. Both loved the fast pace and excitement of Manhattan. As Salty's trainer said, "He was definitely a city dog."

Omar worked for New York's Port Authority, and his office was on the 71st floor of the North Tower. In contrast to Roselle, Salty became very excited, running back and forth, as the building shuddered and swayed at 8:46 am, when the first plane struck the 93rd to 99th floors.

Once in harness, however, Salty settled down, which is typical of service dogs. Off-duty, they relax and even indulge their mischievous sides. In harness, they are like a police officer in uniform—no funny business.

Descending in the stairwell, "I heard people crying, screaming, praying," Omar said. "We passed many people who would not or could not continue."

Around the 35th floor, the stairs became uncomfortably crowded. Worried that Salty might become overwhelmed in the hot, confined space, Omar released him. He dropped Salty's leash and felt him walk ahead alone. But after a few minutes, a familiar furry body pressed against Omar's legs. "At one point he decided: *No, I cannot go without him*," Omar said. "So he came back."

Once the pair reached the street, Omar said, "I didn't see anything, but I heard everything. People screaming, crying. Helicopters, ambulances, fire trucks… a hundred million sounds concentrated in one place."

Then, as the South Tower collapsed, they, too, ran headlong down city streets, Omar holding fast to Salty's leash, and by some grace, the pair survived.

"Trust, that's the most important thing in a relationship with a guide dog," Omar said. "They give everything they have for almost nothing, just for love."

TRAKR THE GERMAN SHEPHERD . . . FINDS THE LAST SURVIVOR

NAME: *Trakr*

SPECIES: *German shepherd*

DATE: *September 12, 2001*

LOCATION: *Ground Zero, New York City*

SITUATION: *People buried beneath collapsed World Trade Center towers*

WHO WAS SAVED: *Genelle Guzman-McMillan, Port Authority employee*

LEGACY: *National hero for finding last survivor at Ground Zero, cloned five times*

After the second World Trade Center tower fell on the morning of September 11, 2001, the police, firefighters, and other first-responders at the scene immediately turned their focus to rescuing anyone who might be alive within the seven-story mountain of rubble and steel that had been, moments before, two of the world's tallest buildings.

Literally within minutes, the first canine search-and-rescue (SAR) teams arrived (see the "Appollo & the Dogs of 9/11" sidebar for more), and K-9 teams kept arriving, hour after hour, each one joining the frantic search for survivors at Ground Zero, which rescue workers came to call "the pile."

Even for these intensively trained animals and their handlers, it was a scene of desolation and destruction no one was prepared for—fourteen acres of broken concrete, twisted girders, and rent metal, riddled with precarious dark voids and smoking, still-burning fires. Everything was covered in ankle- and knee-deep-thick dust.

"It was like walking into hell," said Sonny Whynman, who with his German shepherd Piper was one of the first SAR teams to arrive. "People were running in all different directions. There were dozens of firefighters, and they were all pleading, 'Bring your search dog over here.'"

Ultimately, only twenty people were found alive at Ground Zero afterward. The last person to be rescued was Genelle Guzman-McMillan. She was discovered on the morning of September 12 with the help of the German shepherd Trakr and his handler, James Symington.

JOINING THE PILE

Symington and Trakr were a K-9 team on the Halifax, Nova Scotia, police force in Canada. Symington was then on a leave of absence, and as he watched the tragedy of 9/11 unfold on television, he decided to help. With a friend, he drove fifteen hours to New York City, arriving that night. Without ceremony or protocol, Symington and Trakr simply joined the growing number of SAR teams on the pile.

It was grueling, chaotic work, but the well-trained dogs flew over the wreckage with determination and zeal, unfazed by the nightmare scene. Floodlights lit up the ruins. Generators, bulldozers, and cranes rattled the air with noise. Yet as Rick Lee, a FEMA canine task force handler, said, "Whenever the K-9s were searching, it became very quiet. I would look and all of the rescuers would be watching us work our dogs. It was like someone had turned off the sound. . . . Until that moment, we never realized we had so much responsibility."

Around 7 am, Trakr pawed, sniffed, and sat on one spot, giving a mild signal for a "live hit," or the presence of a living person. "It was very chaotic, very hard to see, very treacherous," Symington said. "But for one quick brief moment, Trakr gave me an indication that someone was buried below."

Genelle Guzman-McMillan was a secretary for New York's Port Authority in the World Trade Center's North Tower. She worked on the sixty-fourth floor, and about an hour after the first plane hit, she and her coworkers started descending a stairwell. She had reached the thirteenth floor when the building collapsed. Then, for more than twenty-four hours she lay buried, alternately sweating, shivering . . . and praying.

Rick Cushman, a volunteer with a Massachusetts emergency team. worked beside Symington and Trakr, and he said,"I am proud to have been involved in this rescue. . . . If Trakr hadn't picked up her scent, we might not have known she was there. They helped save her life."

At the time, no one knew that Guzman-McMillan would be the last person rescued, and Trakr's role in finding her only became notable in retrospect. Indeed, once firefighters took over her rescue, Symington and Trakr moved on. For another two days, the team worked the pile almost nonstop—as did hundreds of others—until Trakr collapsed from smoke and chemical inhalation, as well as burns and exhaustion.

Trakr was treated with intravenous fluids, and on September 14, he and Symington returned to Nova Scotia. Afterward, Jane Goodall presented the pair with an Extraordinary Service to Humanity Award, they were featured in several books, and in 2011, *Time* magazine named Trakr one of America's "Top 10 Heroic Animals" of all time.

APPOLLO & THE DOGS OF 9/11

Estimates vary, but between 300 to 350 canine search-and-rescue teams worked the 9/11 rescue sights, which included the Pentagon. All told, it was the largest call-up of emergency services in US history, and SAR teams arrived from all over the country.

The majority of 9/11 dogs were trained to Federal Emergency Management Agency (FEMA) standards as either live-find or cadaver-search dogs. Numerous police dogs also joined in, some of them cross-trained for this type of disaster work.

Daily shifts were meant to last about twelve hours, but teams often kept going for sixteen hours and more, until they literally dropped from exhaustion. The dogs worked off-leash and barefoot (so they could use their feet for traction), crawling over and into spaces no human searcher could reach.

In New York City, after a shift, SAR dogs were taken to a makeshift decontamination ward in the Javits Center, where dogs had their eyes and ears flushed, had any wounds patched up, and were bathed and fed. While no definitive link has yet been verified, some claim that a disproportionate number of SAR dogs later died due to 9/11-related illnesses.

Off-duty SAR dogs played another role: therapist. Traumatized relief workers often came up to pet the dogs, who freely offered their companionship. According to their handlers, the dogs seemed to understand, if not the nature of the tragedy, then the pain being experienced all around them.

Similar to Trakr, Appollo was another dog widely honored on behalf of all 9/11 dogs. Appollo and his handler, Peter Davis, were an NYPD K-9 team who arrived about fifteen minutes after the second tower fell, making them the first canine SAR team at the site. Appollo and Davis worked at Ground Zero for weeks, and afterward Appollo received the American Kennel Club Ace award and the British Dickin Medal (along with Roselle, page 126).

THE WORLD'S MOST CLONEWORTHY DOG

Trakr's work at Ground Zero made him a national hero, but Trakr's accomplishments were and are often praised as representative of all 9/11 dogs. Hundreds of other trained search-and-rescue teams made similar heroic efforts. It's hard to single out any one animal when every single one braved the same surreal, dangerous conditions while doing the work they were trained for.

And yet, Trakr *was* singled out in a way that makes his story unique: In a 2008 contest run by the genetics firm BioArts, Trakr was selected as the "World's Most Cloneworthy Dog." And in 2009, five puppies cloned from Trakr's DNA were born. Symington named them Déjà Vu (naturally), Solace, Valor, Prodigy, and Trustt, and he planned to train them as search-and-rescue dogs.

In the contest application, Symington also cited Trakr's six years of work on the Halifax police force, during which he helped make hundreds of arrests and found more than $1 million in contraband. He wrote that "once in a lifetime, a dog comes along that not only captures the hearts of all he touches but also plays a private role in history."

Trakr got to meet his genetically identical progeny just before he died in April 2009. For two years, Trakr had suffered from a debilitating illness that was believed to be 9/11-related.

After Trakr died, Symington said, "I am honored to have been Trakr's partner, best friend, and lifelong companion. He possessed a rare combination of uncanny intuition, pure heart, and relentless courage. He'll live in my heart forever."

ROCKY THE K-9 ...
CATCHES AN ARMED FUGITIVE

NAME: *Rocky*

SPECIES: *Dutch shepherd*

DATE: *August 4, 2002*

LOCATION: *Lakewood, Colorado*

SITUATION: *Armed fugitive fleeing arrest*

WHO WAS SAVED: *Police officer Darren Maurer and fugitive*

LEGACY: *Represents the dauntless courage of all K-9s in the face of deadly force*

Today, police K-9 teams are a staple of law enforcement, and it's no exaggeration to say that every day, somewhere, a police K-9 does something to save someone's life.

Police dog programs have been used in the United States since the start of the twentieth century, but they weren't adopted widely until the 1960s. Most of the time, a K-9's typical job description involves tracking and locating suspects, missing persons, drugs, or weapons, and occasionally it means cornering and intimidating a criminal or suspect to keep them from fleeing or using force. In rare cases, it means physically subduing a person engaged in violence.

When the latter happens, dogs put their lives on the line just as surely as their police handlers. The only difference is that an officer knows beforehand that risking injury and death comes with the territory. They can mentally prepare for it.

We don't know if dogs understand this beforehand, but in the moment of a violent encounter, this surely becomes clear.

THE CALL

Very early in the morning on August 4, 2002, in Lakewood, Colorado, police officer Darren Maurer received a radio report about a domestic disturbance at an apartment complex: Someone called to say a young man was shouting, waving a pistol, and threatening his girlfriend and the neighbors.

Office Maurer and his K-9 Rocky arrived at the scene and began searching for the man. As they drove around, Officer Maurer spotted the suspect's pickup truck, but apparently the man saw the police first and fled on foot.

Seeing the man run, Officer Maurer released Rocky, and the then-three-year-old Dutch shepherd took off in hot pursuit. Quickly trapped by the much-faster canine, the man scaled a fence, and "just like in the movies," said Officer Maurer, Rocky jumped and snapped at the fugitive's heels but missed by inches.

"Rocky ran around the building," Officer Maurer continued, "and a gunshot echoed through the night. The guy shot Rocky at almost point-blank range."

Officer Maurer thought the worst as the man emerged from behind the building, running almost directly at the officer. But then he saw Rocky bounding around the corner, still giving chase.

The man aimed his handgun at Officer Maurer, but the policeman fired first, just missing. Then, closing a distance of about seventy yards, Rocky pounced on the fugitive.

"He caught the guy—bit him in the back of the leg," said Maurer.

The man fell to the ground and Rocky held him there until Officer Maurer arrived to put him under arrest.

It was then that Officer Maurer saw that Rocky had been hit: the bullet had shattered his front left paw.

ALL IN A DAY'S WORK

Afterward, a police spokesperson said, "We don't know what the suspect would have done had he not been knocked down, but he didn't want to give up. It's possible the dog saved [the suspect's] life or that of an agent."

Indeed. With two shots fired, more would have been, but Rocky put an end to the pursuit, nonlethally, just as he'd been trained—and despite being shot himself.

It's this, more than anything, that exemplifies the fierce, steadfast devotion of working dogs: Being injured, and the awareness that he could be killed, didn't stop Rocky from continuing to work, nor did it transform him into a revenge-crazed Cujo. Once he was shot, Rocky might have fled or hid, and this would have been understandable, but he didn't.

Why? Most trainers say working dogs perform their jobs to get whatever incentive is used to teach them during training. Often a dog's reward for successfully completing a task is the chance to play with a favorite toy, but sometimes the reward is nothing more than the handler's loving praise. Dogs come to expect the reward as their "pay." In search-and-rescue work, a handler will sometimes reward a dog even after an unsuccessful search because the dog did everything he or she was trained to do. That nothing was found wasn't the dog's fault, and it would undermine the dog's incentive to work if the reward was withheld. The dog would become discouraged.

But praise and playtime don't seem like enough to motivate an injured animal whose life is threatened. Surely something more primal and essential drives them. Perhaps it can't be proved, but it often looks like love—the urge to protect their partner at the other end of the leash.

IT'S A FELONY TO HURT A DOG

Luckily, Rocky got immediate medical attention, and though he lost some pad and some bone, his foot healed completely. Not only that, he seemed unfazed by his brush with death or by the attention and animal heroism awards that followed.

"He was the same dog after as he was before," said Maurer.

The fugitive, meanwhile, was charged with several felony counts, one for criminal mischief for injuring the dog and another for "attempted aggravated cruelty to animals." He was also charged with a misdemeanor for "obstructing a police dog."

Rocky went on to serve in the Lakewood Police Department until 2007, and during his six-year career, he was credited with locating hundreds of suspects and missing persons. After 2007, Rocky officially retired, but in the manner of most high-drive dogs, he kept chasing things.

"He loved to play ball—any kind of fetch, with sticks, Frisbees, anything," said Officer Maurer. "He would play all day."

Then, in 2008, Rocky developed cancer and died. When he was put down, Officer Maurer was with him, holding his longtime partner and beloved companion.

"There's a huge hole in my heart," he said.

Afterward, Officer Maurer expressed a universal sentiment among working dog handlers. Whatever reward-based training is involved, the intimacy of the connection they develop far surpasses it.

"He was more than a dog," Officer Maurer said. "He and I shared the human-animal bond. We had a bond that's impossible to describe."

CHEYENNE THE PIT BULL . . . KEEPS A VET FROM SUICIDE

NAME: *Cheyenne*

SPECIES: *Pit bull*

DATE: *Fall 2002*

LOCATION: *Yorktown, Virginia*

SITUATION: *Combat veteran suffering from PTSD*

WHO WAS SAVED: *Twenty-three-year-old David Sharpe*

LEGACY: *Inspirational companion showed healing benefits of pet therapy for emotional trauma*

One fall night in 2002, David Sharpe, a US Air Force Security Forces Airman, was slumped on his kitchen floor preparing to take his life. He was overcome with despair and "ready to finish the fight with the demons that followed me back from the war," he said.

In the months since the twenty-three-year-old had returned from Afghanistan, his life had spun "out of control," he said. He was a "wreck," and the evidence surrounded him: the holes he'd punched in the apartment walls, the unwashed uniforms, the empty liquor bottles, the bruises from the fights he started "for no reason."

He thought he had nothing to live for, and so he took his .45-calibar handgun, "cocked it back, put it right in my mouth, and I sat there and cried for about a minute or two," David said. "I was this close to pulling the trigger."

Then David's six-month-old pit bull, Cheyenne, came up behind him and licked his ear. David turned, and for a long moment the pair regarded each other. Cheyenne tilted her head with a quizzical expression most dog owners would recognize.

"It was just one of those looks dogs give you," David recalled, as if Cheyenne were saying, "What are you doing, man? Who's going to let me sleep in your bed? Listen, if you take care of me, I'll take care of you."

This wasn't the first time Cheyenne had interrupted one of David's meltdowns. Months earlier, during a violent rage when he nearly ripped the refrigerator door off its hinges, David noticed Cheyenne watching him with a concerned look, wagging her tail.

"I picked her up," he said, "and took her back to my bed, and I just lost it—started crying, bawling. She inched her way up. She knew something was wrong. She just started licking the tears off my cheek. It makes you laugh, it tickles, and I immediately starting feeling relief, because I didn't have anyone [saying] to me, 'How do you feel now? Are you glad you got that off your chest?' She never asked. I told her on my own terms."

In the kitchen, David pulled the gun from his mouth and never threatened himself with it again. In fact, that moment provided the inspiration he needed to turn his life around: He allowed the wordless acceptance and caring of his pit bull to lead him out of his emotional isolation, and he eventually devoted himself to providing companion animals for other troubled veterans.

"There's no doubt about it," David said. "I owe her my life."

PTSD IN DOGS

It's not just soldiers who can develop post-traumatic stress syndrome (PTSD). For many years, combat dogs have sometimes displayed emotional "battle scars," but since dogs can't tell us what's going on inside their heads, we couldn't confirm the condition. However, since 2011, it's been widely recognized that working military dogs can suffer from what's termed "canine PTSD."

As with soldiers, it's a mystery why some combat dogs are traumatized by events that other dogs are able to shrug off. However, troubled dogs display many classic signs: hypervigilance, disturbed sleep, apparent nightmares, unusual aggression or unusual timidity with their handler, avoidance of places or things clearly related to the traumatizing incident, depression, and an inability or unwillingness to do the job they were trained for. It's been estimated that about 5 percent of war dogs develop PTSD.

Dogs are also treated with the same mix of medications and behavioral therapies used with humans, and recovery rates are just as variable. Some dogs go back to detecting bombs and assisting troops, some get transferred to noncombat roles, and some must be retired from service.

Further, it's now recognized that many animals can suffer PTSD-like reactions to just about any dangerous, overwhelming, or life-threatening experience, including car accidents, earthquakes, violent attacks by other animals, physical abuse, abandonment, prolonged confinement in small cages, emergency medical procedures, and so on.

This is worth remembering when reading this book: All of these stories have happy endings. Yet both the people saved and the animals who helped them may suffer lingering emotional scars that can be hard to predict and hard to overcome.

PTSD AND THE TRAUMA OF WAR

In mid-2002, when David Sharpe returned from active duty during the Afghanistan War, he was suffering from undiagnosed post-traumatic stress disorder (PTSD). He had served several tours at bases in Saudi Arabia and Pakistan, but one life-threatening incident early in his first tour traumatized him more than he realized or would later admit.

It was December 2001, and David was deployed as a security guard in Saudi Arabia. One day in the guard shack, a guard he'd been working with began laughing over a newspaper photo of New York City's Twin Towers burning on 9/11. The Saudi soldier revealed himself to be a Taliban sympathizer, and David became angry, told him to shut up, and walked away.

As he did, David heard the click-clack of a machine gun being readied, and he turned around to find the gun pointed at his face. "I froze for a few seconds, but it felt like days. I looked at him and pulled my M-16 up and charged it," David said.

Both men were yelling. A British guard ran in and leveled his weapon on the other guard, then a French guard entered and raised his weapon on the British guard. Eventually, everyone lowered their weapons and no shots were fired.

Later, David was debriefed on the incident and referred to a chaplain for counseling, but he refused to discuss it.

After finishing his deployment and returning home to Virginia, David was a tinderbox of rage. He constantly argued with family and friends, driving them away, and he instigated fights with anyone. He also began having nightmares of the guardhouse confrontation.

"I had visions of the bullet going through my head and coming out the other side," he said. "I woke and I started crying, and then I started calling myself a bunch of names and saying to myself, 'Suck it up. What's wrong with you?'"

One concerned friend suggested that David adopt a dog. In summer 2002, they visited a shelter with a batch of pit bull puppies who had been saved from a fighting ring. At the time, David said, "Hell, yeah, I want to get a fighting dog. I'm a fighter."

Oddly enough, David chose the pit bull sitting by herself in the corner—the only quiet dog. Perhaps David sensed that, in truth, he didn't need an aggressive companion. He needed one capable of ignoring the anarchy of her overeager siblings.

Almost immediately, as David gave in to tiny Cheyenne's affection and started talking to her about his pain, "I felt like a 10,000-pound weight had been lifted off my chest," David said.

This culminated in the night on the kitchen floor. Afterward, David's recovery began.

PET THERAPY

Without realizing it, David was engaging in pet therapy.

"I couldn't talk to anybody—not my father, not the counselors—but I could talk to that dog, and she never judged me," Sharpe said. "She was the force that pulled me back into society."

David's family immediately noticed the change, but the road back was long. In 2005, David quit the Air Force and began professional therapy, and only in 2009 did the Department of Veterans' Affairs confirm the diagnosis of PTSD.

"Pet therapy helps people who have PTSD to reconnect with the world," said Megan O'Connell, a clinical nurse specialist at Fort George G. Meade in Maryland. "One of the problems with PTSD is that it really destroys people's trust. They feel disconnected."

For one thing, caring for an animal forces people to think of someone else's needs. But pets also offer a form of open-hearted companionship that humans can't replicate.

"Especially dogs—they react to body language," O'Connell said. "If your body language is stressed, they want you to stop being stressed, so they pay a lot of attention to you. It makes you feel like they care and they're listening, and that makes you feel comfortable, to want to open up more."

However, trained and certified therapy animals are expensive, so David founded his nonprofit organization Companions for Heroes with the mission to connect veterans and first-responders with shelter animals. After all, David was helped by an untrained, abandoned puppy.

"Most of the vets I've spoken to don't want dogs to do tricks," David said. "We just want companionship. Eighteen vets commit suicide every day in this country, and one animal is put to sleep every eight seconds. They can help save each other."

BETSY THE QUARTER HORSE . . . BOWS TO A CHILD

NAME: *Betsy*

SPECIES: *Quarter horse*

DATE: *2004*

LOCATION: *Austin, Texas*

SITUATION: *Autistic child suffering multiple dysfunctions*

WHO WAS SAVED: *Three-year-old Rowan Isaacson*

LEGACY: *Shining example of equine therapy and intuitive connection between horses and autists*

In April 2004, when he was three and a half, Rowan Isaacson was diagnosed with autism. He displayed the classic signs: He babbled or only repeated memorized words. He was obsessive with toys, lacked interest in people, and exhibited repetitive gestures.

After the diagnosis, Rowan's autistic symptoms steadily worsened. He began throwing monumental tantrums, most likely due to sensory overload; suddenly, out of nowhere, he would thrash wildly and scream uncontrollably. Rowan's father, Rupert, said, "His screaming once even drowned out the noise of a jackhammer crew, who downed tools and just stared in awe."

During these fits, Rowan might slam his head on the ground, projectile vomit, and become incontinent; potty training was useless.

Autism cannot be cured, but dysfunctional behaviors or symptoms can be treated so they are less disruptive, and sometimes even eliminated. Also, autism exists along a broad spectrum, from extremely mild to very severe. However, as Dr. Temple Grandin has shown, some children with severe autism can eventually lead high-functioning lives (see "Thinking in Pictures").

The Isaacsons started treating Rowan with a mix of prescription medicines, vitamins, and homeopathic remedies. They sent him to a range of educational and behavioral therapists. Nothing seemed to improve Rowan, particularly his hyperactive outbursts, except one thing.

Every day, Rupert took Rowan on walks in the woods behind their home in Austin, Texas.

"Immediately his screams would lessen and out he'd fly," Rupert said, "flitting between the trees like some happy woodland elf."

MEETING BETSY

During one walk in August 2004, Rowan ran off, away from his father, and by the time Rupert caught up, Rowan was scrambling under a wire fence into a neighbor's horse pasture.

On the other side, four horses grazed quietly. Rowan laughed, delighted, for he loved animals, and "he threw himself on the ground, belly up, right in front of the alpha mare, the herd leader," Rupert said. "A big bay quarter horse called Betsy."

Rupert, a longtime rider, had once trained horses. He knew Betsy might trample Rowan if she became threatened or spooked, so Rupert approached cautiously as the horses regarded the strange boy. Then Betsy "dipped her head, and mouthed her lips. The sign of equine submission," Rupert said.

"I knew I was witnessing something extraordinary. . . . In all the years that I had been training horses, I had never seen this happen."

Weeks later, intrigued by Rowan's unexpected horse connection, Rupert asked his neighbor if he and Rowan could ride Betsy. The neighbor agreed.

To risk putting his son on the horse, "I broke all the rules," Rupert admitted. Rupert knew Betsy dominated and bullied the other horses, and she could be willful with adults. But he sensed an unusual restraint, even kindness, in her behavior with Rowan.

This became obvious as Rupert readied Betsy for their first ride. Rowan ran wild in the barn, chasing a cat, yelling, hitting the horse with his doll, and racing beneath her belly. Through it all, Betsy "stood like a rock, moving not a muscle," Rupert said.

Then Rupert asked Rowan if he wanted to get up. "I wasn't expecting a response," he said, "but for the first time ever, he gave me an answer to a question. 'Up,' he said. And off we went."

To Rupert's amazement, the conversation continued as they rode. Rowan kept responding to his father's prompts. Rowan mostly repeated his father's words, exhibiting echolalia, but it still "was more cognitive speech than I'd ever heard him utter," Rupert said.

Acting on impulse, Rupert let Betsy run, and Rowan laughed in ecstasy. Rupert was amazed at Betsy's responsiveness. "Already we had achieved a level of instinctive trust . . . that usually takes months, sometimes years, to build."

When the ride was over, Rupert asked Rowan to say thank you to Betsy. Immediately, Rowan hugged her brown head and gave her a kiss. "As he did so, an expression of extraordinary gentleness came over her," Rupert said, "a blissful half-closing of the eyelid."

In that and many moments to come, Rupert said he felt that "something passed between them, some directness of communication that I, a neurotypical human, could never experience."

RIDING AND TALKING

Rupert and Rowan started riding Betsy almost every day, and invariably, Betsy was tolerant, submissive, and calm with Rowan. Further, while riding, Rowan showed the same linguistic, behavioral, and cognitive improvements. The only frustration was that, away from Betsy, the advances disappeared. Overall, Rowan's dysfunctions continued unabated.

As months passed, professional therapists grew pessimistic that Rowan would ever improve permanently, "but with Betsy he was a different kid," Rupert said.

And Betsy was a different horse. During one ride, the cinch broke on the saddle, which swung below her belly, unseating Rupert and Rowan. As they fell, Rupert's foot caught in the stirrup and his head slid under a wire fence.

"I should have been dead meat," he said. Rupert had seen horses bolt or buck in that situation numerous times, kicking and flailing until the loose saddle fell off.

"But again Betsy did not move," Rupert said. "She just stood there, with that soft look in her eye she always had when Rowan was on the ground near her."

Betsy waited patiently as Rupert fixed the saddle and they continued the ride. Had Betsy saved both their lives because of her devotion to Rowan? Rupert thought so.

Once, after a long ride in spring 2005, Rowan threw a fit because he wanted to keep riding. Then, abruptly and unprompted, he stopped wailing, walked up to the horse, and hugged and kissed her foreleg, saying, "I wuv you, Betsy."

"It was the first time he'd ever said the words," said Rupert, and as always, "Betsy's eye half closed as he held on to her."

Still, Rowan's progress on Betsy was inconsistent and didn't translate beyond riding. So, in summer 2005, the Isaacsons hired a teacher to work with Rowan while riding Betsy. For a year, this worked far better than any previous therapies, but permanent gains were elusive. Rowan's tantrums remained a volatile, ever-present storm.

"Our lives were tantrum," Rupert said. "Tantrum and the spaces in between."

Exhausted and feeling their marriage coming apart, Rupert made an admittedly crazy proposal to his wife, Kristin.

THINKING IN PICTURES

Dr. Temple Grandin is one of the world's most famous autists. She is a professor at Colorado State University, a published author, and an acknowledged expert in animal behavior. She was severely autistic as a child, but she improved dramatically because of devoted caregivers and an early connection to horses.

Dr. Grandin said, "Animals think in pictures. So do I. So do many autists. It means we can't connect to other people, who think differently, in words or other mental patterns. Because animals think the same way—visually—autistic people often connect well with animals."

Dr. Grandin has written about this in her book *Animals in Translation*. She says that fear is the main emotion in autism, and its the same for prey animals like horses and cows.

"The brain of the horse is very specific," she said. "If a horse gets a fear memory, it's stored as a picture, a sound, or a feel."

Dr. Grandin compares it to having a slide projector in your mind, in which there are no generalized, generic images.

"Animals and autistic people don't see their *ideas* of things; they see the actual things themselves."

TO MONGOLIA AND BACK

As a travel writer and journalist, Rupert had met aboriginal Bushmen from Africa and seen Bushman shamans perform incredible healings. Once, a Bushman even performed a healing on Rowan, and afterward, for a short time, Rowan's symptoms eased.

"Might there, I wondered, be some way of combining these two things—horses and shamanic healing?" Rupert asked.

The answer was yes, in Mongolia, the birthplace of the domestic horse, where native people still nurtured their ancient shamanic traditions. Rupert's idea was to ride with Rowan across Mongolia on horseback seeking traditional shamans who might heal Rowan's symptoms.

For two years, Kristin had resisted the idea on the grounds that it was insane, but finally she gave in. They were at the end of their rope. Even if it didn't work, what did they have to lose?

So, for a month in 2007, the Isaacsons journeyed across the windswept Siberian steppes, meeting herds of wild horses and engaging in a series of bizarre rituals and strange healings. The last shaman they met, Ghoste, even informed them that he had communicated with Betsy in the spirit world, for he said the horse was Rowan's animal protector. When Ghoste was finished, he said that Rowan had accepted the healing and would be fine.

The Isaacsons didn't know what to believe, but as they made their long way back home to Texas, the shaman's promise was realized. Within days, Rowan's tantrums faded, he began using sentences, and he used the toilet on his own, a practice he then continued. Within a month, Rowan had become social and conversational, and "the tantrums, the hyperactivity, and anxiety . . . had left him completely," Rupert said. To their utter amazement, "we had come back with a completely different child."

Rowan and Betsy kept riding, and by six years old, Rowan was riding her on his own. He was also making friends and reading above his age level. In other words, Rowan had his life back.

"Rowan is still autistic—his essence, his many talents, are all tied up with it," Rupert said, but "he has been healed of the terrible dysfunctions that afflicted him—his physical and emotional incontinence, his neurological firestorms, his anxiety and hyperactivity."

Neither Rupert nor Kristin can explain how this happened. But some change occurred in Mongolia that proved lasting, and it was born in and remained connected to Rowan's intimate relationship with Betsy.

Rowan "has not been cured," Rupert said, and emphasized, "nor would I want him to be."

HEALING ON A HORSE

Today, equine-assisted therapy is used to help people with a range of emotional, psychological, and physical issues, from children with autism, ADD, Down syndrome, and cerebral palsy to veterans with PTSD, adults coping with depression, and more. Simply put, riding a horse can be effective medicine. As with Rowan, it isn't a "cure," but it can help ameliorate a wide range of problems.

Many theories exist about why riding a horse and being involved in horse care are therapeutic. None have yet been proven. In part, interacting with animals in nature just feels good. Another reason has to do with the nature of horses. "Horses are naturally empathetic," said horse trainer Franklin Levinson, who runs programs in England. "The members of the herd feel what is going on for the other members of the herd."

Horses are highly attuned to body language and are extraordinarily responsive to a person's emotions. Stories like Clever Hans (see page 295) and Molly (see page 154) illustrate this well. Interactions with horses can be revealing, useful mirrors for a person's psychological state.

However, the motion of riding, as riders fall in and out of balance, is also thought to open the brain to learning. This may explain why autists show improved language skills. Finally, the physicality of riding tones the muscles and improves posture.

One day, research may explain why riding is therapeutic, but it's doubtful that it will ever unlock the secrets of shamans and the spirit world.

MOLLY THE PONY . . . LOSES A LEG AND INSPIRES HOPE

NAME: *Molly*

SPECIES: *Pony of the Americas*

DATE: *2005*

LOCATION: *St. Rose, Louisiana*

SITUATION: *Three-legged horse with a prosthesis*

WHO WAS SAVED: *Handicapped people and children*

LEGACY: *National icon of New Orleans' post-Katrina recovery, became beloved therapy animal*

In late August 2005, as Hurricane Katrina bore down on coastal Louisiana and Mississippi, many people heeded evacuation orders and scattered north (for the story of one person who didn't, see page 43). In their haste, they left behind many things, including pets and animals they couldn't take with them.

One left-behind animal was fifteen-year-old Molly, a small gray-speckled Pony of the Americas (which is a cross between an Appaloosa and a Shetland pony). Untethered and untrailered, Molly survived the storm unharmed. Afterward, however, her owners were unable to care for her, and they gave her to Kaye Harris, who ran a pony farm in St. Rose, Louisiana. Kaye was rescuing all sorts of abandoned animals in the wake of the natural disaster.

Rather than a happy ending, however, this is when Molly's luck went south.

THE WILL TO LIVE

This story is about the unquenchable spirit of a rare individual, and it begins with Molly's indominatible will to live when she suffered perhaps the worst handicap that can befall a horse.

A few months after Molly's arrival, Kaye returned to her ranch to a horrific sight: One of her rescued animals, a pit bull who had shown no previous signs of aggression, was viciously attacking Molly.

Molly's flank, neck, face, and all four legs were severely lacerated; one leg was chewed to the bone. Kaye immediately intervened, but Molly's injuries were so grave she thought it was too late.

"He gnawed on this pony like a meat grinder," Kaye said.

However, Kaye is not a person to give up on animals. She found another home for the pit bull, rather than euthanize him, and she and her vet, Dr. Allison Barca, worked to heal Molly's wounds.

Everything healed successfully except for Molly's right front foreleg, which was too damaged to recover. The only option was to amputate and fit the horse with a prosthetic. "This is almost never done," said Dr. Barca. "It's so expensive and so hard, and everyone who tries fails."

Nevertheless, they contacted Dr. Rustin Moore, director of the Equine Health Studies Program at the Louisiana State University School of Veterinary Medicine. Dr. Moore was skeptical and said that euthanizing Molly was probably the most humane option.

"We said look, just meet Molly," Kaye said. "It wasn't going to be me who convinced them. It was going to be her."

So Dr. Moore and his team observed Molly and came away impressed. "She's very intelligent," Dr. Moore said, "and she knows how to take care of herself. She made it obvious she understood that she was in trouble."

Dr. Moore approved the surgery, which went off without a hitch. A one-of-a-kind prosthesis was created. The only question was, would Molly accept it?

"Let me tell you," Kaye said, "most horses would feel that thing on and try to get away from it. Not her. She felt it and went, 'Oh, a leg.' Boom, went walking straight off. I just cried because I knew it was going to work."

Ultimately, Molly's prosthesis evolved through three different versions, but throughout the ordeal, Molly amazed everyone. Dr. Moore said, "Molly happened to be a one-in-a-million patient. She's tough as nails but sweet, and she was willing to cope with pain."

A SYMBOL OF NEW ORLEANS

In the wake of Hurricane Katrina, Molly's unusual story made national news.

"To me, she is a symbol of New Orleans," said Kaye in 2006. "You know, if you ask me, New Orleans had its leg chopped off, but it can survive. That is the spirit of New Orleans, and this city can come back. Molly has come back. She's not back to normal; she's gonna be better."

At the time, this sounded like a hopeful boast. Molly's story was heart-warming, but how could life as a lame three-legged pony be an improvement?

Yet that's how it turned out.

First of all, Molly adapted to and adopted the prosthesis as her own. "She asks for it," said Dr. Barca. "She's amazing. She will put her little limb out and come to you and let you know that she wants you to put it on. Sometimes she wants you to take it off, too."

Not only that, she didn't let it slow her down.

"Occasionally she will drag your butt down the levee," Dr. Barca said. "She'll tow you! It can be pretty bad when you can't catch a three-legged horse."

This kind of determination can't be taught, and Kaye knew Molly was special.

"It's important to understand that the will of the animal has a lot to do with it," Kaye said. "The animal has to participate in her own survival. That's very like people. If you don't participate in your own survival, in your own therapy, you're not going to go anywhere. And that's the point about her, she never gave it up."

Kaye feels strongly that all people, all beings, have a duty to give back to society, and she had a sense what work Molly might be fit for.

Again, the only question was, would she take to it?

TENDING TO THE WOUNDED

One day Kaye and Dr. Barca took Molly to a local children's hospital. A group of children coping with various issues was brought to an outdoor courtyard to pet the horse. One encounter stood out from the rest.

A boy who'd recently had a brain operation was wheeled next to Molly's face.

"His head is thrashing wildly and they say, 'Oh, he can't control it,'" Kaye recalled. "He gets up next to Molly. His head goes—whoop. Her eye's right there, and his head stops dead, deliberately. They stay looking at each other for three minutes. Molly doesn't move a muscle."

Dr. Barca reached over and placed the boy's hand on Molly's nose. "Again," Kaye said, "the kid supposedly can't control his limbs. He keeps it there for a whole minute."

When the hospital visit was over, and the kids had gone back inside, Kaye and Dr. Barca led Molly away, only to have her drag them back up the pathway. Kaye yelled at her to stop, figuring she wanted to eat the grass, but

Molly returned to the empty courtyard. Only after a lot of convincing that the kids were truly gone would Molly agree to leave.

In this way, Molly seemed to embrace a new calling. Kaye founded the nonprofit Molly's Foundation, and through it, she brings Molly to visit children and adults coping will all sort of disabilities. In these encounters, Molly dispenses a type of inspirational healing that Kaye half-jokingly calls "Molly magic."

Kaye is emphatic that it's Molly who pursues these interactions. "Things like that have happened to me over and over and over again with her. Where I know it's not just me saying, 'Oh look, you're a celebrity. Let's go.' No. This is her choice. Over and over again in our visits, she chooses to stay. She'll pick out a person, and she won't move until I get that person to come up. I just listen to her."

When people train therapy animals, they select them carefully. They discern which animals have the right temperament and ability for therapeutic work, and they weed out the many who don't display the right aptitude, demeanor, or focus. But perhaps people aren't the only ones choosing. Many stories in this book, like Molly's, involve animals who apparently choose to work with a particular person or in a particular therapeutic way. Perhaps these animals agree to be trained, and are successful at it, because the affinity and desire already exist.

No one trained Molly for therapy work, and no one had to convince her to want to help people with disabilities.

"I think she has that empathy," Kaye said. "And I think she knows. I think there's some wavelength that reaches out from her and touches these people. Cause I see people go to absolute goo when they meet her."

Dr. Moore said, "She survived the hurricane, she survived a horrible injury, and now she is giving hope to others."

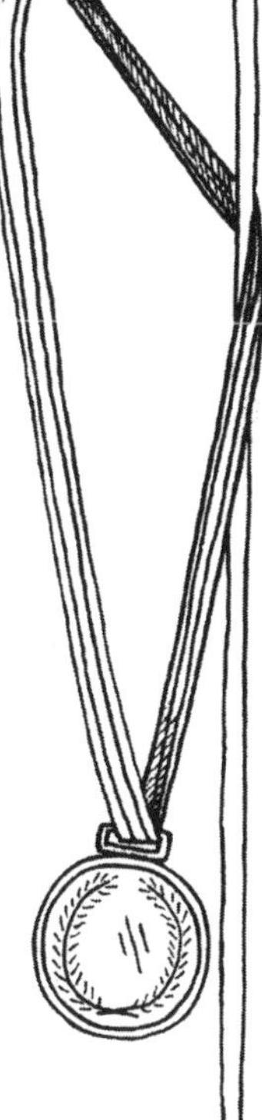

OXYTOCIN: THE BIOLOGY OF GOOD FEELINGS

Why does touch feel so good? How is it possible that simply petting another animal—such as a horse like Molly or a dog like Cheyenne (see page 141)—can have such positive emotional and therapeutic benefits?

One answer is oxytocin. This potent chemical is released whenever we pet an animal, which also releases dopamine and beta endorphins. These chemicals help increase our sense of well-being: They lower our heart rate and blood pressure, and decrease the production of stress hormones. Studies have shown that petting a dog doubles a person's oxytocin levels.

As researcher Meg Daley Olmert writes in her book *Made for Each Other*, oxytocin "makes people more trusting and more trustworthy. It can even relieve some of the antisocial tendencies of autistics."

Further, oxytocin is produced in both the animal being petted and the one doing the petting. This seems to confirm what most of us have known all along: Our companion animals enjoy being petted as much as we enjoy wrapping our arms around them.

Oxytocin has long been recognized as essential to creating our "maternal instincts" (see page 41), but as Olmert writes, it's now believed to be "at the heart of the human-animal bond" and "squarely behind the domestication of animals."

Anthropologist Pat Shipman agrees. In her book *The Animal Connection*, Shipman writes, "I would argue that we love animals and find companionship and joy in their presence because we have evolved to be connected to animals," and that the "main biological ingredient" behind this is oxytocin.

Over millennia, animals have deeply influenced human evolution (see page 244). In the here and now, animals provide healing by their presence and contact alone. That might sound romantic, but oxytocin reveals that there is, Olmert writes, a "physiological reality of why animals can love us, why we can love them, and why that love is so good for everyone it touches."

CHANCER THE GOLDEN RETRIEVER . . . CALMS THE STORM

NAME: *Chancer*

SPECIES: *Golden retriever*

DATE: *January 2008*

LOCATION: *Roswell, Georgia*

SITUATION: *Impaired child suffering fetal alcohol syndrome*

WHO WAS SAVED: *Eleven-year-old Iyal Winokur*

LEGACY: *The world's first certified assistance dog for fetal alcohol syndrome*

In August 1999, unable to have children themselves, Harvey and Donnie Winokur eagerly adopted two undernourished, one-year-old babies—an unrelated girl and boy—from a Russian orphanage. The Winokurs were optimistic that they could create the kind of loving home in which the pair, Morasha and Iyal, would thrive.

After about two years, however, Iyal's increasingly erratic behavior signaled deeper problems. While Morasha remained a bright and curious three-year-old girl, Iyal began having unexpected, raging tantrums; he would alternately hurt other kids and try to kiss strangers.

For a year, the Winokurs saw specialists of all kinds, but no one could diagnose Iyal's issues. Meanwhile, the family was, Donnie said, "living with a constant anticipation of a hurricane." Harvey said, "Iyal's disabilities began to define our family's existence."

Then a pediatrician recognized the signs of fetal alcohol syndrome (FAS), an incurable birth defect, which is caused when a mother drinks during pregnancy. This was the worst-case scenario: Iyal was permanently brain damaged. Across the range of possible fetal alcohol disorders, FAS is the worst, and it would affect Iyal for life.

For several years, the Winokurs tried every known therapy and medication to ease or remedy Iyal's condition. Nothing worked, and Donnie felt increasingly anguished and desperate; the strain of caring for Iyal was destroying their family.

Then in 2007, Donnie heard about the Ohio organization 4 Paws for Ability, which trained service dogs to work with autistic children. Could that work for Iyal? Karen Shirk, the executive director, said no one had ever trained a dog for FAS before, but she'd be willing to give it a try.

TRAINING FOR "INVISIBLE DISABILITIES"

Training dogs to work with "invisible disabilities"—particularly mental disabilities like autism, post-traumatic stress disorder, and other emotional impairments—was, and is, a relatively new idea. While it's been shown to be effective, it takes a very special animal to succeed, since the person being served is, perhaps by definition, unreliable. Their mind isn't right, so in some sense, the dog needs to think for them—anticipating and providing what's needed without request.

For instance, trained dogs thrive on positive feedback, but someone who can't control their emotions can become verbally or physically abusive to the animal, or their violent outbursts might scare the dog. Thus, dogs are trained to intervene when they sense an impending episode, and they must be emotionally strong to persevere when meltdowns can't be stopped.

Jeremy Dulebohn, the 4 Paws training director, paired Iyal with Chancer, a shaggy, unruffled, go-with-the-flow golden with "high self-esteem." Donnie said Dulebohn "taught Chancer three special skills: nuzzling against Iyal at the first sign of agitation; if Iyal was on the floor, climbing on top of Iyal's legs and lying down (the pressure calming him); and tethering." For the last, Chancer and Iyal would be connected by tethered vests, allowing Chancer to keep Iyal from running away.

In January 2008, when the time came for Chancer to join the Winokurs, the initial meeting at 4 Paws seemed disastrous. Chancer's friendly eagerness won over everyone in the family but Iyal, who threw fits and ran off. The pair hardly interacted.

However, on the second day, the Winokurs brought Chancer back to the hotel where they were staying, so the dog could spend the night with them. On a walk, Chancer spotted Iyal in the hotel's hot tub, jerked free from his leash, and dove into the water with a tremendous, ungainly splash.

Iyal was startled and laughed harder than his family had ever heard before. It was a strange scene: Iyal had not been drowning, nor was Chancer trained for water rescues. But Chancer's unnecessary "rescue" sparked a connection that rang out loud and clear.

CONNECTIONS: CHANCER WITH IYAL, IYAL WITH THE WORLD

Initially, Harvey Winokur had vehemently resisted the idea of getting a dog. He didn't think their household could handle the strain of one more being.

But, Harvey said, "The moment [Iyal] walked in the house with Chancer, I knew something had changed. I could feel it instantly, the magnetism between Iyal and the dog. . . . Chancer was an emotional and physical anchor for a kid who was pretty lost in the world."

That night, snuggled with Chancer, Iyal slept through the night for the first time since 1999. Chancer immediately put his training into action and intervened whenever Iyal's rages erupted. The slobbery dog kisses and the warm, furry, ninety-pound body pinning Iyal to the floor were often enough to relax Iyal and change his screams into laughter.

Within two weeks, Iyal was surprising his parents with unexpected cognitive improvements. He started using multisyllable words and expressing never-before-heard opinions, such as what he wanted for lunch. He also quit repeating everything his sister said.

Most startling of all, Iyal began to consider Chancer's point of view. He developed what's called a "theory of mind," which most kids achieve by age four, and in this way he began to develop a self-awareness about his own condition.

One day, Donnie said, "I was in the kitchen, Iyal beside me, petting Chancer. Suddenly he said, 'Mommy, do you think Chancer knows I love him?'"

"Was this for real?" Donnie asked herself. "My son, who had never uttered such a complex sentence, let alone expressed awareness that someone might have feelings different from his own? 'Yes,' I said. 'He knows. And *he* loves you.'"

At other times, Iyal asked, "Did Chancer's birth mother drink alcohol?" and "Why did my birth mother drink alcohol?" The Winokurs had explained Iyal's condition to him in the past, but received no indication that he understood.

Clearly, Iyal's trusting, caring relationship with Chancer helped him to improve where other therapies and medications had not. As with Joe and Fonzie (page 109), what Chancer provided may have been the loving motivation that inspired Iyal to overcome obstacles on his own. As emotionally sensitive and aware as dogs are, it's hard to say what the animal understands—such as whether Chancer knows Iyal is disabled. Whatever the animal knows, the human-animal bond seems to create a cascading positive effect.

NOT UNDERSTANDING THE RULES

Nevertheless, Iyal and Chancer's story points to some of the limits of service animals as well. For all that Iyal has and may continue to improve, he remains neurologically damaged; as Iyal gets older, his psychological and emotional hurdles may grow. Chancer's love and companionship cannot change that, and trainer Jeremy Dulebohn warns clients not to indulge in "the Lassie syndrome." The presence of a service dog can heal in marvelous and unexpected ways, but it won't heal everything or everyone.

Further, it's an open question of what Chancer might do if Iyal told him to do something wrong—for instance, something that could hurt another person, Chancer, or even Iyal himself. As Donnie said, before Chancer came along, "Iyal had trouble remembering instructions from one day to the next. Don't squeeze the cat. Don't go out of the house. Don't crowd your sister."

In fact, animals can be trained in "intelligent disobedience," so that they recognize and refuse a bad request. Seeing-eye dogs must be able to do this; they must evaluate the environment independently and signal their blind companion when a command is dangerous.

Yet a blind person knows the animal is trained to disobey for their own good; someone like Iyal, who suffers bouts of irrational, oppositional behavior, might not. Then, what about instructions that are morally wrong or inappropriate rather than physically dangerous? As some stories in this book suggest, certain species display a basic moral sense, but that doesn't mean they possess ethics that reflect human cultural norms. It's almost certain they don't. If someone like Iyal can't be trusted to know right from wrong, Chancer can't be asked or trained to do this for him.

In other words, though Chancer and Iyal have become inextricably devoted to each other, Iyal can never be Chancer's caretaker.

"He can't even take Chancer for a walk around the block," Donnie said. "He might drop the leash, and Chancer might interpret that release as permission to track a hamburger. Chancer's an amazing service dog, but he is a dog."

Luckily, for both Chancer and Iyal, being a dog is quite enough.

THEORY OF MIND

Animals think, but do they understand that they think and that other animals have their own independent thoughts? For Iyal, this awareness was not automatic, and it may have taken his relationship with Chancer to bring it out. Iyal loved Chancer so much he finally had to know: Did Chancer understand what *he* felt?

Imagining the mind and perspective of another is called "Theory of Mind." For a long time, scientists considered only humans capable of this cognitive leap, but as with so many claims to human exceptionalism, this turns out to be not an exclusive ability.

Empathy—the ability to feel or understand what another animal is feeling—is different from considering the world from their perspective. To do this requires mentally projecting oneself into the mind of another, as well as awareness of one's own knowledge—it allows us to guess someone's intentions and to recognize when we don't know something.

For instance, Chancer certainly senses when Iyal's feeling distressed, but can he ask himself: WWID, what would Iyal do? Or, more specifically, WIITD: what is Iyal intending to do?

According to scientist Marc Bekoff, yes. "My own research on social play behavior in dogs, coyotes, and wolves," Bekoff has written, "has also led me to conclude that they have a theory of mind."

Apes and dolphins have also displayed theory of mind, and some feel that monkeys, elephants, orcas, and parrots also show signs of it. As with mirror neurons (see page 59), the ability to understand that other animals think may be a necessity for highly social mammals.

This matters to us, deeply. Like Iyal, we want to know that our companion animals know that we love them—that there is mutual understanding. Like Donnie Winokur, we want to say "he knows" and believe it.

TREO THE LABRADOR RETRIEVER . . . SNIFFS OUT A BOMB

NAME: *Treo*

SPECIES: *Labrador retriever*

DATE: *August 2008*

LOCATION: *Afghanistan*

SITUATION: *War-time threat from hidden roadside bombs*

WHO WAS SAVED: *Hundreds of Afghanistan-based Coalition Forces troops*

LEGACY: *Medal-winning British military hero, exemplifies gutsy devotion of bomb-detection dogs*

Treo's story begins like that of many working dogs who find themselves suited for the rigors of the military, the police force, or as search-and-rescue dogs. He was, as the British would say, a royal pain in the arse.

A feisty black Labrador retriever, Treo had a highly developed prey drive and an aggressiveness that his owners couldn't control. The one-year-old pup growled at and confronted everyone. Frazzled and frustrated, the owners eventually donated Treo to the British military.

In fact, the military searches for exactly this kind of relentless, overachieving, Type-A canine personality. One British military dog recruiter said, "It is no good having a dog that will chase a ball behind the sofa a couple of times and then grow bored."

PARTNERING WITH A HANDLER

Over a twelve-week training course, Treo's energy was channeled into becoming a working military dog specializing in bomb detection. Then Treo was matched with a military handler—the soldier who would work with him in the field.

Treo was partnered with Sergeant David Heyhoe, who was actually Treo's second handler, but that didn't make their relationship, or their need to connect, any less important. The ultimate success of every canine-human working partnership, no matter what context, often relates directly to the strength of their emotional bond. Pairing the right dog with the right handler is essential.

Sergeant Heyhoe said his experience with Treo was virtually kismet. "I looked at him and he looked at me and that was that—I know it sounds daft, but it was love at first sight," he said.

Then, once partnered, the handler and the dog spend as much or more time together than the person does with his or her own family. For deployed soldiers, this includes a spouse. For the next five years, except for one two-week period, Sergeant Heyhoe and Treo were together every single day. In this way, dogs and handlers come to know each other intimately and can read every nuance of each other's behavior.

"Basically, me and the dog have got to get a rapport," Sergeant Heyhoe said. "We've got to understand each other, and without that we can't be effective on the ground. Everyone will say that he is just a military working dog—yes, he is, but he is also a very good friend of mine. We look after each other."

In the military, the extraordinary closeness of the handler-dog relationship also relates to the inherent dangers of war. As Maria Goodavage, author of *Soldier Dogs*, writes: "Handlers put their lives on the line for their dogs, and the reverse is also true."

FINDING BOMBS IN AFGHANISTAN

In 2008, Sergeant Heyhoe and Treo were deployed to Helmund Province in Afghanistan. They formed part of the British military's contribution to the Coalition Forces during the Afghanistan War against the Taliban insurgency in the 2000s.

Sergeant Heyhoe and Treo were a detection team whose main role was to find improvised explosive devices, or IEDs—that is, hidden bombs along roadsides or near public spaces that are either detonated remotely or on contact. In the Afghanistan and Iraq Wars, the opposition used IEDs rampantly, and locating these remains the most common and important role for working military dogs. It is also the most dangerous, since it "involves searching for arms and explosives out on the ground to the forefront of the troops," Sergeant Heyhoe said.

During their six-month deployment in Helmund Province, Treo found numerous bombs, but two incidents in particular stood out.

In August 2008, Treo found "a daisy-chain that was three or four devices linked together," Sergeant Heyhoe said. "If that would have gone off, it would have killed the whole patrol."

Similarly, a month later, Treo uncovered a second daisy-chain that would have killed another entire patrol.

As a result of these two finds, and six months after he was retired from active duty, Treo was awarded the British Dickin Medal in 2010. The Dickin Medal is England's animal equivalent to the Victoria Cross, which recognizes bravery in battle. The United States has no similar official award for working military animals (which has long been a point of controversy; see page 290).

While Sergeant Heyhoe said he was "very proud" to receive the award, he felt that it really honored all the dogs and handlers working in Afghanistan and Iraq.

"That's what the medal means to us," he said. "Taking it for the rest of the guys and their dogs."

FOUR-LEGGED METAL DETECTORS

In the last decade, working military dogs have become an indelible, and perhaps irreplaceable, aide in battle, particularly for Britain and America. In 2008, Treo was one of twenty-five dogs serving the British military in Afghanistan, while the Royal Army Veterinary Corps (RAVC) currently has two hundred dogs trained for combat.

Today, the US military has approximately 2,700 working military dogs in service worldwide in a range of capacities.

With obvious affection, Sergeant Heyhoe once called Treo "basically a four-legged metal detector." But the truth is, no mechanical device comes close to doing what a dog can do. One RAVC officer said, "A dog is a robust, fast piece of equipment that can work in all areas. Other kit often has far more technical and operating problems."

Most soldiers bristle at the characterization of dogs as "equipment." After all, working military dogs excel at what they do in part because they are unconditionally devoted to the soldiers. They are dogs, after all. This translates directly into lives saved.

Over an eight-year period in Afghanistan and Iraq in the 2000s, IEDs were responsible for approximately 60 percent of all casualties (including deaths and injuries) among Coalition Forces.

Without dogs like Treo, that percentage would have been far higher. Though estimates of lives saved by dogs vary widely, according to Goodavage in *Soldier Dogs*, it ranges "from 150 to 1,800 lives per dog." And according the US Department of Defense, "non-canine detection units" have about a 50 percent success rate at detecting hidden weapons and bombs, while dogs have an 80 percent success rate.

THE NOSE KNOWS, BUT THE HEART FINDS

It's no secret that dogs have a better sense of smell than humans. Depending on the breed, dogs have up to 300 million olfactory receptors in their noses, while humans have a paltry 6 million. Plus, the part of a dog's brain devoted to analyzing odors is forty times larger, proportionally speaking, than in humans.

Because of this, dogs smell anywhere from 10,000 to 100,000 times better than we do. If smelling were a sprint, a dog would be done before we took our first step.

But dogs don't have the *best* noses in the animal kingdom. Bears, sharks, snakes, mice, and even moths are considered better sniffers.

So are pigs, and in the 1970s, military researchers discovered that pigs topped dogs at detecting underground bombs. So why are there no bomb-sniffing pigs—or bears, for that matter?

Well, pigs instinctively root, and they grow quite large, both of which are clear detriments if the underground object you're hunting could explode.

According to Cat Warren in *What the Dog Knows,* researchers also experimented with bomb-sniffing coyotes, deer, raccoons, badgers, wolves, skunks, raptors, and even rattlesnakes. Over the years, they also tried bugs and special ferns (which turn white near dangerous chemicals). All of these can accurately detect bombs, but none of them are suited for bomb detection for a very simple reason: None are motivated to work with humans. Wild animals, being wild, easily become distracted and disinterested, and thus unreliable.

Domestic canines may not be the ultimate sniffers, but they're the only animals who truly want the job. This applies to other areas, like disease detection, as well.

Plus, dogs work cheaply. When they make a find, their "pay" is typically play time with a favorite toy or even just a well-earned hug.

RICOCHET THE SURFING DOG . . . RIDES WITH THE DISABLED

NAME: *Ricochet*

SPECIES: *Golden retriever*

DATE: *August 2009*

LOCATION: *San Diego, California*

SITUATION: *Teenage quadriplegic wanting to walk*

WHO WAS SAVED: *Fourteen-year-old Patrick Ivison*

LEGACY: *The world's only tandem-surfing therapy dog and renowned viral-video star*

Ricochet didn't make the cut.

That's okay. Most dogs don't.

But Ricochet's owner, Judy Fridono, was bitterly disappointed. From the moment the golden retriever was born on January 25, 2008, Judy wanted her to be a service dog for people with disabilities.

Ricochet began training at only thirteen days old—before her eyes were open—and for the next three months, she seemed like "a true prodigy," Judy said.

However, Ricochet loved chasing squirrels . . . and seagulls . . . and every other furry or feathered critter that crossed her path. They don't call the breed "retrievers" for nothing.

"I tried for months to make her something she wasn't but finally had to release her from the program," Judy said. A dog who can't resist chasing birds "could be harmful for someone with disabilities."

Like many a Southern California dropout, Ricochet preferred surfing to working, so . . . wait, *what?*

When did she learn to *surf*?

"I do not train dogs to surf," Judy protested. "Ricochet learned on her own!"

Yeah, but . . .

"I was working with her at balance and coordination," Judy explained. "We started on a body board in a paddling pool, and from that it went into surfing."

In fact, Ricochet loved surfing so much that at around fifteen months old the red-haired retriever entered her first surf-dog competition and came in third.

Why hang ten when you can hang twenty, *amiright*?

Ahem, anyway . . . Judy knew the surfing life wasn't going to be enough. "I still wanted her to do something meaningful with her life," she said. "So I thought about fundraising."

But what sort of fundraising can you do with a lazy, misbehaved, soggy rag of a surfing dog?

Then, in August 2009, Judy and Ricochet met Patrick Ivison, and everything fell into place.

SURFING TO WALK

Patrick Ivison was then fourteen years old. He'd been a quadriplegic and confined to a wheelchair ever since he was fourteen months old, when a car unexpectedly reversed into him. Trapped under the car, Patrick suffered an irreversible spinal cord injury.

However, like Ricochet, Patrick unexpectedly learned to surf, and he loved it. He'd been doing what's known as "adaptive surfing" ever since he was about eight years old, using a customized board on which he'd lie on his belly and hold up his head and shoulders with his elbows.

Further, Patrick had recently made himself a pledge: He wanted to walk across the stage at his high school graduation in three years. To accomplish that, he needed a very expensive program of physical therapy, one that his family couldn't afford.

Ding! A light bulb went on over Judy's head: Ricochet and Patrick could hold a surfing demonstration, raising awareness about adaptive surfing and raising money for Patrick's physical therapy.

Ricochet made the decision easy. Patrick's mother said, "Patrick and Ricki, when they first met, it was like instant love. They instantly clicked. She just met him, and she would run and leap and jump into his lap and sit there."

For the demonstration, the plan was for Ricochet and Patrick to ride the same waves on their separate boards. They did this, cool enough, but then "Rip Curl Ricki," as Judy liked to call her, decided to mix things up: On the beach, she jumped onto Patrick's board, straddling him over his back, and looked at everyone as if to say: *Come on, dudes, who* doesn't *want to ride tandem!?*

None of them had ever done tandem adaptive surfing before, but Patrick was game. So the crew set up the pair for a wave and pushed them into it.

"It worked the first time," Patrick said. "I was kind of surprised. I didn't expect it to go as well as it did."

Now a whole string of light bulbs went on over Judy's head.

Ricochet and Patrick kept at it and did more fundraising demonstrations.

Patrick said that Ricochet "knows how to balance. It's kinda crazy. We were about to fall one time, and she just steps on the other side of the board and evens us out. I barely know how to do that. I said, 'What are you talking about? You're not supposed to be a better surfer than me.'"

Of course, no one surfs without a few spills.

"When you fall off you are at the mercy of the wave and it takes you wherever it wants," Patrick said. "A lot of people would be scared, but I kind of like it." And each time they fell, Ricochet would stick right by Patrick's side.

Within months, Judy and Ricochet had raised $10,000 for Patrick, and one of Ricochet's corporate sponsors awarded Patrick a $90,000 three-year grant, which covered Patrick's physical therapy expenses.

Flash forward three years later, and Ricochet watched from the front row as Patrick received his high school diploma—using a wheeled walker to walk himself across the stage.

THE WORLD'S FIRST *SURF*ICE DOG

What do you know? Ricochet wasn't such a slacker after all.

"It's what she chose to do; she jumped on the board and went surfing," Judy said. "It's her instinct and what she loves. She has total control and is good at what she does."

However, Judy admitted to some doubts the first time Ricochet rode with disabled groms, or novice surfers.

"In fact, that first day I remember saying to the team, 'I will just have to trust my dog,' because we have never done this as outreach. None of the kids had ever surfed, so pretty much everyone put their trust in the dog, and she went for it."

As Judy explained, "Her balance is so good she helps to stabilize the board for the kids who've never done it before. And it makes them feel good to know that Ricochet is there with them, keeping them company."

Judy dubbed Ricochet a "SURFice dog" (a "service" dog who surfs, get it?), and Ricochet rode the waves as a tandem adaptive surfer in support of a succession of causes—in addition to continuing to surf competitively against other dogs! Before long, Ricochet was a media and Internet sensation, with videos of her wave riding going viral. By 2014, she had helped raise over $300,000 for 150 different organizations and brought the joy of surfing, and of canine companionship, to countless disabled and handicapped people for whom mobility is a constant struggle.

For Judy herself, who has wrestled with chronic arthritis ever since she was a teen, this lesson struck close to home.

"Ricochet has taught me to focus on what I can do, rather than what I can't."

RIDING THE WAVES BACK TO SHORE

Most recently, Ricochet has expanded her therapeutic repertoire. She has joined an organization that pairs therapy dogs with veterans suffering from PTSD. One aspect of the program is for dogs to accompany vets into public spaces, such as shopping malls and grocery stores; the dogs help the person stay calm and avoid the triggers that might spark an anxiety attack. They help them ride a different kind of wave, so to speak.

Ricochet teamed with retired Staff Sergeant Randall Dexter, who battles PTSD. "Before I met her I was very isolated, and became depressed and suicidal," Dexter said. "But when I met Ricochet, I finally had a new sense of hope. I definitely feel that Ricochet saved my life."

Once rejected as a service dog, Ricochet is now a certified therapy dog, one who has become as comfortable on dry land as in the water.

"There is something special about her," Judy said. "She bonds with people instantly. She has this sixth sense about her that is able to touch people's hearts. The only thing I do is make one decision—to allow her to be who she is without any expectations. It's all her leading this entire journey."

Or as Judy puts it: "She is an ordinary dog with an extraordinary spirit."

DEFINITIONS: SERVICE AND THERAPY ANIMALS

Animals help us in an ever-growing variety of ways, and the terms used to describe them can get confusing. Very few terms are standardized, and new ones pop up all the time. Here is a quick overview of some major categories:

Service Animals

In 1990, the US government passed the Americans with Disabilities Act (ADA), which legally required all businesses and public institutions to allow service animals. In 2011, the ADA further specified that only dogs are considered "service animals" under federal law. Other animals who perform services, like cats, monkeys, and miniature horses, have limited or no federal rights.

To quote the ADA: "Service animals are defined as dogs that are individually trained to do work or perform tasks for people with disabilities. Examples of such work or tasks include guiding people who are blind, alerting people who are deaf, pulling a wheelchair, alerting and protecting a person who is having a seizure, reminding a person with mental illness to take prescribed medications, calming a person with Post Traumatic Stress Disorder (PTSD) during an anxiety attack, or performing other duties. Service animals are working animals, not pets. The work or task a dog has been trained to provide must be directly related to the person's disability."

Dogs who help partners with emotional or mental issues are also called "psychiatric service dogs"; they are trained to recognize and respond to a person's specific behavior (like Chancer, see page 160). In public, all registered service dogs wear identifying vests.

Therapy Animals

Though not defined federally, several states legally define therapy animals. Typically, this refers to animals brought to public institutions like hospitals and schools, or to disaster sites, to bring cheer and emotional healing to a range of people. This includes "comfort dogs" who help survivors in the wake of public tragedies as well as "animal-assisted therapy," in which an animal is present during therapy with a counselor (like Fonzie, see page 109). These animals are often trained, but they don't perform specific tasks related to one person (and thus are not legally "service animals").

Emotional Support Animals

Animals who provide necessary emotional or mental help solely by their presence are called "emotional support animals" (ESAs). These animals are not trained; they only provide companionship for a partner with documented mental health issues. They are considered neither pets nor official service animals. However, when properly registered, ESAs have the right, under federal law, to be allowed in any residence and on airplanes.

Companion Animals

Quite simply, this is another term for "pet." It confers to no legal status, but today it is often used to describe the animals, trained or not, who share our lives and homes.

DAISY THE LABRADOR RETRIEVER . . . DETECTS BREAST CANCER

NAME: *Daisy*

SPECIES: *Labrador retriever*

DATE: *August 2009*

LOCATION: *Milton Keynes, England*

SITUATION: *Woman with breast cancer*

WHO WAS SAVED: *Forty-five-year-old Claire Guest, cancer researcher*

LEGACY: *One of the world's first trained cancer-detection dogs, saved pioneer researcher*

There are so many uses for a dog's nose that it's hard to keep up. One recent estimate is that there are now 180 different types of detection, and new applications arise every year.

Perhaps none are as potentially life-changing as training dogs to detect human cancer. One day, will every oncology center have resident "bio-detection dogs" to offer their own medical diagnosis? This wild notion is gaining advocates with each new study.

A CALL FOR HELP

One pioneer of this work has been Dr. Claire Guest, from Milton Keynes, England. Dr. Guest got into the field almost by accident in 2001. She had been working for Britain's Hearing Dogs for the Deaf when she heard a radio interview with Dr. John Church, a well-known orthopedic surgeon.

The interviewer asked Dr. Church if he thought animals could help in human medicine. As Dr. Guest recalled, "He said he believed dogs could detect cancer and urged anyone who thought they could train a cancer dog to get in touch."

Dr. Guest had already been wondering the same thing. Over the years, she'd heard a number of anecdotes about this.

She said, "Even a colleague of mine, Gill, told me about how her pet Dalmatian had started licking and sniffing a mole on her leg when she was in her twenties. She couldn't even be in the same room as the dog." When Gill eventually had the mole removed, "a biopsy revealed it was malignant melanoma, the most aggressive form of skin cancer."

Dr. Guest contacted Dr. Church, and they teamed up for a ground-breaking study that was published in 2004: Using a small sample, they found to their amazement that dogs could detect bladder cancer with 56 percent accuracy.

After this, Dr. Guest said, "We started to wonder that if dogs were finding it by chance, then perhaps we could actually train dogs to do this reliably."

The idea was controversial, but in 2008, Dr. Guest decided to try. She founded the nonprofit Medical Detection Dogs to train dogs to detect bladder cancer.

DOWN, DAISY

Among the first dogs that Dr. Guest trained was her own, Daisy, a thick-coated, ginger-hued, one-year-old Labrador retriever.

By summer 2009, Daisy was barely more than a puppy and still in the middle of her training. One day in August, Dr. Guest drove to the park to take Daisy for a walk.

"I opened the back of the car up," Dr. Guest said, "and instead of running off into the park as usual, Daisy jumped on me and nudged my chest."

At first, Dr. Guest was "bemused" by Daisy's exuberance, since "Daisy is usually such a gentle dog."

But Daisy persisted. She seemed anxious rather than playful, and "then she jumped up against me so hard that she raised a bruise."

Dr. Guest said, "It hurt more than it should, and I found a small lump."

Dr. Guest immediately got it checked out, and to her relief, the fine needle biopsy "came back clear." Yet over the next few days, Daisy wouldn't quit her strangely attentive behavior, so Dr. Guest returned for a core needle biopsy and discovered that she had a deep-set tumor exactly where Daisy had bruised her. She had breast cancer.

"I was told it could have been very serious and life-threatening," Dr. Guest said, "because by the time I felt the lump it would have been very advanced."

Instead, Dr. Guest got immediate treatment and the cancer went into remission.

"I wouldn't have known until it was too late if it hadn't been for Daisy. She saved my life."

THE DOG-TER WILL SEE YOU NOW

As they say, if it were fiction, no one would believe it: The cancer researcher saved from cancer by her own dog, who detected a type of cancer she wasn't trained to find.

Dr. Guest said, "It's made me absolutely determined to continue with this work. I feel that Daisy has done something incredible, whether she knew she was trying to do it or not. For me, my relationship with her is all part of why I feel so passionate about the work that I do and what dogs can do for us in the future."

Today, Daisy is the organization's star, one of the first and most accomplished "advanced cancer dogs," or what's called more generally a "medical alert dog."

Daisy is trained to detect bladder cancer in breath samples, but dogs have shown they can detect numerous types, including prostate, colon, kidney, ovarian, lung, and skin cancer. Some cancers are detected in the breath, others in urine (like prostate cancer), and skin cancer by the skin.

Significantly, as with Daisy, dogs are able to detect the very earliest stages of cancer, and early detection often makes the crucial difference in the success of cancer treatments.

A trained dog's accuracy is stunning. Some studies have shown a cancer-detection accuracy rate from 88 to 99 percent, depending on the type of cancer. Mechanical sensors can't compete, at least not yet. So far, some can only match the 60 percent accuracy of an untrained dog. One hope is that current research will lead to creating an electronic sensor with the same accuracy as a dog.

The trouble is, to create a mechanical nose, scientists have to reverse-engineer what a dog's nose does naturally.

One of Guest's researchers said, "It's difficult because, essentially, we are working backward—we don't know yet what it is that they can smell, but finding out they can smell something gets us one step closer to identifying it."

"Of course, no dog is going to be 100 percent," said Dr. Guest, "but at the moment there is no machine out there that can do what the dogs are doing. Cancer detection is extremely invasive, so imagine if it could be picked up simply by a urine sample or blowing into a tube?"

This revolutionary possibility is what drives Dr. Guest and other cancer researchers, since this "has the potential to save thousands of lives," she said.

When that day comes, we can thank Daisy for saving the life of one of the field's pioneers.

CAIRO THE BELGIAN MALINOIS ... ASSISTS NAVY SEAL TEAM SIX

NAME: *Cairo*

SPECIES: *Belgian Malinois*

DATE: *May 2, 2011*

LOCATION: *Afghanistan*

SITUATION: *Secret military raid to kill Osama bin Laden*

WHO WAS SAVED: *Navy SEAL Team Six*

LEGACY: *The most famous exemplar of the military's modern breed of elite combat dogs*

Tragic events often bring out the best in people, and as this book shows, that also holds true for animals. In America over the last fifteen years, no event has been more tragic and life-altering than the 9/11 terrorist attacks and the Middle East wars that followed in their wake.

Working dogs have been present throughout, heroically and prominently saving lives and helping people in dire circumstances: Guide dogs led blind owners from the World Trade Center towers during the attack on September 11, 2001 (see page 120), and search-and-rescue dogs found the last buried survivors at Ground Zero (see page 132). Bomb-detection dogs protected soldiers on the ground in the ensuing Afghanistan and Iraq Wars (see page 166), and service and companion animals helped care for the physically and emotionally wounded veterans who returned (see page 141).

One dog also took part in the 2011 Navy SEAL raid that killed Osama bin Laden, the Al-Qaeda leader who masterminded the 9/11 attacks. This top-secret mission ended a decade-long manhunt. It also turned a spotlight on the elite combat dogs who actively engage the human enemy alongside soldiers.

That combat dog was the only member of SEAL Team Six to be named afterward. His name was Cairo, and like the raid itself, his story remains mostly cloaked in secrecy.

ZERO DARK THIRTY

Cairo is a Belgian Malinois, a type of shepherd originally bred in Belgium and today extremely popular in the military for their intelligence, extreme drive, sense of smell, durability, and aggressiveness.

Cairo joined twenty-three Navy SEALs on Team Six, who were divided among two Black Hawk helicopters. Taking off from Afghanistan, the team infiltrated Pakistan, arriving at the Abbottabad compound where bin Laden was believed to be hiding early in the morning of May 2 ("zero dark thirty" is military slang for anytime between midnight and dawn).

As the first helicopter started to land, unexpected turbulence from its own down draft caused it to crash in a far corner of the large compound. The SEALs were unhurt and quickly began their mission to infiltrate bin Laden's living quarters.

The second helicopter, containing Cairo, landed in a grassy field across the street. Cairo, four SEALs, and a translator dressed like a Pakistani police officer then patrolled outside the compound, while the other six SEALs on the second helicopter broke inside and joined the rest of the team.

The group that remained outside had a two-fold job: to deter and send away curious onlookers and to ensure that no one tried to attack the team from outside. Cairo would intimidate, protect, smell, and attack if necessary. If someone wearing a hidden suicide vest approached, Cairo would scent the explosives and apprehend them. Then, if bin Laden wasn't found inside, Cairo could be sent in "to search for false walls and hidden doors," according to Nicolas Schmidle in the *New Yorker*.

From what has been reported, no incidents occurred outside the compound. A few locals approached, but they went away quietly. Presumably, on this mission, and similar to his fellow team members outside the compound, Cairo fulfilled his duties with his presence alone, one that surely radiated with the intensity of his training and his readiness to engage.

Meanwhile, inside the compound, the rest of Team Six completed the mission: They found bin Laden and killed him. While Schmidle described this raid in a *New Yorker* report, and the movie *Zero Dark Thirty* dramatized the events, significant details of how it was accomplished have never been publicly and officially confirmed.

CAIRO: ONE IN A THOUSAND

Most military dogs are trained for only one or two jobs, like bomb detection, but a very small cadre of elite dogs are trained as "multipurpose dogs." As the name implies, they can handle a variety of duties and combat situations, and they are used primarily by Special Operations.

Cairo was a multipurpose dog. In his book *Trident K9 Warriors*, former Navy SEAL and military dog trainer Mike Ritland said that finding a dog with the necessary abilities and resilience is "a one-in-a-thousand (or more) proposition."

Even among the high-prey-drive shepherd breeds the military prefers, these are atypical dogs. Their prey drive and detection skills must be off the charts

A PIECE OF EQUIPMENT MEETS THE PRESIDENT

After WWII, the US military decided to classify working military dogs as "equipment," the same as tanks, guns, and boots. This classification still exists today, though it feels like an anachronism of a bygone era—from a time when the suggestion that dogs were thinking beings with individual personalities was routinely dismissed. Now, that basic assumption informs most training techniques.

In general, soldiers don't agree with the military's accounting system. They feel the designation belittles the contribution of these heroic animals, and it leads to some postmodern ironies, such as that, as a piece of equipment, Cairo was not considered an official member of SEAL Team Six. In addition, he was the only piece of equipment to meet President Obama.

During his briefing at Fort Campbell, Kentucky, after the raid, President Obama met SEAL Team Six and the other officers and personnel who were involved. The SEALs presented the president with a signed American flag, and officers walked the president through the entire raid. When Cairo was mentioned, President Obama was surprised.

"There was a dog?" he asked.

In fact, Cairo was waiting, muzzled as a precaution, in another room.

Obama asked to meet him, and an official joked, "If you want to meet the dog, Mr. President, I advise you to bring treats."

and combined with extraordinary environmental toughness—meaning they are unfazed by gunfire, explosions, rappelling, helicopter rides, tactical vests, "doggles" (canine protective eyewear), mounted cameras, and more.

Finally, what makes these dogs even more rare is their willingness, really their eagerness, to be aggressive to humans. This goes against the very domesticity that canines evolved to possess and that usually makes dogs such ideal human companions.

These dogs aren't just annoyingly assertive. Ritland said, "Without the proper training and the control of a well-trained handler, these dogs would be a potential threat to folks."

Nevertheless, these elite dogs are not trained to kill, which has been and remains controversial. In what's called apprehension work, they are trained to subdue and capture; this neutralizes the threat and allows the enemy to be interrogated afterward. Bullets and bombs can't make such distinctions. This is why Ritland characterizes elite combat dogs as "a very highly skilled nonlethal force."

A DOG IS STILL A DOG

In his book, Ritland describes a dog named Cairo who was the first Navy SEAL canine warrior to be deployed, sometime in 2008. Coyly, Ritland does not confirm whether or not this is the same Cairo involved with the 2011 bin Laden raid. Given that the dog has the same name, we might presume he is the same dog, but Ritland deliberately leaves this Cairo's specific deployments unclear. All Ritland says is that this Cairo first served in Iraq, mostly for IED detection, and he saved many lives that way.

Even if this Cairo is not *the* Cairo, Ritland's description of him is universal to all elite combat dogs.

Most of all, Ritland makes clear that Cairo's effectiveness, as with all working dogs, depended on his relationship with his handler, Lloyd. The same handler-dog dynamics of trust, intimacy, communication, companionship, and love applied. In other words, even elite dogs are still dogs, just as elite soldiers are still human.

"Cairo was inspirational," Lloyd said. "To see how tirelessly he went after it, running and searching night after night and day after day, you felt like you had to keep up with him. . . . Maybe this is a bit of an exaggeration, but for me, even if Cairo hadn't had any finds or apprehensions, he would have been a valuable asset for us. Just having him as a companion, one bit of home out there, was huge for us. And I don't mean just for me. Cairo was great with all the other team members. You're out there. You're hungry. You're tired. A dog comes up to you, and you feel better."

Today, Cairo is retired, and he lives at home with Lloyd and Lloyd's other two dogs. Cairo still likes to work, and so he helps Lloyd haul lumber and put away the groceries, "and for as powerful as those jaws are," Lloyd said, "when he carries a carton of milk or whatever, he never busts through the package."

Then, as if to drive home the point that a dog is always still a dog, Lloyd said Cairo lets Lloyd's beagle get the best of him in wrestling matches and he carries a blanket with him "all the time."

"He's had it for years now," Lloyd said, "and I guess having it makes him feel secure."

TRAINING GUIDE DOGS: THE SEEING EYE

In 1928, Morris Frank and his guide dog Buddy returned to America after training in Switzerland to become the first guide-dog team in the United States. They arrived in Manhattan and, in front of amazed crowds, demonstrated how a trained dog could help a blind person safely cross a street.

In 1929, Frank cofounded The Seeing Eye, which is today the oldest guide-dog school in the world. Based in Morristown, New Jersey, The Seeing Eye has paired more than 16,000 dogs and people who are blind, using methods that have changed remarkably little over the past eighty or so years.

I spoke with one of the Seeing Eye's current managers of instruction and training, Doug Bohl, about how dogs are trained, what dogs know, and the guide-dog partnership. Doug has worked for The Seeing Eye for twenty-seven years—twenty-two as a trainer and five as a manager. By his own estimate, he's trained over six hundred dogs, "and I remember almost every one."

Doug said, "I love training dogs, but the reward is the students. During a class, you see the dog change and you see the person change. And what they become is one team."

Jeff Campbell: How does training start?

Doug Bohl: You go through a period of four months training the dogs, and then the fifth month is the class of blind students. We teach the dogs six basic commands. There are other commands, but the basic ones are forward; left; right; hup-up, which means to go faster; steady, which means to go slower; and pfui, our correction word.

JC: Is this reward-based training?

DB: Yes, positive reinforcement. Basically, what our dogs work for is verbal and physical praise. Training a dog is similar to raising a kid in teaching right and wrong. I think that some of the best students I've had over the years are mothers. An adult dog is at about the intellectual level of a two-year-old. We always teach the student to praise the dog every time the dog follows a command because that's how the dog gets paid.

JC: Are dogs thinking for themselves? What about "intelligent disobedience," where dogs are trained to disobey when necessary?

DB: We do a lot of intelligent disobedience. What we teach the dogs is to follow the commands but to think for themselves as they do it. In other words, if the student tells the dog "forward" and they start walking down the sidewalk, the dog will go until there's a reason to stop. That's their command. If anything comes up, then it's up to the dog to take over and say, "Uh, there's a garbage can. We have to go this way."

The biggest thing we do is traffic. For this, we have changed our training to meet the needs of students. When I started in 1970s, there was no right-on-red law, so 99 percent of the time you could tell the dog "forward" and cross the street. Not so much now.

JC: How does the dog communicate this?

DB: We teach the student to learn what is normal for their dog. For instance, after working with a dog a couple of days, the student will learn how much the dog normally pulls. If the student knows what's normal, they can pick up what's abnormal and look for a reason why. If there's an audible signal like a car, then you know a car's there, but you can't always hear things.

JC: How do you match a person with an animal?

DB: There are some simple things. Like, we all have our natural walking speeds. You can speed us up or slow us down a little bit, but not much. Dogs are the same. If I made you walk too fast or too slow, you'd be uncomfortable. You want to walk the way you want to walk. So that is the first thing. Matching the walking pace of the dog and the person.

Aside from pace and pull, alot of it is the environment where the student lives. If I have a student who lives in New York City, I have to give them a dog with a solid temperament, where the noise and confusion of the city won't bother them. While other dogs I might place with someone who lives in Wichita, Kansas, because there's not so much going on. Both dogs are good dogs, but it's about matching the person's needs and the dog's needs.

When the students arrive, the instructor works with the person to see how they are, and then we make the match with the dog, and that takes about two days.

JC: That's fast. How often does a relationship stick?

DB: Most of the time. In a class of twenty students, it's not uncommon to have to switch one dog, but that's about it. It's a funny thing. I equate this a lot to dating between two human beings. Only here you have a dog and a person.

JC: Do the dogs understand they are being matched with someone?

DB: The dog doesn't. During the four months of training, the dogs get attached to the instructors. That's a normal thing. When the student comes in, and you give the dog to the student, the only thing the dog knows at that point is, "Where's my buddy, the instructor? Who's this person?" That's why the students are here for four weeks. It takes time for the dog to switch its allegiance from the instructor to the student.

JC: How important is the emotional rapport between the person and the dog?

DB: That's the most important thing that makes our teams work. They have a bond. If somebody hasn't had a dog before, that's when I compare it to a human relationship. I tell students, you know, in a lot of human relationships, you may have a bad first date and still end up getting married. The first time you work the dog, it may not go real smooth, but it's getting used to each other, and it all takes time.

JC: Do you feel that it's a two-way street—that the dog is also in some sense choosing the person?

DB: Not really. Dogs are more easy-going than that. That would be a human reaction. Dogs pretty much like everybody. I always say that if humans were like dogs, there would be no war. You don't have to prove anything to a dog. Dogs like people.

JC: Do the dogs understand that the people are blind?

DB: You know, I still haven't decided on that. My basic answer is yes, but. The best explanation is, the dog may not understand the person is blind, but what the dog knows is, if they don't do something for them, the student can't do it for themselves. Like in the example of walking down the sidewalk. The dog knows, "There's a garbage can ahead. I have to steer this person around because they can't get around by themselves."

However, a lot of our staff have taken home retired guide dogs, and almost all of us have had this happen: You take the dog home, you're in the kitchen, the dog walks right over to the counter and takes something off the counter, and when you yell at them, they look at you like, "You can see me?" So, yes, in all practical senses, I think the dogs figure it out.

JC: Do you sense that the dogs want to help, and that's why they succeed at this type of work?

BD: I don't think to help. I think the dogs are willing by nature. They like to do it because it's their nature to please. That's why we use the dog breeds that we do—golden retrievers, labradors, and German shepherds—because they're more willing than some other breeds.

JC: In my book, I tell the story of Michael Hingson and Roselle on 9/11. In your experience, how unusual was Roselle's behavior? Do you have any stories of guide dogs saving people or going beyond the call of duty?

DB: Oh god, I've got a lot. Certainly, Michael Hingson is an exceptional story. One happened just about a year ago. Great guy, a student who's had several dogs over the years. He lived in an apartment building in Philadelphia, on an upper floor. The building caught fire in the middle of the night when he was asleep. The dog came over to the bed and nudged the guy until he woke up. Once the guy was awake, he smelled the smoke. And all he did was get the dog, put the harness on the dog, pick up his cell phone, walk out the door, and say, "Forward." That's all he said, and the dog just took him out of the building.

Back in the eighties, I had a student who lived in Florida. Nicest lady in the world. She'd been home for six months, and she called me up one day and said, "I've got to tell you what my dog did. I was walking down the sidewalk in my neighborhood and the dog stopped and wouldn't go. I told her go; she wouldn't go. I corrected her; she wouldn't go. I praised her; she wouldn't go. And a guy came out of a house and said, 'Lady, there's an alligator on the sidewalk in front of you. And it's not leaving.'"

And I said to her, "I didn't teach the dog that."

JC: In stories like these, it seems like the dog is helping in creative ways that have nothing to do with the reward.

BD: Adapting to new situations is pretty normal for our dogs, but what that dog did in the fire wasn't the result of our training. It was the result of the dog figuring out the situation, knowing it wasn't good, and thinking, "This is my master. I have to get him out."

JC: At that point, it's just devotion.

BD: Yep.

JC: How do you feel at the end of a training when you see a team go off?

BD: Wonderful. Absolutely wonderful. And that never changes. I just got out of my seventy-ninth class, and I don't feel any different than I did in my first. We're here for the people, and the joy they experience . . . They keep in touch. I'm still in touch with someone from my first class in June 1976. I've had students in my class get married. They met in my class, and when they had their first kid, I called them up and said, "What? You didn't name him after me? Who got you two together?"

How are you going to replace that? It's the emotions of this job. You can't find this anywhere else.

Nothing gets our attention faster than when a wild animal comes to our rescue. After all, why would a wild animal care whether a human lives or dies? Don't they know that the "law of the jungle" is "survival of the fittest"?

Apparently, the animals in these stories didn't get the memo. They rescued perfect strangers when it would have been much easier to walk, or swim, away. Though rare, life-saving rescues involving wild animals are extremely significant. At times they have prodded scientists to expand our understandings of what other animals are capable of. Nature can certainly be "red in tooth and claw," to quote Tennyson, but as these stories illustrate, empathy and compassion exist, too.

For instance, consider wild animals in captivity. Zoo keepers never forget that, no matter how friendly their charges might become, they remain potentially dangerous. Stories of zoo animals attacking people also get our attention, and those episodes of violence highlight what makes these rescues so remarkable. We know that captive wild animals will, on rare occasions, try to hurt their human caretakers, yet in these stories, when a human was in trouble, the animals chose to respond by helping.

JAMBO THE GORILLA . . . COMFORTS A FALLEN BOY

NAME: *Jambo*

SPECIES: *Lowland silverback gorilla*

DATE: *August 31, 1986*

LOCATION: *Jersey Zoo, island of Jersey, England*

SITUATION: *Injured child falls into gorilla enclosure*

WHO WAS SAVED: *Five-year-old Levan Merritt*

LEGACY: *Famous "Gentle Giant" showed the world that King Kong had a heart of gold*

Born in a Swiss zoo in 1961, Jambo, a lowland silverback gorilla, was the first male gorilla to be born in captivity. His name is Swahili for "hello," and that friendly greeting would come to perfectly suit Jambo, who, one sunny summer day in 1986, displayed an act of kindness that helped change forever the belief that gorillas were inherently violent and aggressive.

The 1933 movie *King Kong* had something to do with the "killer ape" reputation. But also, into the 1980s, many scientists still regarded apes, and indeed most animals, as instinct-driven, unthinking, unfeeling brutes. One of the few who didn't was primatologist Jane Goodall, whose controversial, groundbreaking research on chimpanzees in Tanzania's Gombe National Park started the year before Jambo was born. Goodall proposed that apes and monkeys had feelings, were capable of rational thought, and even exhibited individual personalities. For decades, Goodall was roundly disparaged and dismissed as engaging in romanticized anthropomorphism.

After all, King Kong fell in love with Fay Wray, but that only happened in the movies.

A BAD FALL

On August 31, 1986, the Merritt family visited the Jersey Zoo on Jersey, the largest of the Channel Islands off England's southern coast. When they arrived at the gorilla enclosure—a landscaped outdoor greenspace unmarred by protective bars—Stephen Merritt hoisted his five-year-old son, Levan, on top of the chest-high protective barrier. The exhibit's seven gorillas were at the base of the wall, and Levan couldn't see them.

Then Stephen turned to pick up his other son, Lloyd, and in that moment's distraction, Levan fell.

The boy struck the concrete wall on the way down, landing twenty feet below, face down and unconscious, with blood visible on the back of his head. "When I looked down," Stephen Merritt said, "I thought he was dead."

At first, the gorillas jumped back, but then several moved toward Levan to investigate. These included a male named Rafiki, the female Nandi with her child, as well as Jambo. As they got close, Jambo suddenly positioned himself between the boy and the others in what appeared to be a protective gesture, as if he were saying, "Do not touch."

Afterward, what Jambo intended with this behavior was hotly debated. It could be that Jambo wasn't protecting Levan, but was protecting his gorilla family from an intruder. Or perhaps he was establishing dominance so he could investigate first. Either way, Jambo then sat next to the boy for about ten minutes, occasionally stroking his back very gently and carefully with his fingers, and once sniffing them for scent. At one point, Jambo also looked at the crowd with a curious expression, which one witness interpreted as asking, "What is he doing here?"

"Instead of tearing him limb from limb," Stephen Merritt said later, "the gorilla was being caring. Then, as the six other gorillas moved in, he stood guard and wouldn't let any of them near my son. It was tenderness that I would never have thought possible."

HYSTERIA AND HOBBIT

Meanwhile, chaos reigned among the zoo visitors who were watching. The growing mass of onlookers was crazy with fear that the gorillas would hurt the child. Levan's mother, Pauline, was screaming so hysterically she had to be pulled away. Others wanted to throw rocks to scare the gorillas off. This idea was squelched, but the wild shouting and shrieking continued.

Zoo personnel knew they needed to rescue Levan quickly; for one thing, if he didn't wake up soon, he might slip into a coma. None of the options for subduing the gorillas—such as driving them away or tranquilizing them—could be done quickly and without risk of making the situation worse.

Then, after about ten minutes, Levan woke up on his own and started screaming. This shocked the gorillas, and they all immediately moved across the enclosure toward their covered living quarters, with Jambo leading the way. As they did, zoo employees jumped in and herded the gorillas inside.

But just when the situation seemed under control, another gorilla, a seven-year-old male named Hobbit, broke away.

In stark contrast to Jambo, Hobbit was agitated and excited as he peeled off from the group. Hobbit raced aggressively back and forth across the grassy slope, while two zookeepers stood their ground near Levan, driving Hobbit away each time he swooped by. Hobbit gave every impression of wanting to approach or grab the boy, and his actions grew increasingly bold. Hobbit even threw rocks in their direction. Now that Jambo was gone, the situation deteriorated.

As this was happening, ambulance worker Brian Fox jumped in and began tending to Levan in the enclosure. The boy's spine seemed okay, and he was capable of being moved. Brian gathered up the child, tied a lowered rope around himself, and together they were pulled out to safety to the accompaniment of wild applause.

Levan was immediately taken to a nearby hospital, where he was treated for a broken arm and fractured skull. He eventually made a full recovery.

"THE GENTLE GIANT," A NEW FILM STAR

As luck would have it, amateur videographer Brian LeLion was there the day Levan Merritt fell into the Jersey Zoo gorilla enclosure, and he captured almost the entire rescue on tape. This home movie, made in the days before cell phone cameras and "selfies," turned Jambo into "the gentle giant," the biggest celebrity ape since King Kong stormed the Empire State Building.

Even without video, Jambo's story would have made world headlines, but with it, TV news broadcasts across the globe ate it up. Once people saw the clips, they found it hard to dismiss the apparent compassion in Jambo's behavior as he stroked the unmoving child at his feet and kept the other gorillas at bay. Plus, Hobbit's behavior made clear that the boy needed protecting. Not every gorilla would necessarily respond the same way.

Indeed, in just the ways Jane Goodall had proposed, Jambo was an exceptional gorilla, one with the seeming ability to problem-solve, make individual choices, and provide real care. Today, science has largely vindicated Goodall: All four great ape species—gorillas, orangutans, bonobos, and chimpanzees—are credited with displaying self-awareness, empathy, compassion, and a high degree of social intelligence.

Great apes are capable of viciousness as well; Goodall also famously documented deadly violence among chimpanzees. Just like humans, apes can choose when to be kind and when to be cruel. But as well-respected primatologist Frans de Waal has written, "The male gorilla, despite his ferocious King Kong reputation, is a born protector. The horrifying tales of gorilla attacks with which colonial hunters used to come home were designed to impress us with human rather than gorilla bravery. But in fact, a charging gorilla male is prepared to die for his family."

Film of Jambo's kindness helped change pop culture and slow the knee-jerk skepticism of the scientific community. Yet it came as no real surprise to the person who knew Jambo best, his keeper, Richard Johnstone-Scott.

"He reacted in just the way I would expect him to," said Johnstone-Scott. "He has the strength of ten men but the heart of a lamb."

DARWIN'S STORY: PROTECT THE KEEPER

Humans, apes, and monkeys are all primates. In broad terms, monkeys are distinguished from apes (and humans) by their smaller size and tails. Also, many scientists do not think that monkeys, despite their obvious intelligence and sociability, exhibit the same level of self-awareness as apes.

Like apes, and us, monkeys have the capacity for both cruelty and kindness. They may even be capable of brave altruism. Scientist Charles Darwin, who developed the theory of evolution, certainly felt monkeys were capable of courage and compassion. To illustrate, he repeated this story of a life-saving rescue that had been told to him:

"Several years ago a keeper at the Zoological Gardens showed me some deep and scarcely healed wounds on the nape of his own neck, inflicted on him, whilst kneeling on the floor, by a fierce baboon. The little American monkey, who was a warm friend of this keeper, lived in the same compartment, and was dreadfully afraid of the great baboon. Nevertheless, as soon as he saw his friend in peril, he rushed to the rescue, and by screams and bites so distracted the baboon that the man was able to escape, after, the surgeons thought, running great risk to his life."

UGANDAN VERVET MONKEYS . . . ADOPT A RUNAWAY

NAME: *Unnamed*

SPECIES: *Green vervet monkeys*

DATE: *1991*

LOCATION: *Uganda*

SITUATION: *Runaway toddler in the African jungle*

WHO WAS SAVED: *Three-year-old John Ssebunya*

LEGACY: *Proved that benevolent, life-saving jungle creatures were no myth*

In 1991, as some versions of this story go, a woman named Millie from a Ugandan village near Bombo was foraging in the forest when she encountered a group of monkeys. This was not unusual. Monkeys are populous, and they hang near farms so they can steal food by "crop raiding." Many Ugandans consider the monkeys annoying pests.

Then Millie noticed that one of monkeys didn't look right. It was too big, and it had no tail . . . and scared out of her mind, she ran back to the village for help.

A group returned and found the strange creature, which frightened some so much they wanted to kill it. But a man named Benedict, who later claimed to be among the group, argued that it wasn't a monster. It was a malnourished boy who needed to be rescued or he would probably die.

"The boy looked funny, very funny," Benedict said. "The boy looked like a monkey. His face was covered with hair. All over his body he has hair."

The boy resisted capture, and the monkeys screamed ferociously and threw sticks at the villagers, trying to drive them off. Benedict threw sticks back, scattering the monkeys, and the men grabbed the boy and took him to their village.

The boy looked and acted like a wild animal. He had scars all over his body. His knees were calloused from moving on all fours, and he had long curled nails. He could not speak; he could not tolerate cooked food; he hated being bathed; he preferred squatting to standing; and he was infested with tapeworms. Then, there was his hypertrichosis, or excessive body hair.

The villagers gave him to a local school that helped troubled kids, but the boy frightened the teachers and the children alike. He was "totally different," the school's headmaster, William, said. "You could see he was scared. He didn't have trust of people. He didn't have proper speech." He rarely made eye contact, and if he wanted something, "he'd pop out his hand."

Eventually, the boy was taken to the Kamuzinda Christian Orphanage run by Molly and Paul Wasswa. The Wasswa's took the boy into their home. Through their care, they healed and nurtured him and taught him to speak, if haltingly. They recovered the boy inside, and eventually, they gleaned his story.

As with all cases of feral children, it is a tale that tests the limits of our beliefs.

JOHN'S STORY

The boy was identified as John Ssebunya. Apparently, when he was about three years old, he witnessed his alcoholic father murder his mother. Afraid for his life, John ran headlong into the forest and did not return. Some years after this, John's father apparently hung himself.

What happened next? Years later, in several newspaper and TV interviews, John described his experiences in extremely broken, usually monosyllabic Swahili, which was translated into English by those who understood his stuttering speech.

"It was very frightening," John said about the first few days. "I stayed in the middle forest. I saw monkeys, and they came over to me. They gave me bananas and cassava roots."

He also ate sweet potatoes, nuts and roots, and other fibrous plants. At first, the monkeys were uncertain around him, but after a few weeks they seemed to accept him. They allowed John to travel with them, and they taught him how to forage and climb trees.

"I didn't sleep very well," he said. "Head down, and bottom in the air. Or I would climb a tree. But I didn't sleep well."

John was emphatic that the monkeys cared for him. He learned and often participated in their favorite game, a monkey version of hide and seek.

"The monkeys used to love me," he said. "We played together all of the time. It is how I remember it, and it is the truth."

He made the experience sound oddly happy, rather than traumatic, but John was still glad he had returned to human society.

"I am grateful, yes, I am. . . . Not because of love from them, from the monkeys. But because what they did made it possible for me to be loved by other people, by humans."

A SKEPTICAL WORLD

Human history is rife with stories of abandoned children raised by wild animals. Most of these stories are only legends, folktales, or hoaxes (see page 277). Yet a few stories, like John's, turn out to be real.

About eight years after he was found, John's story emerged, and an amazed but skeptical world came calling. Scientists, reporters, and filmmakers questioned every claim and detail. While some observers still remain doubtful, the consensus is that, not only could John have survived in the way he has described, but he is sincerely telling the truth—at least, the truth as he remembers it.

"It's very complex because you're dealing with childhood memories," said Douglas Candland, a psychology professor who interviewed John to verify his story. "Memory itself is a very unreliable witness."

First, it's impossible to say how long John was in the bush, how old he was then, or even his age today. His experience lasted at least a year, and possibly three years, and he was between the ages of four and seven when he was found.

Next, John's monkey-like physical and social behavior—vestiges of which continued for years and are still evident—indicated a close association with monkeys no child could fake. John mimicked certain telling mannerisms, such as avoiding eye contact, and he later interacted with green vervet monkeys with preternatural ease.

Further, green vervet monkeys will tolerate a human presence, they travel slowly enough for a young boy to keep up, they tend to gather more food than they need (discarding the extra), and through crop raiding, their diet is amenable to a human.

Was John really covered with hair? This is a standard detail in feral child stories and could be an exaggeration. However, one commentator said that hirsutism can be a response to chronic malnutrition, and so it might have occurred.

CARING VERSUS TOLERANCE

Given all this, we can say with some confidence that a troupe of vervet monkeys did indeed save John's life.

Yet a controversy remains, possibly the biggest, and it is the hardest one to answer: Did the monkeys actually care for John? Did they intentionally feed him and emotionally nurture him—in essence, accepting and "adopting" him into their troupe as one of their own?

Or is that only what John believed because, as a frightened, isolated toddler, he needed to? Unthreatened by the boy, perhaps the monkeys simply tolerated his unwanted presence, letting him steal scraps like a scavenging mutt and unconcerned whether he survived.

When Candland asked John about his relationship with the monkeys, John said, "They fed me." Then John mimicked how he was fed, by squatting on all fours and grabbing something from the air.

Vervet monkeys are known to toss away a good portion of the food they examine. Further, primate experts note that vervets almost never exhibit food sharing (as chimpanzees sometimes do). Thus, it's possible John misinterpreted their behavior. He believed he was being "given" food, but the vervets, who never "feed" even each other, were discarding it.

Still, that doesn't negate the possibility that the monkeys eventually felt compassion for John. As the weeks became months, and then perhaps years, might "tolerance" have become something more? John experienced their interactions as playful and loving, and by the time he was found, the monkeys seemingly fought for and defended John.

In the end, the one undeniable truth is that John Ssebunya survived, and his life has become an unforgettable lesson in compassion. His adoptive parents, Molly and Paul Wasswa, raised the once-wild boy with so much love he was able to overcome his horrific start to life. Among many other things, the Wasswas taught John to sing and made him a member of their touring Pearl of Africa Children's Choir. John may never quite fit in, or speak properly, but he can at least give voice to the gratefulness in his heart.

MODERN-DAY MOWGLIS: RUNNING WITH DOGS

They sound like Victorian-era Rudyard Kipling "Just So" stories, but even in our modern world—wired to the teeth and blanketed with satellites—abandoned, feral children still emerge from the wilderness with alarming regularity.

Sometimes they even emerge out of the wilderness of urban life. In 1998, six-year-old Ivan Mishukov was found roaming outer Moscow streets with a pack of feral dogs. Ivan had run away from abusive, neglectful parents, joining a virtual legion of homeless, urban Russian children. Ivan, however, shared his acquired food with a group of homeless canines, and they formed a bond. Working together for two years, they kept each other fed during the day and warm and protected at night.

Once Moscow police learned of Ivan, they had a devil of a time catching him. Ivan's pack viciously defended him, and the boy escaped each time. Finally, police separated Ivan from his pack by baiting the dogs with meat in a restaurant kitchen.

Sounding a common note, Ivan said later, "The dogs loved and protected me."

Here are three more stories:

- In 2001, in Talcahuano, Chile, a ten-year-old boy named Alex was captured after living with a pack of fifteen feral dogs for more than two years. They scavenged together and, he claimed, the dogs even suckled him. He told police, "The dogs are my family. Please let me go back to them."
- In 2002, in Romania, seven-year-old Traian Caldarar was rescued and reunited with his mother after living for at least two years in Transylvanian forests. Traian escaped an abusive father; authorities believe, given his condition and behavior, that Traian survived only by joining wild dogs.
- In 2004, authorities in the Siberian region of Altai discovered Andrei Tolstyk, a seven-year-old boy who'd been abandoned as an infant by his parents and only survived because the family dog took care of him. Andrei behaved like a dog and knew no language.

BINTI JUA THE GORILLA . . . CONSOLES AN INJURED CHILD

NAME: *Binti Jua*

SPECIES: *Western lowland gorilla*

DATE: *August 16, 1996*

LOCATION: *Brookfield Zoo, Illinois*

SITUATION: *Unconscious boy fallen into gorilla exhibit*

WHO WAS SAVED: *A three-year-old boy, name unknown*

LEGACY: *One act of motherly love made her the most famous female gorilla in scientific history*

Almost exactly ten years after Jambo (see page 195) shocked the world by displaying kindness for a fallen, injured boy, it happened again. While Jambo opened people's eyes to the possibility of animal empathy, Binti Jua truly rattled scientific assumptions about animal compassion. This incident represented a "paradigm shift," said scientist Marc Bekoff. Or as primatologist Frans de Waal put it, "It wasn't until an ape saved a member of our own species that there was a public awakening to the possibility of nonhuman humanness."

After Binti Jua, the debates about primates were never the same.

A PROTECTIVE URGE

August 16, 1996, was a typical, bright summer day at Illinois's Brookfield Zoo.

A group of nine children and three adults entered the zoo's "Tropic World" exhibit and approached the holding pen for the western lowland gorillas. Excited to see the animals in action, a three-year-old boy ran ahead of the group and climbed atop the low stone wall. Not satisfied, he continued climbing over the three-foot fence, where he slipped and fell some eighteen to perhaps twenty-four feet into the enclosure.

As the boy tumbled, he scraped his face, broke his left hand, and hit the concrete floor so hard he was knocked unconscious. Witnesses screamed, some running for the exits, and the exhibit's seven gorillas scattered in surprise.

One gorilla, though, returned and approached the still body. It was Binti Jua, a 160-pound, eight-year-old female whose name means "daughter of sunlight" in Swahili. Binti Jua had recently given birth to a daughter, Koola, and the mother shifted her infant on her back and picked the boy up in her arms.

At this point, several things happened at once. One zoo visitor recorded video as Binti Jua carried the boy to a different spot. Meanwhile, Craig Demitros, one of the gorillas' keepers, signaled staff that the zoo had a life-threatening emergency.

"Another gorilla walked toward the boy," said Carrie Stewart, a zoo visitor who witnessed the encounter, "and [Binti Jua] kind of turned around and walked away from the other gorillas and tried to be protective."

But was she? No one knew what she would do, or how any of the gorillas might act. A shudder of horror energized watchers, who feared the worst, and zoo staff urgently strategized how to safely recover the boy.

"She carried him . . . through the river, made a right turn, . . . [and] went over to that log," Demitros said. "She was gently kind of rocking the kid in her right arm."

Zookeepers decided to spray water into the exhibit. This was a standard signal for the gorillas to move to an indoor habitat, and staff hoped to separate the other gorillas from Binti Jua. As the staff did this, to their dismay, Binti Jua got up and joined the other gorillas while still carrying the child.

"He just lay limp in her arms while she carried him," Carrie Stewart said, "and after she got to the cove, she very gently laid him down."

Binti Jua carried the boy about forty feet and left him by a familiar staff access door before continuing out of the exhibit. Paramedics immediately rushed in, and the boy was taken to the hospital. Though the boy's injuries were serious, he made a full recovery. To this day, he and his parents have chosen to remain anonymous.

For Binti Jua, anonymity was something she would never enjoy again.

UPROAR OVER AN ACT OF KINDNESS

Within days, Binti Jua was an international celebrity as the story of the loving gorilla who saved the injured child rocketed around the world. *Newsweek* readers voted her 1996's "Hero of the Year," she won an American Legion medal, and the zoo was inundated with Binti Jua fan mail. Over the next few months, the feel-good story was retold literally thousands upon thousands of times in newspapers, magazines, and TV and radio programs.

Naturally, her fame was helped enormously by the grainy video taken of the rescue that allowed people to see the truth with their own eyes: King Kong's mother was just a big softy.

But not everyone agreed about what Binti Jua's actions meant. Even as the rescue made headlines, an intense debate arose among commentators and animal experts. In fact, as luck would have it, the rescue occurred at the same time that 1,400 primatologists were gathered for the International Primatological Society's annual symposium at the University of Wisconsin in Madison.

"Everybody was very excited that there was an incident that focused attention not only on gorillas, which are an endangered species, but on the issue of animal thinking, which is what we were at the meeting for," said H. Lyn Miles, a primatologist at the University of Tennessee.

So: Was Binti Jua displaying compassion, a mothering instinct (see page 41), zoo training, or an unthinking curiosity that contained no conscious intention to help?

Melinda Pruett-Jones, Brookfield Zoo's curator of primates, downplayed the popular notion that Bintu Jua was "protecting" the child from the other gorillas. "They were just paying attention to what their keepers were telling them to do," Pruett-Jones said. "None of them were aggressive. They were probably frightened and confused."

Binti, meanwhile, was merely displaying "predictable" gorilla behavior, according to Kenneth Gould from Atlanta's Yerkes Research Center. "Gorillas normally do not approach a strange individual aggressively. They are going to be curious. Usually they are quite gentle in their approaches."

Nevertheless, scientist Marc Bekoff felt that Binti Jua "put herself in danger by protecting the boy." For instance, Bekoff said, "if she'd left the boy there, I think the boy would have gotten torn apart. I really do. You get these frenzies, too. What she did saved the boy's life from all of them."

TAUGHT TO BE A MOTHER

Maybe the most debated point was whether Binti Jua was just mindlessly repeating zoo training.

Before Binti Jua gave birth in 1995 to Koola, the zoo trained her extensively in how to be a nurturing mother. They did this because, when Binti Jua was born, she herself was rejected by her own birth mother and was hand-raised by zoo staff. Thus, even for a captive gorilla, Binti Jua was particularly acclimated to humans, but this had a downside.

As Craig Demitros said, "If the mother is hand-reared, a lot of times they don't mother properly. A lot of this behavior is learned."

Brookfield Zoo staff taught Binti Jua, among other behaviors, how to cradle a stuffed animal as if it were an infant and how to practice a babysitting technique known as "retrieval." Some said that Binti Jua was just automatically repeating her training with the unconscious boy.

Others felt this explanation was inadequate. Binti Jua couldn't have confused the boy with a doll, and her behavior exhibited more than mere curiosity; she made a choice to approach and pick up the boy, to be gentle, and to leave him where she knew zoo staff could recover him.

"I don't think you can train a gorilla to save a baby," said animal expert Jeffrey M. Masson. "I think it's genuine compassion. . . . I think [Binti] made the connection between [her] baby and this baby that is in trouble. It came straight from the heart."

Primatologist Frans de Waal commented, "That Binti's behavior caused such surprise among humans says a lot about the way animals are depicted in the media. She really did nothing unusual, or at least nothing an ape wouldn't do for any juvenile of her own species."

De Waal said that Binti Jua's behavior is today known as "consolation," which is "one of the most common responses among apes. We recognize this behavior because apes do it in a way identical to ours. The empathic response is one of the strongest there is."

One thing, at least, is certain. Binti Jua became "a very good mother," said Demitros. Not only did she raise Koola with all the care and attention zoo staff hoped for, but in 2005 Binti Jua gave birth to a son, Bakari, whom she also raised "beautifully."

Today, the Brookfield Zoo remains hopeful that Binti Jua will mate and give birth again. Whatever the world thinks, she is the undisputed star of the zoo's successful breeding program for this endangered species.

A MORAL DILEMMA

One reason Binta Jua caused such a stir among scientists was that her actions suggested a basic moral impulse: She wanted to help an injured boy. Yet circa 1996, the general scientific consensus was that humans alone possessed the cognitive hardware necessary for compassion, fairness, and justice—for ethics and morality, in other words.

Still today, what morality is and which animals have it is hotly debated. But research has shown that some animals do possess a moral sensibility. In other words, "morality is not as much of a human innovation as we like to think," writes primatologist Frans de Waal.

To begin with, morality is essentially a social concern. It arises in relation to others. To be capable of morality, then, an animal must possess empathy and sympathy. This basic "prosocial" formula is embodied by the "golden rule": Do unto others as you would have them do unto you.

De Waal calls this "gut level" morality. He writes, "Evolution has equipped us with genuinely cooperative impulses and inhibitions against acts that might harm the group on which we depend. We do apply these impulses selectively, but are affected by them nonetheless."

That is, we can choose whether to be kind or cruel, helpful or hurtful, but we always understand the difference.

Scientist Marc Bekoff says that, today, animals displaying moral behavior include many primates, social carnivores like wolves and coyotes, elephants, dolphins, whales, and some rodents, such as rats and mice. While it's possible that morality is restricted to mammals, more research is needed to make any definitive conclusions.

Finally, this doesn't necessarily mean that all animals operate by the same moral codes, nor is this "gut level morality"—which the latest research indicates humans might be born with—the same as ethical reasoning or following cultural norms.

The urge to comfort a fallen child? That seems to come naturally. What to wear, and what to say, when meeting your future in-laws? That takes some thought.

DONNA NOOK GRAY SEALS . . . KEEP A WOMAN AFLOAT

NAME: *Unnamed*

SPECIES: *Gray seals*

DATE: *February 1, 1999*

LOCATION: *Donna Nook nature reserve, England*

SITUATION: *A woman drowning in the freezing North Sea*

WHO WAS SAVED: *Thirty-year-old Charlene Camburn*

LEGACY: *Celebrated local saviors, showed that dolphins aren't the only kind sea mammals*

On February 1, 1999, Charlene Camburn visited the Donna Nook nature reserve with her seven-year-old son, Brogan, and her boyfriend, Chris Tomlinson. Donna Nook protects 6.5 miles of sandflats and grassy marshes along Britain's east coast, bordering the North Sea, and one of England's most popular wildlife spectacles is observing the gray seal colony that resides there.

During breeding season, in November and December, access is restricted. People gather at specific viewing points to watch as the bull males preen and fight and as mothers give birth and care for their pups.

However, by February, breeding season is over, so Charlene, Brogan, and Chris struck out freely, wandering across the extensive, intertidal sand dunes to get a closer look at the four-hundred-member gray seal colony and the flocks of migratory seabirds. What they didn't realize was that the fog wasn't the only thing rolling in during the late afternoon.

The tide was, too.

ADRIFT IN THE NORTH SEA

Around 4:30 pm, as the day's light was failing, the trio decided to return, but they found their way to shore blocked by the frigid North Sea.

They wandered along the sand dune looking for a dry path, but as far as they could tell, they had become surrounded by water, and with each passing minute, the sea was rising. Only Charlene knew how to swim; her son and her boyfriend would drown if they weren't rescued before their sandbar submerged completely. So Charlene did the only thing she could think of. She stripped to her underwear and bravely started swimming toward shore, intending to get help.

Within ten minutes, Charlene became lost in the gloom and disoriented by the North Sea's strong current, and she soon shifted her prayers for help onto herself. Then a group of six gray seals appeared. They surrounded her in the water and made her even more nervous. She was at their mercy, alone in their element. Would they consider her a threat? All gray seals are powerful, territorial predators who can inflict harmful bites, and mothers can be extremely protective around their pups.

But the watching seals didn't attack. In fact, after a few moments of treading water, Charlene got the impression that they meant for her to follow them. Scared for her life, Charlene decided to put her faith in the animals. She resumed swimming, doing the breaststroke, and tried to follow the seals.

TWO DAYS ON A SEA TURTLE

Maybe it's not such a stretch to imagine that social mammals like seals, whales, and dolphins might, on occasion, feel a compassionate urge to keep a fellow mammal—like ourselves—from drowning.

But sea turtles?

On June 2, 1974, a passenger ship carrying 277 people sank off the Philippines. According to news reports, 243 people were plucked from the sea and rescued afterward. One of the last was fifty-two-year-old Candelaria Villanueva, who was found two days later by a Philippine navy vessel, the *Kalantia*.

"I would not have believed it if I had merely heard it," said an officer on the Kalantia. "The truth is I was an eyewitness myself, together with practically everyone else aboard."

In their official report, the navy said they found Mrs. Villanueva clinging to what appeared to be a "huge oil drum." But as Mrs. Villanueva grabbed the thrown life ring, the oil drum sank, quickly reappearing and revealing itself to be a giant sea turtle.

"The sea creature even circled the area twice before disappearing into the depths of the sea, as if to reassure itself that its former rider was already in good hands," the officer said.

Apparently, Mrs. Villanueva didn't want to talk about it. Her experience at sea was too far-fetched even for her, and she gave "the impression she did not believe it ever happened at all."

"All I could see were their faces around me," Charlene said. "Not one of them faced away, and they were barking and squealing. I will never forget the seal in front of me. He was there all the time, swimming backward and staring at me. It was a dreamy feeling."

A CIRCLE OF CARING

Meanwhile, Brogan and Chris kept searching for an escape route. They ran for two miles along the fog-shrouded sand dune, and they eventually threaded a narrow dry path all the way back to shore. They kept running, knowing they needed to help Charlene. Around 5:30 pm, they were able to contact the coast guard, who immediately sent out a helicopter and rescue boat.

However, after more than ninety minutes of battling the current and getting nowhere, Charlene was succumbing to the effects of hypothermia. She was also beginning to despair. She felt certain that, by then, her son and boyfriend must have drowned; she had failed them and would soon die herself.

The only thing that kept her panic at bay was the constant, calming presence of the chattering seals.

"I kept going under toward the end, and it seemed easier to die than stay alive," she said. "But I could feel the seals going under my feet. They were nudging my legs and kept diving beside me, and I kept bobbing back up."

After about two hours had passed, Charlene saw the distant lights of a boat, but her voice was too weak to shout. When the boat disappeared, "I thought that was it," she said. "I kept going under constantly, and I had given up hope."

Charlene slipped into unconsciousness, but the seals kept her afloat. Then, some minutes later, the rescue boat's lights stabbed through the dark, illuminating Charlene along with the surrounding seals. Charlene woke long enough to realize she'd been saved, then she passed out again.

Charlene was airlifted to a nearby hospital, where she was treated for extreme hypothermia. That she remained alive after two hours nearly naked in the frozen North Sea was remarkable enough, but she wouldn't have survived without the presence of the seals.

Charlene's boyfriend, Chris, said, "I am convinced that without the seals creating a circle around her she would have drifted three to four miles further out."

By following the seals, Charlene kept herself closer to shore, and the seals actively kept Charlene from sinking. But did the seals understand what they were doing? Did they intentionally lead her and comfort her, nudge and lift her, in order to keep a human alive?

Gray seals are social mammals—like dolphins, dogs, and people—who are intelligent, emotional, and sensitive. The seals didn't confront or ignore Charlene, so curiosity might have been one motivation. They were familiar with the presence of people, but maybe they had never seen one in the water.

Still, curiosity doesn't seem to explain everything. The seals remained with Charlene constantly for two hours, and yet they only touched her when she needed physical help—when she was too weak to swim and falling unconscious. Perhaps the seals were only disinterested observers nudging her for their own reasons, but Charlene herself didn't feel toyed with. She felt the seals' efforts were connected to what was happening with her. In the end, if the seals weren't compassionately trying to keep her afloat, they mimicked helping in a near-miraculous way.

For Charlene, these questions ultimately don't matter.

"Whether they were with me accidentally or intentionally," she said, "I owe them my life."

LULU THE KANGAROO . . . SAVES A FARMER

NAME: *Lulu*

SPECIES: *Eastern grey kangaroo*

DATE: *September 2003*

LOCATION: *Moe, Australia*

SITUATION: *Man knocked unconscious by a tree branch*

WHO WAS SAVED: *Fifty-two-year-old Leonard Richards*

LEGACY: *The only Australian kangaroo known to help anybody (besides TV's fictional "Skippy")*

Farmer Leonard Richards doesn't remember what happened on this particular afternoon in September 2003. He doesn't remember the falling tree branch that knocked him unconscious or the actions of the animal who saved his life.

"I was walking down to clean up the limbs around the tree," he said. "The next thing I knew, I was in the Alfred hospital."

What happened, though, was like a scene straight out of the Australian children's TV show *Skippy the Bush Kangaroo* (see page 103), and it made a national celebrity out of Lulu, the family's adopted, hand-raised kangaroo.

NOT PUSHING UP DAISIES

About four years before, Len's son had found Lulu as a joey in the pouch of her dead mother. He "brought her home, bottle-fed her, and it just went from there," Len said. "She's been part of the family since."

Lulu wandered freely around the ranch and occasionally knocked on the door for a treat. "She thinks she's a dog," said Len's daughter Celeste. "Lulu and Dad are very close, and she follows him around, but we all just love her so much."

Apparently, Lulu noticed when Len was knocked out, and she came rushing to him. The rest of the family was in the house, several hundred yards away, and unaware of a problem. So Lulu raised the alarm.

"I heard Lulu," said Lynn Richards, Len's wife. "She has this bark, and it's a very loud bark that she gives out." The yipping sound that a distressed kangaroo makes is unique; Lynn described it as somewhat like a barking dog.

The Richards family estimated that Lulu must have barked for fifteen to thirty minutes before anyone emerged. However, "she was obviously trying to get our attention because she never acts like that," Celeste said. "So we went outside to investigate, and we saw Lulu standing upright with her chest puffed out over Dad's body."

When the family ran over to their unconscious patriarch, they found Len on his side with vomit coming out of his mouth. Apparently, Lulu had "actually saved me from choking," Len said. "She looked like she'd rolled me over . . .

to keep my airway clear, but we'll never know for sure."

Richards was flown by helicopter to a Melbourne hospital and made a full recovery. Yet it was a close call, and the entire family credited Lulu with the outcome.

"If it wasn't for her," Lynn said, "I don't know how long it would have been before we actually found him." Len was more succinct. "I'd be pushing up daisies if it wasn't for Lulu."

A ROO DID WHAT?

To say that Australians were surprised that a kangaroo had saved someone's life would be an understatement. Outside of fictional TV animals, no one had ever heard of an altruistic roo before.

"It's just totally abnormal behavior," said Peter Jarman, a kangaroo expert from Australia's University of New England. "Kangaroos don't even help out other kangaroos . . . except their own injured young."

Local wildlife expert David Middleton said, "There is zero chance a wild kangaroo would act like that. I have never heard of a wild kangaroo doing anything helpful to a human, so some kind of trusting relationship with this kangaroo and the family must have developed over the years."

That appears to have been the case.

In May 2004, the Australian Royalty Society for the Prevention of Cruelty to Animals presented Lulu with its annual "Animal Valour Award." According to the RSPC, the award acknowledges "an animal that displays exceptional courage in the face of danger, thereby greatly benefiting a human or humans."

It was the first time a kangaroo had ever won. "Certainly the vast majority of recipients have been dogs," said RSPC executive Jenny Hodges. But, she added, "What [Lulu] did was really exceptional."

A KANGAROO BLANKET

Lulu certainly seems to be one-of-a-kind. Then again . . .

In early August 2013, seven-year-old Simon Kruger got lost in the wilderness near Adelaide, Australia. The kill-me-with-cuteness reason? Simon was picking flowers for his mother during a family picnic and wandered too far off to find his way back.

By dusk, the Krugers were frantic. August is Australia's winter, and Simon wasn't dressed for the freezing overnight temperatures. Authorities sent a forty-person search party into the bush, and two rescue helicopters crisscrossed the sky, but Simon wasn't found until the next morning.

"Dad, I'm okay," Simon said when he was reunited with his parents. "I slept under a tree, and there were kangaroos."

Simon's father later explained the boy's incredible tale to news reporters: "A kangaroo came closer to him and ate the flowers from him, and the kangaroo fell asleep next to him."

A wild kangaroo snuggling a lost boy, thereby keeping him warm and probably saving his life? Crikey, mate, did he sing songs and tap dance, too? Yet Simon seemed too adorably sincere to make up a *Jungle Book*-type fiction just to impress his parents—or escape punishment.

Naturally, his mother didn't need convincing.

"I think it was a miracle," she said. "When I smell his jacket, it's kangaroo—bush and kangaroo."

BOTTLENOSE DOLPHINS ...
ROUND UP THE LIFEGUARDS

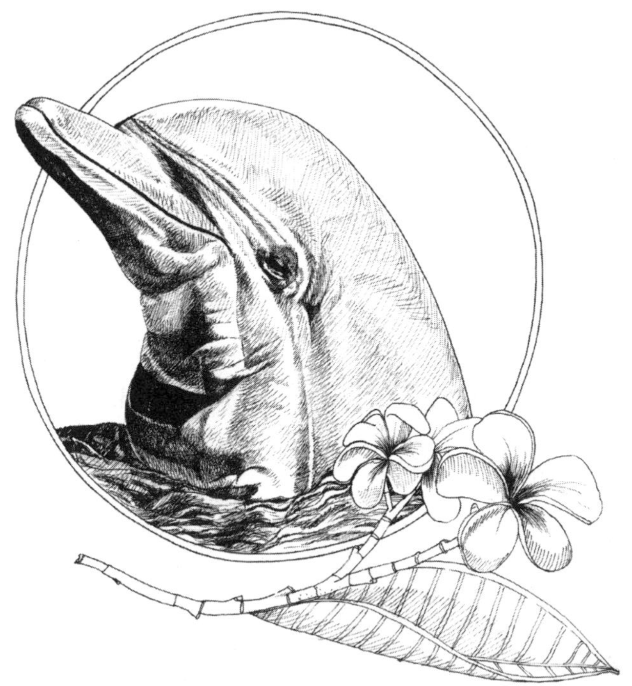

NAME: *Unnamed*

SPECIES: *Bottlenose dolphins*

DATE: *October 30, 2004*

LOCATION: *Whangarei, New Zealand*

SITUATION: *Swimmers threatened by great white shark*

WHO WAS SAVED: *Four New Zealand lifeguards*

LEGACY: *Renowned incident of life-saving dolphin helped confirm their exalted reputation*

Almost no one who has ever been saved by a wild animal in the wild can ever quite believe their own experience. When he was saved by a pod of bottlenose dolphins, Rob Howes, a forty-seven-year-old veteran lifeguard, said, "I did not know quite how to handle it."

After his experience, Howes spent three weeks speaking with dolphin experts and wrestling with his doubts. At first he refused to share his story publicly. When he finally came forward, it was only so he could warn others of the great white shark prowling local waters.

"I didn't want anyone to get chomped," Rob said.

HERDED LIKE SHEEP

On October 30, 2004, Rob Howes and three teenage girls—his fifteen-year-old daughter Nicola and Nicola's two friends, Karina Cooper and Helen Slade—went swimming off Ocean Beach, near Whangarei, along New Zealand's northeast coast. All were trained lifeguards, and they swam about a hundred yards past the breaking surf.

Almost immediately, a pod of seven dolphins sped up to them and started circling in a bizarre, agitated, aggressive manner. Dolphins are common at Ocean Beach, but they usually approach slowly and keep their distance.

"The dolphins started herding us up," Rob said, "pushing all four of us together and doing tight circles around us, rather like a sheepdog rounding up sheep."

The dolphins were less than an arm's length away, and "the girls were screaming with fright," Rob said. "I didn't know what to make of it either." He wondered if perhaps the dolphins were protecting one of their own babies.

Rob waved to a passing lifeguard boat, but the lifeguard thought they were just being friendly; the driver waved back and moved on. After this, the dolphins became even more agitated, "slapping the water with their tails," Rob said, which unnerved the swimmers.

For almost forty minutes the dolphins kept them trapped like this. Howes knew they were in danger, but not from what. Deciding to escape and get help, and maybe identify what was upsetting the dolphins, Howes swam hard through an opening and broke away from the group.

A single dolphin charged after him and submerged. Fearing he was about to be hit from below, Howes looked into the "crystal clear" water. Just a body's length away, a ten-foot great white shark turned to avoid the speeding dolphin.

HELP FOR THE HELPLESS

"I'll never forget watching that shark's long, sleek, pale gray body glide past for what seemed like the longest time," Rob said.

The shark continued swimming straight toward the girls. "My heart went into my mouth because one of them was my daughter," he said, but the dolphins "went into hyperdrive." They did this, Rob believes, in order to create "a confusion screen around the girls. It was just a mass of fins, backs, and . . . human heads."

At this point, the lifeguard patrol boat returned. Lifeguard Matt Fleet had seen the ruckus and come to investigate. Fleet said, "I had a clear sighting of the shark and could see that it wasn't ready to take on the dolphins."

Perhaps because of the boat's arrival, the shark then left. When it did, the dolphins relaxed but still remained close, and the four lifeguards took the opportunity to swim to shore.

Not wanting to scare the girls more than they already were, Rob didn't tell them about the shark until the next day. "I came out of that water," he said, "and I was stunned."

The scientists Rob spoke with said that, though rare, stories of dolphins saving people from sharks are not unheard of.

Dolphins will attack sharks to protect themselves, said whale expert Ingrid Visser, and "they could have sensed the danger to the swimmers and taken action to protect them."

"They like to help the helpless," said marine mammal researcher Rochelle Constantine of Auckland University. "It is an altruistic response, and bottlenose dolphins in particular are known for it."

NINGNONG THE ELEPHANT . . . RUNS FROM A TSUNAMI

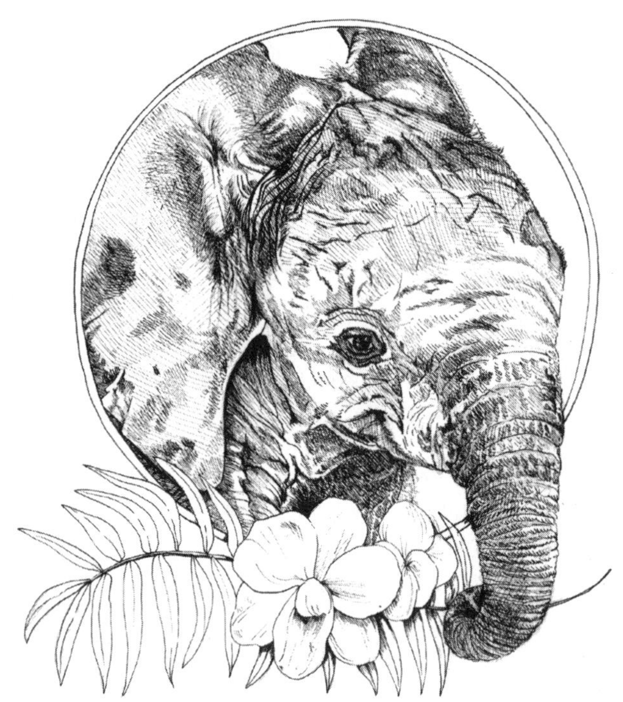

NAME: *Ningnong*

SPECIES: *Asian elephant*

DATE: *December 26, 2004*

LOCATION: *Phuket, Thailand*

SITUATION: *In the path of a tsunami*

WHO WAS SAVED: *Eight-year-old Amber Mason*

LEGACY: *One of numerous tales of animals communicating danger before the Thailand tsunami*

Eight-year-old Amber Mason was enjoying a family beach vacation at a holiday resort in Phuket, Thailand. By far her favorite activity was taking tourist rides on the resort's Asian elephants.

Amber visited the same pachyderm every day—the four-year-old elephant Ningnong—and on the morning of December 26, 2004, or what is traditionally Boxing Day in Amber's native England, the girl raced to the beach as usual and hopped on her best friend.

A WALK ON THE BEACH

Ningnong's owner and handler, Yong Chalamtaisong, led the pair as he gathered stranded fish along the beach, for the tide was curiously low that morning.

"The sea had gone out really far," Amber said, and "Ningnong was behaving really weird. He kept running the other way to walk off the beach."

Yong kept pulling the elephant back so he could collect fish for his lunch, but Amber said, "I think Ningnong thought something was wrong."

Something was. Earlier that morning, a 9.3-magnitude earthquake had struck off the coast of Indonesia, triggering a series of deadly tsunamis throughout Southeast Asia. The enormous waves were making landfall without warning, and at around 10 am, the tsunami reached Phuket. As it did, the receded ocean charged back up the beach as if it were filling a bathtub without stopping.

Yong released Ningnong and yelled at him to run. With Amber on his back, Ningnong "turned away from the incoming sea and ran for both our lives," Amber said.

The wave was faster than the elephant, and as it crashed into them, Ningnong "stood really still and braced himself against the water," Amber remembered. "I love Ningnong so I wasn't scared for one minute. He saved my life."

Amber's mother, Sam, had been enjoying breakfast at the hotel when the first wave hit. After it passed, she ran to the ocean, screaming, "Where's the elephant?"

"FOLLOW THE DOLPHINS"

In 2005, the PBS program *Nature* presented several eyewitness accounts of the 2004 Indian Ocean tsunami. One witness, Chris Cruz, described how an apparent warning he received from dolphins saved his life.

A scuba diving instructor, Chris was leading a diving trip near an island north of Phuket on December 26. Around 10 am, the waters started swirling strangely, and to avoid tangling, a number of boats cut their anchors. Then, suddenly, dolphins appeared very close in front of their boats, acting in a way Chris had never seen.

No one knew then about the tsunami. Acting on intuition, Chris radioed nearby boats and suggested that they "follow the dolphins." Many agreed, and soon seven to ten boats were traveling together behind the dolphins, who were, Chris said, "jumping and jumping and jumping and jumping. . . . We realized the dolphins at that point were trying to lead us westward, farther away from the island."

This shift in position saved their lives. The boats had been too far out to sea to be hit by a breaking wave, but if they'd remained where they were, the tsunami's swell would have swept them into the island, wrecking all the boats.

Chris is familiar with Philippine folktales of dolphins saving humans, and he believes that the dolphins "were telling us something. . . . A number of people, like me, believed the dolphins saved us and communicated with us."

Chris said it was "almost a miracle" they survived. But the miracle depended on having a certain attitude, one that valued, Chris said, "following your instincts, understanding your surroundings, being in tune with nature, also cooperating and having a symbiotic relationship with other creatures of the sea."

Sam knew her daughter would be riding him, and when she saw Amber and Ningnong at the far end of the beach, she said, "I was almost hysterical with relief."

Sam then grabbed Amber and raced back to the hotel just before the second wave hit. This wave traveled even farther than the first and destroyed several rooms on the resort's first floor.

Sam believes Ningnong saved her daughter. "If she had been on the beach on her own or with us on the beach, she would never have lived. The elephant took the pounding of the wave."

WHAT THE ELEPHANTS KNEW

The 2004 Indian Ocean tsunami was a devastating tragedy that is considered one of the deadliest natural disasters in modern world history. Over 227,000 people are estimated to have died in fourteen countries.

In the days that followed, numerous stories emerged about people being saved by heroic elephants, the ones used for tourist rides. Some of these stories may be apocryphal; others are impossible to verify. Amber Mason's story is one that's known to be true. Another is of two elephants who, carrying five Japanese tourists between them, ran up a mountainside despite their trainer's efforts to stop them.

In some cases, the mahouts, or elephant guides, told their elephants to run. The elephants were following instructions, and all were accustomed to having people on their backs, so it's impossible to say if the elephants knowingly intended to save their riders. Perhaps it was just a lucky break that Amber Mason was riding Ningnong as he acted to save himself.

What is clear is that the elephants knew to flee long before the tsunami arrived. Early in the morning, hours before the earthquake even struck, elephants were described as screaming and making "such a horrible noise" they woke people up. Elephants also screamed after the quake, and again minutes before the tsunami hit, at which point some even broke their chains in order to run to higher ground.

Scientists do not know how they knew—perhaps they felt the earthquake's shock waves or the low-frequency vibrations from the oncoming wave.

Or, perhaps, the elephants were themselves rebroadcasting a warning they understood from other animals. In the hours before the wave hit, people described witnessing strange, agitated behavior in all sorts of creatures—songbirds, bats, dogs, monkeys, flamingos, antelopes, and more. Many animals were seen fleeing low-lying coastal areas for the hills.

Afterward, in contrast to the shockingly large loss of human life, investigators in many affected areas found virtually no, or startlingly few, animal carcasses, either among wild or domestic animals.

In short, elephants and many other animals knew what was coming and communicated a warning. Next time, perhaps people will listen more closely.

ETHIOPIAN LIONS . . .
RESCUE A GIRL FROM KIDNAPPERS

NAME: *Unnamed*

SPECIES: *Ethiopian lions*

DATE: *June 9, 2005*

LOCATION: *Southwest Ethiopia*

SITUATION: *Girl abducted by kidnappers*

WHO WAS SAVED: *A twelve-year-old girl, name unknown*

LEGACY: *Unique, near-legendary encounter with seemingly compassionate lions*

To Western ears, it's unclear which aspect of this life-saving rescue sounds more surreal: That three wild lions would help protect a twelve-year-old girl from kidnappers, or that, according to the United Nations, over 70 percent of marriages in Ethiopia are the result of abductions.

Kidnapping seems like a lousy way to start a marriage, but tragically, it's no joke: Abductions of young girls are rife in rural areas, and this method of betrothal has existed for so long in some communities that it's become a regrettable but entrenched custom, despite the violence and pain it inflicts. According to Ethiopian police, "Often these young girls are raped and severely beaten to force them to accept the marriage."

So, in an Ethopian village in early June 2005, seven men kidnapped an anonymous twelve-year-old girl on her way home from school, intending to force her to marry one of them against her will.

For a week, the men kept on the move, eluding the pursuit of the police and the girl's family across the Ethiopian countryside, about 350 miles southwest of Addis Ababa, the capital. Then, with authorities on their trail, the men ran into something even more fierce than themselves: a small pride of three lions.

Afterward, the girl said that the lions scared the men away and then stayed with her for about half a day. She was shocked, traumatized, and crying when police finally arrived. She said she'd been beaten by the men but was entirely unhurt by the lions. Police said that as the authorities approached, they witnessed the lions get up and back away slowly from the girl.

"They stood guard until we found her," said Sergeant Wondimu Wedaj. "And then they just left her like a gift and went back into the forest."

THE MIND OF A LION

This much, most accounts agree with. What people disagree about is interpreting the lions' behavior.

"Everyone thinks this is some kind of miracle because normally the lions would attack people," Sergeant Wondimu said.

Officials estimate that there are only about a thousand Ethopian lions left in the wild. Famous for their large black manes, they are Ethiopia's national symbol, but their territory and numbers are dwindling, and they are still hunted illegally by poachers. Pressured on all sides, wild lions are regularly reported attacking farm animals and even people.

Thus, one game hunter said it was most likely that the lions "were probably preparing to eat her but were intercepted by the police."

We all know house cats sometimes play with mice before killing them, but if the lions were hungry, they didn't need to wait. They could have killed the girl immediately, as well as any of the men they chose. A human on foot is easy prey for even a single lion.

Yet the lions harmed no one. Later, four of the men were captured by police, while three remained on the loose.

Another explanation was offered by a government ministry wildlife expert, Stuart Williams: The girl was found crying uncontrollably, and "a young girl whimpering could be mistaken for the mewing sound from a lion cub, which in turn could explain why they didn't eat her. Otherwise they probably would have done."

Is it possible that lions would confuse a girl with a cub? Or that human tears would give them pause if their intent was to eat? Both scenarios seem unlikely, leaving us with the least likely explanation of all—that these intimidating predators felt empathy for the traumatized girl, drove the men away on purpose, and then, as police described, "stood guard" afterward.

Most often, wild lions avoid humans entirely, so we can only wonder why, after the men ran away, these three would lie down with such a lamb—and for a brief moment embody the biblical metaphor of ultimate compassion.

BOTTLENOSE DOLPHINS . . . STOP A SHARK ATTACK

NAME: *Unnamed*

SPECIES: *Bottlenose dolphin*

DATE: *August 28, 2007*

LOCATION: *Marina State Beach, Monterey, California*

SITUATION: *Surfer attacked by a great white shark*

WHO WAS SAVED: *Twenty-four-year-old Todd Endris*

LEGACY: *In the annals of dolphin rescues, few match this one for altruistic, steel-hearted bravery*

The great white shark hit just before 11 am on a foggy, dismal Tuesday morning.

Twenty-four-year-old surfer Todd Endris had been in the water only half an hour, just long enough to catch one wave and return to his favorite spot over a shallow sandbar about fifty yards out from Marina State Beach, near Monterey, California. Almost immediately, swift and unseen, a fourteen-foot predator caught the two-hundred-pound surfer in its gaping mouth, lifted him high out of the water, and slammed back down.

"There was no pain on impact," Todd said later. "There was a bottom jaw underneath my board and the top jaw pretty much like clamped on my thigh."

The shark, he said, "was so powerful and graceful, and it was so fast and effective."

DON'T PISS OFF THE DOLPHINS

Four other surfers were also in the ocean with Todd that morning, along with a large pod of dolphins, who at first were notable only because they were swimming so close it made surfing awkward.

"They were swimming around us and swimming in front of and underneath us in a couple feet of water," Todd said. Despite this, Todd thought that "they were just being playful, you know, like normal. Here they have no fear. They catch waves right in front of you and surf underneath you. It's not that big a thing."

Wes Williams, who was surfing with Todd that day, agreed: "This isn't odd. We surf with dolphins all the time, and I didn't think anything of it."

In fact, common surfer wisdom is that the presence of dolphins means you don't have to worry about shark attacks. That truism, however, doesn't always hold in what's known as the Red Triangle, an area of the California coastline within the Monterey Bay National Marine Sanctuary that is notorious for shark attacks.

In retrospect, it's clear that the dolphins were not playing. They must have known the shark was nearby. In fact, another of Todd's friends, an abalone farmer, said he'd seen the great white basking at the surface a few hours earlier and a couple miles away.

At first, Wes Williams didn't realize what was happening to his friend. He'd just watched another friend, Brian Simpson, finish a ride, heard Todd scream, and looked back to see Todd off his board. "The dolphins were still circling around him and thrashing," Wes said. "I thought, 'What did he do to piss off the dolphins?'"

Almost immediately, though, he saw the shark whipping Todd back and forth in the water, his blood staining an ever-larger circle around him. Todd was fighting for his life, kicking at the great white with his free leg and hitting it with his left fist. "I was getting nowhere," Todd said. Twice the shark let go and bit again.

Overwhelmed with panic, the four other surfers instinctively fled, paddling for the shore. Surfer Joe Jansen said, "My immediate thought was to get the hell out of there."

Meanwhile, "the dolphins were doing these big tail slaps on the surface of the water," Wes said, "and it was so bloody. . . . All of a sudden, one dolphin leapt full out of the air and swung its tail around, missing Todd's head by two inches. That would have killed him if it hit. It looked like a cartoon."

Suddenly, unexpectedly, the shark released and didn't bite again. Up to then, Todd had been barely aware of what the dolphins were doing, but in that moment his impression was that the circling dolphins had formed "a wall between me and the shark where he couldn't get back to me."

Todd yelled out, "Help me!"

SURFERS TO THE RESCUE

Barely a minute had gone by. Hearing Todd call out, Joe Jansen stopped, turned his board around, and bravely stroked into the bloody attack zone. He rationalized that, having given up, the shark probably wouldn't strike again.

Joe paddled right next to Todd and yelled, "Grab your board! Grab your board!"

Todd did, and with Joe's help they caught the next swell to the beach. There, Wes and Brian helped drag Todd out of the water and onto the sand.

The carnage was gruesome. Todd's back was a serrated flap that exposed his spine and internal organs, and his right leg was punctured to the bone. He was ashen white and hemorrhaging unbelievable amounts of blood, but still, for all that, he was incredibly lucky. Somehow, the shark's teeth missed rupturing his pleural cavity and his femoral artery, either one of which would have meant sure death.

Wes and Brian did what they could: They applied pressure to Todd's wounds, and using a surfboard leash, Brian wrapped a tourniquet around Todd's upper thigh. Above all, they kept Todd conscious and calm until, minutes later, paramedics arrived. Then a medevac helicopter landed and took Todd to the nearest hospital.

In the end, Todd lost half of his blood by the time he reached the surgery room, and the initial surgery required six hours and involved five hundred stitches and two hundred staples.

ROLL CALL OF HEROES

Afterward, during his long recovery, Todd jokingly took to calling himself "Shark Boy," but he considered it a genuine miracle that he survived.

"I was the luckiest guy to have those three out there," Todd said of Joe Jansen, Brian Simpson, and Wes Williams. Of course, he also credited the "truly remarkable dolphins" who came to his aide.

It bears emphasizing that everyone involved in Todd Endris's rescue displayed remarkable bravery. Without warning, everyone's worst nightmare came to life in the middle of a nondescript Tuesday morning. Initially, the surfers panicked, but it's important to remember how fast the attack happened. Almost as quickly, the surfers shook off their terror and responded with steadfast courage.

As for the dolphins, they acted as if they knew danger lurked all along, and the moment the shark struck, "the dolphins went absolutely nuts," Todd said, "like they were my best friend. They tried to protect me at the cost of their family members and their babies."

Presumably, the dolphins experienced the same primitive fight-or-flight response that the surfers did, and at least initially, their defensive behavior may have been solely to protect their own pod. If so, then what are we to make of the fact that, once the shark chose a human victim, the dolphins didn't swim away? And not only that, but once the shark stopped attacking Todd, the dolphins stopped attacking the shark. As with Rob Howes (see page 221), the dolphins' behavior seemed intended to protect the surfer, rather than to kill the shark, and they did this even at the risk of their own lives.

In the end, whomever they meant to protect, the dolphins embodied our ultimate definition of altruism, and Todd believes they understood this.

"They're as smart as humans, and I believe they're capable of empathy," Todd said. "When I was being attacked that day, maybe they were trying to protect their young or acting on instinct. But they drove the shark away. If they hadn't, there's no doubt in my mind it would have come back."

ALTRUISM INSPIRES ADVOCACY

In the days and months that followed, Todd Endris's survival story riveted the public. Oprah Winfrey called, and he was featured in dozens of newspapers, magazines, and TV shows, such as *Good Morning America*, the *Today Show*, and *Inside Edition*. Surf companies offered Todd freebies and asked him to endorse their products.

In both positive and negative ways, the traumatic event forever changed Todd Endris's life. "Good things have come out of it," Todd acknowledged. "You can't be happy or sad."

More important than the media attention was Todd's physical recovery. As a goal, he focused on getting back in the ocean and on a surfboard. After six weeks, he felt well enough, and he headed straight for Marina State Beach.

"You really have to face your fears," he said about returning to the site of the attack. "I'm a surfer at heart, and that's not something I can give up real easily. It was hard. But it was something you have to do."

FLIPPER IS ONE TOUGH DUDE

Shark attacks on humans are rare. Rarer still are shark attacks in which dolphins save a human's life, but Todd Endris's story is not unique.

For instance, in July 1996, twenty-nine-year-old Englishman Martin Richardson was saved by dolphins during a scuba diving trip in the Red Sea near Jerusalem, Israel. At one point, when his chartered boat stopped to admire some dolphins, Richardson swam alone with them.

"Suddenly we heard him scream," the boat's captain said. "We thought it was a joke at first. Dolphins never attack humans. Then we saw him leap in the air and blood stained the water all around him."

In a Zodiac boat, crew members raced to Richardson as three dolphins came between man and shark, slapping the water with their tales and driving off the shark, which gave Richardson time to reach the boat and escape.

Then there is the story of surfer Adam Maguire. On New Year's Day 1989, near the beach town of Ballina in Australia, Adam and his two teenage buddies were surfing on a gorgeous summer day when a pod of perhaps fifteen dolphins appeared—and started swimming very closely under and around them just like with Todd Endris.

"Looking back," Adam said, "it seems like they were trying to warn us. I saw what I thought was a dolphin charge at me. When it was a few feet away, I realized it was a shark."

As the shark grabbed Adam, the dolphins went crazy. Again, the dolphins arced out of the water and slapped with their tales till the shark released the surfer.

Ultimately, we can't know what the dolphins understood. But there is one thing they can't have known: that life-saving medical technology awaited Adam, Martin, and Todd. If not for that, each man was doomed to die from his injuries even though the dolphins chased away the shark.

Apparently, this didn't matter. The dolphins fought anyway. Sometimes, seemingly, dolphins will stop a shark attack because it's just plain wrong.

In addition, Todd began working on behalf of dolphin preservation, such as joining organizations that protest the slaughtering of dolphins in Japan for food, which was the subject of the 2009 documentary *The Cove.*

Then he helped lead a group called the International Shark Attack Research Fund, a nonprofit aimed at understanding human/shark encounters. In part, Endris wanted to help develop an affordable shark attack prevention system for surfers, one that would repel sharks without harming them.

Amazingly, Todd considers protecting sharks as important as saving dolphins. Sharks, after all, have "been on earth millions of years," he said. "A whole lot longer than we have."

MILA THE BELUGA WHALE . . . LIFTS A DROWNING DIVER

NAME: *Mila*

SPECIES: *Beluga whale*

DATE: *July 28, 2009*

LOCATION: *Polarland Aquarium, China*

SITUATION: *Diver drowning in a pool*

WHO WAS SAVED: *Twenty-six-year-old Yang Yun*

LEGACY: *The only whale to be photographed in the act of rescuing a drowning person*

Some job applications are more difficult than others.

For instance, if you want to be a whale trainer at the Polarland Aquarium in Harbin, China, you have to swim with the whales. Could be fun, right?

Except that you must compete against other applicants to see who can free dive (without breathing apparatus) to the bottom of a twenty-foot-deep, arctic-cold tank and stay down the longest, all while the two resident belugas—Mila and Nikola—circle around with seemingly bemused smiles on their faces.

On July 28, 2009, twenty-six-year-old job applicant Yang Yun stood at the edge of the tank and filled her lungs with air.

"Maybe I was too nervous," she said. "I never dive into water so deep and so cold."

About three-quarters of the way to the bottom, Yang Yun's right leg cramped in the frigid water, becoming essentially paralyzed. Not only couldn't she swim, but "I began to choke and sank even lower," she said. "I thought that was it for me—I was dead."

"We didn't notice the problem," an aquarium official said, but Mila did. Suddenly, Yun said, "I felt this incredible force under me driving me to the surface."

Mila grabbed Yun's leg in her mouth and pushed her to the top of the pool—while photographers madly snapped away, capturing images of the incredible tableau.

"[Mila is] a sensitive animal who works closely with humans," an aquarium official said. "I think this girl owes Mila her life."

Perhaps because of Mila's small teeth, or simply because she was gentle, Yang Yun emerged from the pool unharmed. In fact, after recovering from her near-drowning, and perhaps as a way to thank the kind belugas, Yun dove back into the tank and took the test again.

Reports don't say whether she got the job.

DEFINITIONS: DOMESTIC VERSUS TAME

When discussing wild animals in aquariums and zoos, it's important to remember that a "tame" animal is not the same as a domestic animal. Many wild animals in captivity can become very acclimated to humans. Sometimes wild animals are even kept as house pets, such as capuchin monkeys and chimpanzees. But no matter how socialized, docile, cooperative, and loving a wild animal may be, that animal will always remain wild.

One critical distinction is that socialized wild animals do not pass on learned behaviors to their offspring, who are born wild even if they are born in a zoo. A domestic animal has evolved into a different species whose very genes have altered through contact with humans over many generations. Anthropologist Pat Shipman writes, "The very term implies that a domesticated animal lives with humans, in their home, not for a single generation but forever."

Gorillas like Jambo (see page 195) and Binti Jua (see page 206) grew up with humans. They were highly socialized (which is the term scientists prefer instead of "tame"). But these gorillas couldn't share a person's home like a dog or cat. Inevitably, juvenile chimpanzees kept as pets become truly wild and unpredictably dangerous when they reach sexual maturity.

Domestication is a mysterious process. No one knows how long it takes, and in fact, relatively few wild species have ever been shown capable of domestication, though it could still happen. One intriguing possibility is the dolphin.

Among other things, in order to become domesticated, a wild species must already display an affinity for humans. The animal has to like us and want to be with us. As the rescue stories in this book show, dolphins display this natural friendship readily.

Might there one day be a domestic dolphin species? Stay tuned.

LIFEGUARDS OF THE SEA

Scientists consider marine mammals, such as dolphins and whales, to be highly social, intelligent, empathetic, and most likely self-aware. Though this is the only known story of a beluga whale saving a person, dolphins are legendary for saving drowning swimmers. The oldest story in this book, in fact, involves a dolphin rescuing a doomed Greek musician (see page 249). In the category of "most common animal rescue not involving a dog," no other life-saving scenario comes close.

And yet, when you're drowning, it's typically just you, the sea, and any last requests. Skeptics love dolphin stories because they usually can't be proved. The only evidence is the person's word. Despite the popularity of the folklore, or perhaps because of it, we still often question whether a dolphin would really, actually, legitimately come to someone's rescue. If the person isn't actually lying, perhaps they were just imagining that a curious but ultimately indifferent dolphin cared a whit about their plight.

That's why Mila's story is so compelling. Dozens of witnesses saw it. They took pictures. As an equivalently intelligent marine mammal, Mila adds to the evidence that dolphins can and would save drowning swimmers. She helps confirm that these stories are quite possible. Other evidence includes stories of dolphins preventing shark attacks (see pages 221 and 232) and the affinity dolphins display for humans in therapeutic contexts (see page 109).

You might say, our troubles accepting dolphin rescue stories rests mostly with ourselves—verifying the teller and trusting our own experience.

Here are a few additional modern stories:

- ✩ In October 1997, teenager Jamie Hirst was swept a mile or more off the coast of Naples, Florida. He tried to swim to shore, but as night fell, he was exhausted. Four dolphins arrived; all through the night and until dawn, they circled and nudged him, keeping him awake and afloat. Hirst was rescued the next day by a passing boat.
- ✩ In November 1999, when the Cuban boy Elian Gonzalez was rescued off US waters, dolphins were seen surrounding him. Elian claimed

the dolphins broke waves for him and kept him afloat after the boat he was in sank and he had to cling to an inner tube to survive.

- In August 2000, teenager Davide Ceci was rescued by "Filippo," a friendly, well-known wild dolphin who frequented the waters off Manfredonia, Italy. Ceci, a nonswimmer, fell out of his boat and started drowning. Filippo swam up, let him grab his fin, and carried him back to his vessel.

- In December 2008, fisherman Ronnie Dabal's boat capsized in Puerto Princesa Bay in the Philippines. For twenty-four-hours he clung to a piece of foam; then, just as he was losing strength, a pod of dolphins arrived. "Lots of them," Dabal said. "Then a pair of whales started swimming on both sides." Flanking him, the animals used their fins to slowly nudge Dabal toward shore, a process that took so long he passed out along the way and woke up on the beach.

- In November 2010, actor Dick Van Dyke revealed that, as a young man, he once fell asleep on his surfboard and "woke up out of sight of land," he said. As he started paddling with the swells, he said, "I start seeing fins swimming around me and I thought, 'Well, I'm dead.' They turned out to be porpoises and they pushed me all the way to shore. I'm not kidding."

EVOLVING TOGETHER: HOW ANIMALS MADE US HUMAN

The human-animal bond isn't just something we enjoy; it's also something that helps define us as a species.

Think about it: No other animal lives with and interacts with other species as extensively as we do. Animals of all kinds entertain us, comfort us, heal us, feed us, transport us, work for us, play with us, and share our homes. In turn, we spend enormous amounts of money and energy caring for them. Only humans have built lives so thoroughly and intimately connected with such a wide range of other species. Our cultivation of the human-animal bond is one of our signature traits.

Why is that? In recent years, scientists and researchers are coming to the conclusion that the ancient human relationship with animals directly influenced our own evolution as a species. Today, this may help explain why we so often crave the company of animals: They made us who we are, evolutionarily speaking, and being with them helps us feel human.

HUNTING, AND TALKING ABOUT, ANIMALS

"Living with animals is indeed a human characteristic and it is both very old and profoundly important," writes Pat Shipman in her book *The Animal Connection*. "When anthropologists field questions about what makes humans human, they do not say 'Our connection to animals,' but I think they should."

Shipman traces this connection through the three biggest leaps in human evolution: the development of tools, the development of language, and the domestication of plants and animals. Since the advent of tool use extends so far back—at least 2.6 million years—Shipman suggests that the human-animal bond is now probably encoded in our genes just like any other species-defining trait.

For instance, the earliest known tools were developed largely to hunt animals and to process them as food, clothing, and further tools. By becoming such extraordinarily skilled toolmakers, humans transformed themselves and their environment in ways no other animal has ever done.

Shipman proposes that early humans became so obsessed with animals, and were so desperate to share critical, essential information about them, that this spurred the development of language. Apparently, after a while, grunting and pointing just weren't cutting it.

As proof, Shipman cites the explosion of figurative cave art around 40,000 years ago. Cave art is mysterious, but "the overwhelming majority of prehistoric art that we can understand in any way depicts animals," Shipman writes.

While no one knows when language developed, it stands to reason that if early humans were drawing animals, they were discussing them. As any reader of this book can appreciate, talking (and writing) revolutionized human life. Indeed, with the advantages of tool use and language, humans became the world's "top predator" and its dominant species.

LIVING WITH ANIMALS

Domestication of plants and animals—the last great leap in human evolution—profoundly revolutionized human life. As most of us learned in social studies, domestication finally allowed humans to settle down. We no longer had to hunt, gather, and migrate with the seasons. Once humans established villages, and then cities, we got busy creating human civilization with a capital C, yet we were able to do this only with the help of animals.

Yet the assistance of cooperative animals changed us in perhaps an even more significant way: It changed our perspective. Humans were no longer either the hunter or the hunted. We were also caretakers. Through domestication, we gained an evolutionary advantage by working *with* other animals—but to do this we had to understand their needs, communicate with them, care for them, and cultivate a mutually beneficial relationship.

Wolves evolved into the first domesticated species, *Canis familiaris*, the domestic dog, anywhere from 14,000 to perhaps 32,000 years ago. We don't know how or why this happened, but it likely occurred more than once in several different places. Humans certainly couldn't have planned it. Over thousands of years, close contact must have occurred between wolves and ancient humans. They lived in similar social groups, hunted similar prey, and must have found reasons to cooperate. Humans and these early "socialized" wolves, dog expert Mark Derr writes, "helped each other out, and they adapted together to a changing world." If the evidence of the modern dog is any indication, they also found pleasure in each other's company.

The dog was a remarkable occurrence that predated all other domestic species by at least two thousand years, and maybe much more. Domestic plants, and the advent of agriculture, slowly arose around 12,000 years ago. At that point, new domestic animal species appeared once or twice every thousand years.

With animals, domestication is a two-way process. Though individual wild animals can be socialized, it's extremely rare for a domestic species to evolve (for more on this distinction, see page 239). The collection of necessary traits is fairly restrictive—the species must be hardy, grow fast on a cheap diet, live in a flexible social hierarchy, breed often, and be useful to humans. Last, and perhaps most important, the species must have a fondness or affinity for people. You can't force an aggressive species to become domesticated. Shipman says, "Both participants had to cooperate or domestication did not happen."

Further, keeping animals is a lot of work. It typically means caring for their entire well-being, from birth to death. If humans learned to select for the traits they preferred in a domestic animal, then domestication itself selected for the traits that humans needed to be successful at it. Only a happy wolf would become a dog who would stay with you and help you hunt and protect your home. Only a happy aurochs would become a cow.

How did this process change ancient humans? Shipman writes, "Our increasingly intimate interactions with animals have . . . driven us to become more observing, more empathetic, better at communicating, more tolerant, and more able to compromise or negotiate."

All this leads to a radical conclusion: "It was animals who taught us that others—even other species—have emotions, needs, and 'thoughts,'" Shipman writes. "It was animals who selected for the vital skills of empathy, understanding, and compromise in the human lineage."

In other words, we can't help but experience the human-animal bond, since we evolved to nurture it, and it accounts for some of the best parts of being human.

Stories are problematic for scientists, who prefer to isolate objects of study so they can measure and define them. But what's important about a life-saving rescue exists in context: in the relationship of those involved, in their history, and in the nature of the danger and the animal's reactions. If we don't tell the whole story, it diminishes our understanding of what the animal does.

Yet stories are open to interpretation, and they have a way of growing and evolving with each telling. Few circumstances (except perhaps fishing) illustrate the inescapable pull of narrative as much as a life-saving rescue. We almost can't help ourselves: We naturally interpret, edit, embellish, and connect events to bring some meaningful order to the chaotic, swirling river that comprises our lived experience.

The stories in this section all mix real life with exaggeration; they shape events to capture emotional truths or to fit the expectations of folklore. Discerning where myth leaves off and fact begins can be tricky. These stories go back seventy to several thousand years, and they now form part of our cultural bedrock. They help define our popular image of life-saving animals.

MEDITERRANEAN DOLPHINS . . . GIVE A GREEK POET A RIDE

NAME: *Unnamed*

SPECIES: *Dolphin*

DATE: *Seventh century BC*

LOCATION: *The Aegean Sea*

SITUATION: *Rich singer robbed and thrown into the Mediterranean*

WHO WAS SAVED: *Arion, legendary Greek musician*

LEGACY: *Earliest story of a life-saving animal rescue, immortalized dolphins as human helpers*

The myth of Arion and the dolphin is a well-known ancient Greek legend. It is perhaps the oldest surviving version of a tale that's extremely common in folklore worldwide.

And yet, long-buried beneath layers of myth, this story may contain a few kernels of truth. Arion himself was probably a real person. The ancient writers Herodotus, Erasmus, and St. Augustine thought so, and he was presented as a real Greek poet by the nineteenth-century mythologist Thomas Bulfinch.

In his time, around the seventh century BC, Arion was considered one of the best poets and lyre players in Greece. He was famously credited with inventing the dithyramb, a type of chorus-based musical composition used in the worship of Dionysus. Arion was originally from Lesbos, but he taught and played in Corinth, where his artistic patron was the tyrant ruler Periander (who lived from 627 to 585 BC).

The story may also reflect some truths about dolphins. The ancient Greeks were experienced seafarers, and images of dolphins appear in their earliest artworks. Could it be that observed dolphin behavior, and even actual life-saving events, fed the excited myths that the ancient Greeks used to describe their god-infused world?

ARION'S ITALIAN TOUR ENDS IN TRAGEDY

As the story goes, Arion had just concluded a very successful and lucrative musical tour across Italy, even winning a high-profile contest in Sicily—a sort of classical age *American Idol*.

Now richer and more famous than ever, Arion was returning home on a Corinthian ship. Once at sea, however, Arion discovered that the crew meant to kill him and steal his money. Would this have happened to Kelly Clarkson? *No!* Arion pleaded with the mutinous men: He would give them all of his gold if only they'd spare his life. No go, choir boy, they said. They were from Corinth, too, and how could they get away with their crime if Arion remained alive to tell of it?

"Grant me, then, a last request," Arion said, as Bulfinch's rendition tells it. "Since nought will avail to save my life, that I may die, as I have lived, as becomes a bard. When I shall have sung my death song, and my harp-strings shall have ceased to vibrate, then I will bid farewell to life, and yield uncomplaining to my fate."

Very noble, the crew probably sniggered, but why not? After all, if Elvis promised you one last song before you pushed him off the plank, wouldn't that be worth hearing?

So Arion dressed in his minstrel garb, took up his lyre, and sang a heartbreaking ode in honor of Apollo, the patron of Delphi. When he finished, he dutifully jumped off the stern of the ship, and the nefarious crew left him to drown in their wake.

However, Arion's beautiful music had drawn a group of admiring dolphins, and one of the dolphins hoisted Arion onto his back and swam with him all the way to shore at Taenarum. From there, Arion walked home across the countryside, full of gratitude and song, until he reached Corinth and told Periander, the king, of the sailors' crime and the dolphin's kindness.

No gullible rube—perhaps he'd known too many entertainers—Periander was immediately suspicious of Arion, and he put the musician under guard. When the Corinthian ship eventually arrived, the king had the crew brought before him. He questioned them about the missing lyre player. The crew rolled their eyes and said: Oh, *Arion*? That flake is still in Italy, living the life and soaking up the glory.

Then Arion jumped out from his hiding place, shocking the crew and unmasking their plot. Periander banished the men from Corinth forever, and Arion's miraculous rescue was immortalized with a bronze monument in Taenarum.

DOLPHINS IN GREEK MYTHOLOGY

Dolphins swim prominently in a number of Greek myths. In particular, dolphins play transformative roles in famous stories related to Apollo and Dionysus. Since Arion was connected to both gods, this may explain why dolphins were the life-saving vehicle in his story, which emphasizes the Greek musician's favored status.

Homer tells the story about how Apollo founded the temple at Delphi, which the Greeks considered the center or navel of the world. After killing the dragon who previously guarded the site, and after spending many years at sea (Greek stories are never short), Apollo turned himself into a dolphin and hijacked a Cretan ship. As a dolphin, the sun god ordered the terrified crew to become his priests in his Delphic temple, thus supplanting the old religion with a new (and improved) one.

In the Dionysus story, the god of wine and ecstasy was traveling in disguise on a pirate ship. Not knowing they had a god aboard, the pirates decided to sell Dionysus into slavery, and so they tied him to the mast. Bad move. Thus angered, Dionysus caused the wooden ship to sprout vines of ivy, driving the men mad, and as the crew dove overboard to escape, they were turned into dolphins.

These stories are often cited as reasons for the well-known Greek prohibition against killing dolphins. Not only were dolphins venerated by the Greeks and closely associated with these important gods, but the stories provided a mythic explanation of the animal: Dolphins were originally human. As the Greek poet Oppian wrote, "Diviner than the Dolphin is nothing yet created for indeed they were aforetime men and lived in cities along with mortals."

What else, after all, could explain why these social, seagoing mammals were so humanlike? The similarities were not lost on the Greeks. Dolphins breathe air, give birth to live young, nurture their young, and play with evident abandon. Dolphins are attracted to ships to jump in the bow waves (see page 267), and they chatter and "sing" in apparent communication. As we know from modern-day dolphins in captivity, they will willingly give rides to humans, and in the wild, dolphins even occasionally save drowning swimmers (see page 239).

Does Arion's myth, then, reflect an accurate portrait of dolphin behavior? All it would take would be one real-life episode in which dolphins playing in a ship's bow waves saved some everyday Greek sailor from drowning. Once this remarkable story made the rounds, ancient poets would naturally want to use, and preserve, the tale in mythic form, one that involved gods and celebrities.

And as storytelling shorthand for divine intervention and blessing, this is the way life-saving, human-carrying dolphins appear in folklore (such

as in Plutarch). Even the histories of five early Christian saints include dolphin rescues.

Then again, the reverse also occurs. Once an idea is planted in a culture, no matter how fantastical, we tend to see it where it doesn't exist. Any close encounter with a dolphin becomes a "life-saving rescue," and so the myth is perpetuated. This might explain why there are so many stories of life-saving dolphins today: People are culturally primed to believe them.

In the end, folklore is fed by both storytelling impulses. However, Arion's myth probably struck a lasting chord (pun intended) precisely because it contains some known truths about dolphins.

GELERT THE WOLFHOUND . . . SAVES THE BABY

NAME: *Gelert*

SPECIES: *Wolfhound*

DATE: *Early 1200s*

LOCATION: *Beddgelert, Wales*

SITUATION: *Baby attacked by a marauding wolf*

WHO WAS SAVED: *Prince Llywelyn's infant son*

LEGACY: *Treasured Welsh fable of canine devotion, ongoing inspiration for Hollywood movies*

In Wales, the best-loved and most famous animal rescue story is that of Gelert the wolfhound. The tale goes like this:

Early in the thirteenth century, Prince Llywelyn of North Wales had a palace in the town of Beddgelert. Prince Llywelyn was extremely fond of hunting, and he often led hunting parties through the countryside accompanied by his favorite dog, Gelert.

One day, Llywelyn sounded the horn for a hunt, and all his hunting dogs came running except for one, his faithful wolfhound. Puzzled and disappointed by Gelert's strange absence, Prince Llywelyn carried on with the hunt, anyway—accompanied by his wife, and leaving his infant son in the care of a nursemaid.

Later that day, the hunting party returned, and Prince Llywelyn and his wife were greeted by Gelert, who bounded to meet them with joyful strides. Yet as he drew closer, they saw that the wolfhound's muzzle was smeared and dripping with blood.

Horrified, the prince and his wife rushed to the nursery. There, they found the aftermath of a violent struggle: Their baby's empty cradle was overturned, and blood-covered sheets and clothes were strewn everywhere.

Mad with grief, and thinking that Gelert had viciously killed his son and heir, the prince immediately drove his sword into Gelert's side, piercing his heart. Gelert howled in agony. Yet as his cries died away, another cry arose.

Hidden beneath the cradle under the bloody sheets, Llywelyn's son was alive! And next to the child, also hidden, lay the dead body of an enormous wolf.

Llywelyn immediately realized the truth: His ever-faithful Gelert had saved his son from this marauding predator. The innocent dog had raced to meet them out of well-earned pride.

Overcome with remorse, Llywelyn buried Gelert beneath a mighty cairn of stones and marked his grave so that all would remember Gelert's bravery and the tragic lesson of that day. Afterward, it was said Prince Llywelyn never smiled again.

TALES OF THE "FAITHFUL HOUND"

Prince Llywelyn was a real person, but Gelert's story is a fake. It is considered a variation of a popular folktale known as the "Faithful Hound" that appears in many cultures.

Apparently, in a bid to drum up tourism, an eighteenth-century innkeeper, David Pritchard, adapted the folktale to fit the town in which he lived, Beddgelert (which means "Gelert's grave"). Pritchard invented the name Gelert for the dog and added Prince Llywelyn to imbue the story with some local authenticity. It worked quite well. Ever since, English poets and writers have immortalized Gelert, turning him into a Welsh icon, and even today, tourists seek out the sleepy Wales village to visit Gelert's supposed burial mound, which is marked by a plaque telling his story.

The oldest version of the "Faithful Hound" folktale likely comes from India. In the *Panchatantra*, a compilation of animal fables from the third to fifth centuries, there's the story of the mongoose and the black snake. In this rendition, a husband and wife leave their baby in the care of a mongoose, who kills a predatory black snake while they're away. When they return to their bloody home, they make the same error as Prince Llywelyn: In their grief, they kill the mongoose, only to discover too late the dead snake and their safe child.

Other versions—involving different combinations of animals—hail from China, Malaysia, Egypt, and Germany. In the United States, Hollywood has used this evocative scenario several times: In the animated movie *Lady and the Tramp* (1955), Tramp is at one point falsely accused of attacking the baby. The dog is saved from death only when Lady reveals a dead rat in the bloody nursery.

The movie *Babe* (1995) also includes a moment when Babe the pig is mistaken for a sheep killer. The farmer takes Babe's bloody snout as evidence that Babe murdered the sheep, when Babe actually fought off the real attackers—a pack of feral dogs. The farmer takes Babe to the shed to kill him, but—perhaps sensing the lesson of Gelert that rash acts of grief only lead to irrevocable, tragic consequences—the farmer has a change of heart and lets the faithful pig go.

MOUSTACHE THE POODLE . . . JOINS THE FRENCH REVOLUTION

NAME: *Moustache*

SPECIES: *Poodle*

DATE: *1799 to 1812*

LOCATION: *Europe*

SITUATION: *French army trying to dominate the world*

WHO WAS SAVED: *French soldiers*

LEGACY: *National hero for fighting in Napoleon's army, awarded French medal for bravery*

Dogs have participated in human wars ever since canines were domesticated. In those endless conflicts, they have played many roles—standing guard, providing moral support, scouting the enemy, tending to the wounded, carrying messages, sniffing out bombs, and even fighting alongside soldiers.

One of the first and most famous individual war dogs to be recognized was Moustache, a black poodle who accompanied Napoleon's army for almost twelve years, from the end of the French Revolution through the Napoleonic Wars. We may think of poodles as high-strung prima donnas today, but they were originally hunting and retrieving dogs, and their presence on battlefields goes back to the seventeenth century. None proved the breed's moxie better than Moustache.

That said, none of Moustache's supposed exploits are free from the taint of fabrication and conflicting accounts. We cannot know today what, or how much, of his legend is fictionalized. Like the proverbial fish that got away, war stories tend to get more dramatic with each retelling.

But Moustache was real, and he accompanied troops to war, and his efforts, inflated or not, are still representative of the contributions of military dogs of his era.

JOINING THE FRENCH REVOLUTION

Moustache was born in Normandy, France, in 1799. When he was six months old, as one historian tells it, he apparently decided to tag along behind a parading regiment of French grenadiers, or elite attack infantry. Lacking a dog, the regiment, in turn, adopted Moustache, who had no particular training but apparently adapted to and enjoyed military life.

This was not uncommon in the French army. As M. Joupin, a nineteenth-century French historian, once observed, "Dogs militarize themselves almost of their own accord."

And so, in spring 1800, when the regiment was sent to Italy to fight Austria at the end of the French Revolution, Moustache went, too.

If so, then Moustache must have accompanied Napoleon's army on its march through the St. Bernard Pass in the Swiss Alps that May. While it's doubtful that Moustache met Barry, the original life-saving St. Bernard (see page 262) who was then only a pup—who knows? Perhaps they exchanged the traditional canine salute!

In any case, Moustache's first reported heroics occurred at the ensuing Battle of Marengo in June 1800. He is credited with barking to alert sleeping

NAPOLEON'S TEARS

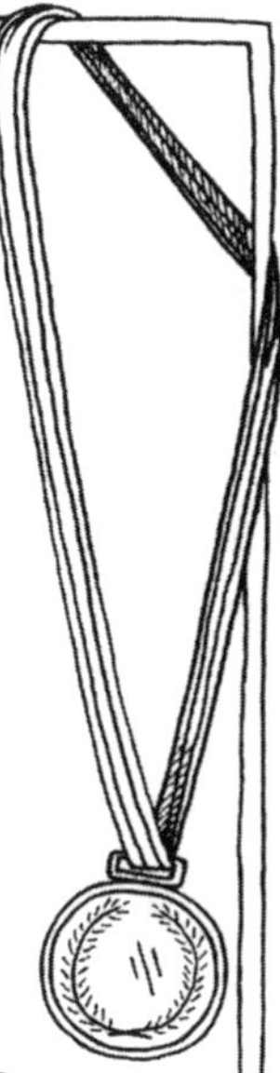

Few military leaders in history match Napoleon's reputation for cold-hearted ruthlessness. Yet he was a sucker for dogs.

The most famous episode occurred in 1796, a few years before Moustache came along, and it seems to prove the ironic truism that dogs humanize war. Napoleon was inspecting the carnage after the Battle of Castiglione, and he came across a dog mourning a dead enemy soldier. The dog was moaning and licking the dead man's hand, and when he saw the general approach, he tried to lead Napoleon over.

Later, Napoleon wrote:

"Perhaps it was the spirit of the time and the place that affected me. But I assure you no occurrence of any of my other battlefields impressed me so keenly. I halted on my tour to gaze at the spectacle and reflect on its meaning.

"This soldier, I realized, must have had friends at home and in his regiments; yet he lay there deserted by all except his dog. . . . I had looked on, unmoved, at battles which decided the future of nations. Tearless, I had given orders which brought death to thousands.

"Yet, here I was stirred, profoundly stirred, stirred to tears. And by what? The grief of one dog. I am certain that at that instant I felt more ready than at any other time to show mercy."

troops to a sneak attack by Austrian soldiers (or perhaps to a single Austrian spy), as well as engaging an Austrian pointer in direct combat. We'll never know whether Moustache would have prevailed over the stronger dog, since a musket shot killed the pointer and also injured one of Moustache's ears.

At Marengo, the Austrians were defeated and driven from Italy, marking a victory for Napoleon.

GLORY AT THE BATTLE OF AUSTERLITZ

Historians debate the official end date of the French Revolution, but by 1805, the ensuing Napoleonic Wars for control of Europe were fully engaged. On December 2 of that year, Moustache cemented his legend at the Battle of Austerlitz, a nine-hour dust-up that became one of Napoleon's greatest victories.

In the heat of battle, the French regiment's standard-bearer found himself surrounded by Austrian troops and was mortally wounded. To save the flag, the standard-bearer wrapped it around himself before collapsing dead to the ground. At that moment, Moustache raced to his side and held off the attacking Austrians. Then, before he could be bayonetted himself, Moustache supposedly ripped the bloody standard from the dead French soldier and raced with it triumphantly back to the French camp.

Moustache did not escape unharmed, suffering a leg wound; according to one source, that leg eventually had to be amputated. However, his heroics earned him not only an official ribboned medal for bravery to hang around his neck but full regimental privileges, including food rations and pay. Topping it off, Moustache was afterward presented to Napoleon himself, who apparently enjoyed Moustache's most-famous trick: At the mention of France's enemies, he would lift his leg as if to pee.

ROMANCE AT THE BATTLE OF ESSLING

Variously wounded and possibly three-legged, Moustache remained undaunted. When he accompanied troops to the front lines at the Battle of Essling in May 1809, he also proved himself a true Frenchman. Spotting a female poodle on the opposing side, Moustache wooed her back to the French camp, where they mated and, within the next year, had puppies. *Vive la France!*

DEATH AND DEFEAT AT THE SIEGE OF BADAJOZ

The Siege of Badajoz, which occurred in Spain from March to April 1812, was one of the bloodiest battles of the Napoleonic Wars, and it constituted a terrible defeat for France. It presaged Napoleon's eventual undoing, and it proved to be Moustache's undoing as well.

During France's Spanish campaign, Moustache continued to lead regiments and bark warnings of hidden or advancing enemy troops. But at Badajoz, the twelve-year-old poodle allegedly took a direct hit from a cannonball and was killed. Moustache was buried with his medal, and his gravestone was carved with the tribute: *Ici repose le brave Moustache* ("Here lies the brave Moustache").

After the war, however, the Spaniards destroyed the stone and, directed by the Inquisition, dug up the dog's bones and burned them.

Perhaps they'd heard about Moustache's notorious "lift the leg" trick.

BARRY DER MENSCHENRETTER . . . SAVES TRAVELERS IN THE SWISS ALPS

NAME: *Barry der Menschenretter*

SPECIES: *St. Bernard*

DATE: *1800 to 1814*

LOCATION: *St. Bernard Pass, Switzerland*

SITUATION: *Lost travelers caught in avalanches*

WHO WAS SAVED: *Around forty people*

LEGACY: *Pop culture icon for all life-saving animals, champion of the St. Bernard breed*

Over time, good stories often get embellished until they become great, unforgettable stories. The details get richer, grander, more dramatic. That's certainly the case with Barry der Menschenretter, the most famous St. Bernard ever to save snow-buried hikers in the Swiss Alps. While Barry was a real dog, and he really saved numerous lives, most of what's known about him is pure hokum.

THE DANGEROUS GREAT ST. BERNARD PASS

Barry's story, and that of the St. Bernard breed, starts with a particular mountain pass in the Swiss Alps, the majestic range of towering peaks that divides modern-day Switzerland and Italy.

This pass became an important military and trade route beginning around AD 43, when the ancient Romans expanded it during their efforts to conquer the northern tribes. However, travelers found it a difficult crossing: At 8,000 feet, not only was it snow-packed most of the year, but it was plagued by brigands and robbers. Around 1050, Saint Bernard of Montjou founded a monastery and hospice there, providing travelers with food, shelter, medical care, and protection from attack. Eventually, the pass took the monastery founder's name.

In the mid-seventeenth century, the first dogs were kept at the monastery, most likely as guard dogs. The monks weren't particularly picky, and they took in the big mixed-breed dogs then common on Swiss farms. These were often called "Küherhunde" (cowherd's dogs), and they had short patched coats of red, reddish-brown, and white hair.

In the 1700s, the dogs would accompany the *marroniers,* or mountain guides, who accompanied travelers over the pass. The broad-chested animals would clear paths through the snow, and their sense of direction and smell proved invaluable in storms or for finding people who got lost or buried in avalanches.

Eventually, the dogs became such experts at finding and rescuing people that they were sent out on their own, typically in twos or threes. When a person was found, one dog would stay with the person, licking them awake and lying on them for warmth, and the other dog would return to the monastery to get help.

This system of dog-assisted *marroniers* grew to be so effective that when Napoleon crossed the pass in May 1800 with an army of 250,000 men, not one soldier lost his life. Indeed, no soldier was lost over a twenty-year period from 1790 to 1810.

Afterward, French soldiers began spreading the word about the remarkable dogs of St. Bernard Pass, and popular interest grew. As it happened, this coincided with the service of the greatest dog the monastery ever produced.

THE MANY LEGENDS OF BARRY

Barry der Menschenretter was born in 1800, and it's not clear when he began working as a rescue dog. Nor is it clear exactly how many people he saved, who those people were, or what he did to help. The monastery didn't keep records of rescues, and indeed, no dog but Barry ever achieved individual recognition. Not only that, the St. Bernard wasn't even a recognized breed at the time.

Barry is usually credited with saving "over forty" people, though his cemetery plaque rounds it off to an even four-zero. What we do know is that Barry retired in 1812, and that he weighed about a hundred pounds, or about fifty to eighty pounds less than a St. Bernard today.

However, one particular rescue made Barry famous the world over and led to his enshrinement as perhaps *the* iconic life-saving animal. Barry was credited with finding a young boy, unconscious and nearly frozen, in an icy crevasse. Barry licked the boy awake, and then encouraged the child to grab hold of his coat and climb onto his back. Then, on his own, Barry carried the boy back to the monastery, where his heartsick parents were waiting.

The only hitch is that it didn't happen, or at least the museum that displays Barry's taxidermied body denies the rescue ever took place. Cooked up by a writer—a certain P. Scheitlin—the story distilled the achievements of the monastery's dogs into one heroic image. And as any ad exec will tell you, a good image sells. The story spread and accrued the patina of legitimacy, and that image of the red-coated dog with a boy on his back came to adorn postcards and household products of every description, from cigars and clocks to elixirs and more.

Nor did Barry, or any monastery rescue dog, ever wear a wooden barrel of liquor around their neck, which was another flight of fancy.

Nor was it true that Barry died while in the middle of what would have been his forty-first rescue. Since no hero can be allowed to leave the stage quietly, someone concocted the tale of Barry tracking a lost soldier. Following a two-day-old scent, Barry eventually found his man in a snow bank. He dug and dug, uncovered the man, and licked his face till consciousness returned. However, the startled and disoriented soldier mistook Barry for a wolf and, in a moment that echoes the "faithful hound" tales of yore (see page 254), stabbed him to death with his bayonet.

No matter. By 1814, when Barry *actually* died (of old age in Bern), his breed was still seventy years away from being officially recognized, but it already had a champion.

BIRTH OF THE MODERN BREED

Suffice it to say, Barry was no Beethoven, the slobbering, long-haired, goofy giant from the movies.

Life in the mountains was hard, and the monastery dogs did not live long, typically from six to eight years. Sometimes, the monastery almost entirely ran out of dogs and had to replenish them from surrounding valleys. At times the monks tried to breed for certain characteristics, but with mixed success.

In the 1830s, they bred the short-haired dogs with Newfoundlands, hoping that longer hair would keep the dogs warmer, but instead this only encouraged ice to form on their coats.

Further, others began selling any old red-and-white Swiss farm dog as a genuine monastery dog, while others bred the dogs willy-nilly, as suited their tastes. In particular, the English preferred heavier heads and greater size and bred them with mastiffs, and this strain came to represent the breed we know today, though it didn't come from the Alps.

Through the nineteenth century, the breed was called a variety of names—Hospice Dogs, Swiss Alpine Dogs, Alpine Mastiffs, or most often, Barry Dogs. In 1880, the Swiss Kennel Club recognized the name St. Bernard, and the breed, with official standards, was formally recognized in 1887.

Then, only a decade later, in 1897, the monastery's St. Bernards made their last rescue, saving a twelve-year-old boy who'd fallen into one of those famous icy crevices. In the end, monastery dogs saved an estimated two thousand people. Today, the monastery still breeds and maintains St. Bernards, but the rescue work is done primarily by helicopter.

And yet, Barry's story has one final, amusing coda.

In 1923, the Natural History Museum in Bern decided that Barry's stuffed body, which they'd displayed since 1815, needed a makeover. The real dog had become unrecognizable compared to the quintessential St. Bernard of popular imagination, so they reposed Barry's body to make it more regal, changed the coat (which had disintegrated), added the wooden keg, and enlarged and adjusted the skull to better resemble the massive modern version.

Even in death, the poster dog for all St. Bernards needed help to look like a St. Bernard!

PELORUS JACK . . .
GUIDES SHIPS THROUGH ROCKY STRAITS

NAME: *Pelorus Jack*

SPECIES: *Risso's dolphin*

DATE: *1888 to 1912*

LOCATION: *Admiralty Bay, New Zealand*

SITUATION: *Hazardous passage through rocky waters*

WHO WAS SAVED: *Numerous steamships*

LEGACY: *Worldwide tourist attraction, the most famous dolphin in New Zealand history*

The conflation and exaggeration of folklore rides the bow waves with Pelorus Jack, the most famous dolphin in New Zealand history.

Pelorus Jack was a rare, albino-white Risso's dolphin—a beakless cetacean who looks similar to a pilot whale—who for twenty-four years accompanied ships across Admiralty Bay in New Zealand. Several photos were taken of Pelorus Jack, and his (or her) distinctive coloring and species made the animal easy to recognize. Actually, the dolphin's sex was never determined, but "he" was always considered male, and he grew to be about fourteen feet long.

Some said that Pelorus Jack was a savior, and that he appeared next to steamships to help them navigate a particularly dangerous, rocky passage. Others said that Pelorus Jack was simply having fun. He was a lone dolphin, presumably orphaned, who met up with passing ships because he loved to ride their bow waves—the faster, the better.

Whatever Pelorus Jack was doing, it's also true that during his tenure, from 1888 to 1912, only one ship was lost in that part of the bay. And as his reputation grew, Pelorus Jack's reliable presence turned him into a worldwide celebrity and tourist attraction, one who was promoted in guidebooks and on postcards. People booked passage along the route just to see him, including Mark Twain. Songs were written about him, and a candy bar and a ship were named after him. Today his image is the logo of New Zealand's interisland ferry.

Whether Pelorus Jack actually saved anyone is doubtful, or perhaps it's a matter of interpretation. However, Pelorus Jack himself was saved in 1904 when, due to his celebrity status, he became the first individual sea creature to be protected by law.

Then, after twenty-four years, Pelorus Jack suddenly stopped appearing next to ships. Various tales surfaced about how someone had shot or harpooned him, but none of these are regarded as particularly credible. Instead, Pelorus Jack likely died of old age, while his amazing story lived on to feed the life-saving reputation of dolphins.

THE REWARDS OF MERCY

Pelorus Jack first appeared in 1888. The traditional story is that he accompanied the schooner *Brindle* as it crossed Cook Strait and approached the treacherous French Pass: This narrow strait south of D'Urville Island was, and is, infamous for its jutting rocks and surging currents, which have wrecked many a ship traveling between New Zealand's two main islands and the principal towns of Wellington and Nelson.

Upon seeing the dolphin in front, the *Brindle*'s crew wanted to harpoon it, perhaps confusing it with a whale. The captain's wife convinced them not to, and as if in gratitude for this mercy, Pelorus Jack supposedly remained ahead of the ship for the next twelve hours, seeming to guide it safely through the dangerous passage.

After this, Pelorus Jack appeared regularly in front of ships. He arrived night and day, sometimes several times a day, almost as if he were a copilot lying in wait for ships to arrive. He seemed to prefer larger steamships, and he would sometimes rub against the steel plates. One local who delivered mail to the steamers said Pelorus Jack was so friendly he would rub against his dinghy, nearly capsizing it.

Always, Pelorus Jack darted and leapt with startling quickness and evident joy, while at other times he appeared to sail unmoving in the pressure wave. Though steamer captains didn't pretend to "follow" Jack, they still regarded his presence as a good omen.

In 1911, James Cowan wrote a contemporary account of Pelorus Jack that described his "uncanny, almost human sociability" and how he would appear "like a sea-god at the steamer's bows."

Nevertheless, local eyewitnesses said Pelorus Jack never actually entered French Pass. The dolphin accompanied ships only up to the pass's north entrance (or joined them after they exited), and he typically plied the same six-mile stretch of Cook Strait, remaining with boats for about twenty minutes or so.

In other words, from what we can tell, Pelorus Jack was inordinately fond of passing ships, but not necessarily in any different way than any other dolphin who rides a boat's bow waves as it traverses the dolphin's home waters.

THE WRECK OF THE *PENGUIN*

Legends, though, are born from tragedy, and the tragic fate of the steamer *Penguin* became one of the telling anecdotes of the Pelorus Jack canon.

In the early 1900s, possibly in 1904, the story is that a passenger on the *Penguin* took a shot at Pelorus Jack, hitting him. According to some accounts, the passenger was drunk; in others, it was the ship itself that bumped the dolphin.

Either way, Pelorus Jack survived, but from that day on, and for years afterward, the dolphin never accompanied the *Penguin* again. Until, that is, the day of February 12, 1909, when the *Penguin* sank in the Tory Channel due to a heavy storm.

All seventy-six passengers on the steamer died except for one, Ada Hannam, who said she had felt anxious and uneasy earlier that day when she spotted Pelorus Jack unexpectedly leaping in front of the *Penguin*'s bow.

Why, people wondered, had Pelorus Jack appeared on this particular day? Was it a coincidence? Or was he warning the *Penguin*—or dooming it? This story captured the unnerving possibility that the famous Pelorus Jack might actually possess what everyone said: godlike powers of foresight, help, and retribution.

MAORI LEGENDS

In fact, New Zealand's Maori peoples believed Pelorus Jack *was* a god. According to their myths, the ocean god Tangaroa created many *taniwhas,* or sea deities. *Taniwhas* live in the ocean and might offer help or cause trouble. One *taniwha,* Kaikai-a-waro, was assigned to protect and guide their canoes as they crossed Cook Strait and navigated its perils. The Maori believed that Pelorus Jack was one of Kaikai-a-waro's embodied forms.

According to James Cowan, the Maori tell many stories, going back hundreds of years, of Kaikai-a-waro aiding Maori in distress, either rescuing them from drowning or guiding their canoes safely to shore. When summoned respectfully, Kaikai-a-waro can emerge at any time from the underwater cave where it lives.

In addition, the Maori believed that, as an embodied *taniwha*, Pelorus Jack was divinely protected. One risked self-destruction to harm or kill the animal.

The popular and ancient stories about Pelorus Jack have some remarkably similar elements, leading us to wonder if perhaps the Maori myths influenced the popular imagination. Or perhaps the similarities reflect a universal human desire to feel protected by divine nature and her creatures, which inspires a moral obligation to protect them in turn.

Certainly, the behavior of dolphins suggests that they possess a conscious intelligence and a sense of empathy that can, on occasion, lead them to help humans in trouble. As with Arion (see page 249), it may only take one exceptional animal or one life-saving moment to set the wheels of human myth-making in motion.

Today, as James Cowan wrote, we may also share "a feeling akin to the old Maori belief that the lone dolphin of Pelorus has something of the supernatural about him. Certainly he is no ordinary creature of the sea."

SERGEANT STUBBY . . . SNIFFS OUT GAS IN WWI

NAME: *Stubby*

SPECIES: *Pit bull*

DATE: *1917 to 1926*

LOCATION: *France*

SITUATION: *World War I*

WHO WAS SAVED: *American soldiers*

LEGACY: *"Grandfather of American War Dogs," most-honored canine in US military history*

The "Grandfather of American War Dogs" was an untrained stray who was smuggled to the battlefront solely to boost morale. While Stubby became a true life-saver, his origins were telling. Today, working military dogs are intensely trained for a range of very specific jobs (like bomb detection, see page 166), and yet, invariably, handlers and soldiers say they would treasure these dogs for their companionship alone.

This experience seems to be universal. Dogs don't just humanize war, they humanize the warrior. And the gratitude military personnel express for the presence of dogs (for instance, see page 76) is probably one reason why war dog stories often feel, and sometimes are, exaggerated. A dog's individual efforts often do directly save soldiers' lives, but a dog's unflagging companionship always provides soldiers with relief from the trauma of battle.

LEARNING TO SALUTE

America officially entered World War I in the spring of 1917. One day that summer—as the 102nd Infantry of the 26th Yankee Division was training at Yale University in New Haven, Connecticut—a stray, short-tailed pit bull puppy wandered onto the parade grounds, fascinated by the soldiers. Private J. Robert Conroy adopted him, named him Stubby, and taught him the drills, the bugle calls, and even how to salute, so that on command Stubby placed his right paw over his right eye.

Though dogs were forbidden in camp, Stubby was allowed to stay because the soldiers enjoyed him so much. In October, when the division shipped out to join the war in France, Conroy smuggled Stubby aboard the *SS Minnesota,* hiding him in a coal bin.

Not long after disembarking in France, Conroy's commanding officer discovered this unauthorized member of their unit. As legend has it, the disapproving CO was won over when Stubby performed his crisp salute, and he immediately approved the dog as their official mascot.

GAS ATTACKS AND GERMAN SPIES

In February 1918, the 102nd Infantry was sent to the front lines in northern France. Within days, Stubby acclimated himself to the violence of battle, but a poison gas attack nearly killed him. Stubby was sent to a

THE MERCY DOGS OF WWI

In WWI, Red Cross "mercy dogs" performed a service that was specific to that conflict's warfare: They were trained to scour the deadly no man's land between the opposing, unmoving trenches to find and tend to wounded soldiers.

Every European nation used mercy dogs, which the Germans called "sanitary dogs"; only America did not, since they arrived late to the war and had no dog program in place. Some estimate that as many as ten thousand mercy dogs were used in all, and they saved uncounted thousands of lives, though this represented only a tiny fraction of that war's millions of casualties.

Mercy dogs typically wore a saddlebag containing medical supplies and small canteens of water and liquor. Working mostly at night, and trained not to bark, they would sniff their way across the pitted, smoking land, ignoring the corpses.

Once a mercy dog found a wounded man, the soldier could, if he was conscious and mobile, tend to his own wounds and then follow the dog back to the trenches. If the man was immobile or unconscious, the dog would take some article, like a helmet or piece of clothing, return with it to the trench as a signal, and then lead paramedics back to the wounded man.

In addition, large dogs transported wounded soldiers from the front lines to rear medical stations by pulling two-wheeled carts. Dogs were uniquely suited for this role, much more so than ambulances or horses: dogs could travel independently, presented small targets, and were cheap to maintain. Plus, they required no spare parts.

Occasionally, individual mercy dogs achieved recognition for their extraordinary feats. A French dog named Captain once located thirty wounded men in a single day, while a French dog named Prusco was credited with finding a hundred men during the course of a single battle.

hospital to recover, but soon returned to his unit, now with a new skill: an extreme sensitivity to gas.

Afterward, Stubby became the division's early warning system, alerting soldiers to the presence of poison chemicals and giving them time to don their gas masks—while soldiers also fit Stubby with his own. One time, during a predawn gas attack, Stubby alone saved the sleeping troops by running along the trench, barking and nipping and waking everyone in time.

Stubby frequently left the trenches as well. He proved adept at finding wounded soldiers while on patrol in the no man's land between the opposing sides. Apparently, upon recognizing the sound of spoken English, he would go to the soldier, then either bark to guide paramedics to the location or help the soldier find his way back to the trenches.

On one such patrol, Stubby came across a German spy mapping the Allied positions. Identifying the enemy, Stubby barked furiously and attacked, biting him in the leg (or in some versions, the butt) and not letting go. Attracted by the ruckus, American troops arrived and captured the spy, and afterward the commanding officer of the 102nd promoted Stubby to the rank of "sergeant"—making Stubby the first dog to achieve any rank in the US Army.

A BLANKETFUL OF MEDALS

In April 1918, Stubby accompanied the 102nd Infantry during a raid on the German-held town of Schieprey. This time, as Stubby jumped out of the trenches to join the fight, a grenade exploded nearby, peppering his chest and legs with shrapnel.

Stubby survived, but required several surgeries, and as he recovered, he visited other wounded soldiers, bringing them the unique salve of canine comfort. Then, once healed, he returned to the 102nd Infantry and continued to support his unit in combat.

After helping recapture Chateau-Thierry, Stubby was presented with a fitted blanket made by the town's grateful women. From then on, the blanket was used to hold his growing number of medals, badges, and mementos—such as the confiscated Iron Cross from the captured German spy.

By war's end, "Sergeant Stubby" had participated in seventeen battles over the course of eighteen months, and he returned home a bona fide war hero. US newspapers, which had already excitedly publicized his exploits, now fueled a postwar fame that no dog had ever known and which no dog may ever experience again.

Stubby was showered with medals for heroism, including one presented by General John Pershing, the commanding general of the US forces during WWI. Stubby visited the White House twice and met three presidents: Woodrow Wilson, Warren G. Harding, and Calvin Coolidge. He was also made a lifetime member of the American Legion, the Red Cross, and the YMCA. Hardly a military parade was held without Stubby leading the troops wearing his blanketful of medals.

After the hoopla died down, Robert Conroy went to Georgetown University to study law, and Stubby went with him, becoming the mascot of the school's football team. One story claims that Stubby's on-field antics during each halftime became the inspiration for modern football's halftime show.

Stubby died in 1926, but he remains a national treasure. His preserved body, wearing his famous blanket, is now a permanent part of the Smithsonian's WWI collection in the National Museum of American History.

WOLVES IN INDIA . . . RAISE TWO GIRLS IN THEIR DEN

NAME: *Unknown*

SPECIES: *Wolves*

DATE: *1920*

LOCATION: *India*

SITUATION: *Stolen or abandoned children in Indian forests*

WHO WAS SAVED: *Amala and Kamala, two young girls*

LEGACY: *Either the most-amazing wolf-child story ever or the most-famous animal-rescue hoax*

In nineteenth-century India, stories of wolf-children were legion. Hundreds, if not thousands, of infants and children were reported stolen from rural villages by wolves every year. If the stories were to be believed, most were dragged into the forests and eaten, never to be seen again. However, some were actually cared for and protected by the wolves. When rescued, these wolf-raised children acted like wolves, exhibiting an incredibly similar collection of traits.

Westerners dismissed these tales of wolf-children as nothing but folklore or primitive superstition. At best, they were supernatural explanations for the unsettling behavior of children suffering from autism or other developmental disabilities.

Then, in the 1920s, the story emerged of an Indian Christian missionary, Reverend J. A. L. Singh, who had supposedly found two such wolf-children living in a wolves' den. Since then, scientists and journalists have skeptically poked and prodded the missionary's tale. Was Reverend Singh telling the truth, or was his story just a massive hoax?

Even today, people still argue the evidence, and so this story is as much about the credibility of Reverend Singh as it is about whether wolves actually raised these two abandoned children.

THE GHOSTS OF GODAMURI

Here is the story as Reverend Singh told it, and largely as he recorded it in his diary, which was first published, with extensive expert commentary, in 1942:

In 1920, during one of his missionary trips through rural India to convert heathen tribes, Reverend Singh heard a story of "ghosts" running with a wolf pack near a forest village, Godamuri. Village leaders pleaded with Singh to exorcise or kill the demons, and with much reluctance, he finally agreed to investigate.

The ghosts had been seen sporadically in the past, but during the previous four months, they had appeared much more frequently and closer to the village. Frightened locals brought Singh to the place where the pack lived: An abandoned, weathered termite mound, perhaps twelve feet high, in which several groomed, narrow openings indicated tunnels.

On two visits there, Singh saw nothing and wrote in his diary, "I thought it was all false." But he suspected the spirit beasts might actually be some new species that he could kill as a hunting trophy, so he had locals build a shooting platform above the termite mound.

On October 9, 1920, Singh and four other men waited on the platform at dusk. This time, in the fading light, three wolves and two cubs were seen exiting the mound, one at a time. Then, Singh wrote, "close after the cubs came the ghost—a hideous-looking being." Quickly, "there came another awful creature exactly like the first, but smaller. . . . I at once came to the conclusion that these were human beings."

Two men raised their rifles to shoot, but Singh stopped them. The next day, the men returned and witnessed the same scene, which convinced everyone but the superstitious villagers that the "ghosts" were really children. For Reverend Singh, he felt it was his Christian duty to save them and restore them to human society.

RESCUING THE CHILDREN

A week later, Reverend Singh returned with a group of men to capture the children. Since the Godamuri villagers were too afraid, Singh recruited people from a distant village who hadn't already heard of the ghosts.

More than fifty years afterward, Lasa Marandi—a man who claimed to help Reverend Singh that day—said, "Some of the older men were saying they would rather stand unarmed against the charge of a tiger than come face-to-face with the ghosts . . . but we also felt [they] would succeed in killing the ghosts with their guns and rid the place of them once and for all."

A group of diggers began excavating the mound, protected by bowmen and others with guns. Soon, two wolves scooted from tunnel openings and ran away. Then, a third wolf, the she-wolf, emerged. She attacked the diggers, who scattered, and then she raced side-to-side, "growling furiously and pawing the ground," Singh wrote.

When she attacked the diggers a second time, the bowmen shot her dead. After that, the digging proceeded easily, and soon the structure collapsed, revealing a sunken, central cave. Singh wrote, "The two cubs and the other two hideous beings were there in one corner, all four clutching together in a monkey-ball."

After a great deal of wrangling, the men managed to separate the cubs from the children and hold them in separate sacks.

Before leaving, Singh examined the den. To his surprise, he wrote, "the place was so neat that not even a piece of bone was visible anywhere, much less any evidence of their droppings and other uncleanliness."

Charles Maclean, in his 1975 book *The Wolf Children*, captured this ironic dilemma, which dogs Singh's story to this day: "They were looking at the only material evidence of the children's life among the wolves, an empty hollow that gave away no secrets."

AMALA AND KAMALA

Reverend Singh brought the two children back to his orphanage in the town of Midnapore, where he optimistically expected to rehabilitate them. He decided that their identity as wolf-children must be kept hidden, or else their lives, and his own, would descend into that of circus sideshow freaks and their keeper.

They were two apparently unrelated girls. At first, Singh put their ages at eight and one and a half, but at other times described them as nearer to six and three. Singh's wife named the older girl Kamala (or "lotus") and the younger Amala, the name of a yellow flower.

Singh could only speculate as to how they had come to be with the wolves. He and others made inquiries about whether anyone knew of any abandoned or stolen girls, but no one came forth. Considering the ages of the girls, Singh was stunned to consider that the she-wolf must have decided to foster human infants twice.

The girls had clearly been with the wolves a long time, for their wild, inhuman behavior was so ingrained that it was nearly impossible to alter. Their actions also fit the quintessential profile of feral children:

They reacted violently to being touched or to being bathed. They moved only on all fours, refusing to stand, and their knees, elbows, and heels of their

THE FERAL CHILD: REAL AND ROMANTICIZED

Stories of children raised by wild animals have always populated world cultures. They are sprinkled throughout Greek and Roman mythology. For instance, Romulus and Remus, the founders of ancient Rome, were famously suckled by a she-wolf.

In medieval folklore, endangered children were continually being rescued by wild and domestic creatures, and the ubiquitous trope of wolf-children in nineteenth-century India inspired Rudyard Kipling to create Mowgli in *The Jungle Book*—which in turn inspired Edgar Rice Burroughs to create Tarzan (see page 103).

What's intriguing is that real cases of feral children exist (see page 200). Interspecies suckling does happen; even humans have been known to do it with other animals.

And yet, feral-child myths typically turn reality on its head. The central tragedy of abandonment is transformed into a necessary right of passage that molds the child into a hero now fit to rule. This message contains a certain guilty hopefulness, a bit of cultural wish-fulfillment: That nature is more merciful than we are, and wild compassion will redeem our civilized cruelty, which leads us to neglect our children in the first place.

Most often, real feral children have been horrifically isolated, perhaps because they showed developmental problems. They sometimes come to mimic animal behaviors even when no animal ever cared for them. Scientists have long been fascinated by what these unsocialized, wild children tell us about human nature, but the sad truth is that real feral children recover haltingly and slowly, if ever, from their traumatic beginnings.

Metaphorically, feral-child stories express a desire to balance an inner duality, a healthy merging of our wild and civilized natures. In reality, the wild is a crippling place for a solitary human infant to grow up.

hands were thickly calloused. Their bodies were covered in scratches and scars. They did not speak; they only uttered rare guttural vocalizations or howled at night. They wouldn't eat cooked food, only raw meat, and they lapped milk or water from bowls. Most of all, their blank expressions were seemingly devoid of emotion, and they avoided all social contact, either with the Singhs or the other orphanage children.

Reverend Singh also insisted on another attribute: their eyes in the dark occasionally exhibited a blue glare. The girls' senses were preternaturally acute, and Singh claimed this included night vision signaled by glowing animal eyes.

THE LIES AND CONTRADICTIONS OF REVEREND SINGH

The story of Amala and Kamala became famous precisely because it was the first to include an eyewitness of feral children in the company of wolves. As such, its authenticity turns on whether you believe the main witness, Reverend Singh. Many commentators do not, and with good reason: His story is full of contradictions and flatly unbelievable details, like the glowing eyes.

One person who believed that Singh's story was "true, though perhaps not the whole truth," was Charles Maclean. "Unfortunately," Maclean wrote, "Singh's tendency to exaggerate is common to all his writings. His letters and reports, written in the convoluted and extravagant style of Indian English, are full of hyperbole and . . . histrionic inflation."

Further, Singh himself told multiple versions of the story. Sometimes he said the children were merely abandoned and neglected and he did not mention the wolves; in other versions, the already-rescued children were brought to him by villagers, who then told him the wolf story. Perhaps, as Maclean believed, these were false accounts meant to protect the children, and Singh's own reputation, from infamy. Supporting Singh, Maclean later found corroborating eyewitnesses, like Lasa Marandi.

Or perhaps the diary and the story it tells are an elaborate, deliberate hoax that Singh concocted after the children died to gain fame and perhaps profit. This is what French surgeon Serge Aroles concluded in his 2007 book *L'Enigme des Enfants-Loup* ("Enigma of the Wolf-Children").

In other words, here is another instance where distinguishing reality from folklore becomes a tricky business. Legends of wolf-children may have inspired Singh, and then encouraged others to believe him, or perhaps those fantastical legends are, on rare occasions like this one, true.

Sadly, the two people who could have definitively solved this mystery did not live long. Amala died in 1921, and Kamala died in 1929 (both of kidney problems). By that time, after eight years in the orphanage, Kamala could speak a few words, stand properly, and behave in a friendly manner, free of any obvious mental handicaps.

But she remained mute on the topic of her alleged canid upbringing.

TOGO THE SIBERIAN HUSKY . . . GOES THE EXTRA MILE

NAME: *Togo*

SPECIES: *Siberian husky*

DATE: *1925*

LOCATION: *Alaska*

SITUATION: *Transporting medicine across Alaska during a blizzard*

WHO WAS SAVED: *Residents of Nome suffering from diphtheria outbreak*

LEGACY: *Legendary sled dog gave rise to "the greatest dog story ever told" inspired the Iditarod*

On January 22, 1925, the following telegram was sent from Nome, Alaska, to Washington, DC:

> *"An epidemic of diphtheria is almost inevitable* STOP *I am in urgent need of one million units of diphtheria antitoxin* STOP *Mail is only form of transportation* STOP *I have made application to Commissioner of Health of the Territories for antitoxin already* STOP"

At that point, Nome already had twenty confirmed cases of diphtheria, a highly contagious and deadly childhood disease, and they had run out of antitoxin. Without more medicine, there was no way to heal the sick or stop the outbreak from spreading.

During winter in 1925, the only way in or out of icebound Nome was by dogsled. Nome is closer to Siberia—fifty-five miles across the Bering Sea—than it is to the nearest Alaskan town, and winter near the Arctic Circle lasts seven months.

Some politicians argued that airplanes should transport the serum, not dogsleds. Planes would be much faster, but only if they made it. Airplane technology at that time still struggled in Alaska's extreme cold; engines seized up, and pilots froze in their open cockpits. Planes were the obvious future of travel in interior Alaska, but right then, at that moment, the only dependable method was the oldest: The partnership of dog and human.

Dogsled teams carrying the mail typically made the 675-mile Fairbanks to Nome run in about twenty-five days. They would need to do better. If they took that long now, everyone in Nome, all 1,400 people, might be infected or dead by the time they arrived.

Five days after the telegram was received, on January 27, the epic Nome serum run began, and it would become known as the greatest dog story ever told.

SEPPALA AND TOGO

Twenty sled drivers and about 150 dogs participated in the serum run. They relayed the case of diphtheria antitoxin from team to team during a hazardous blizzard that brought the coldest weather to Alaska in twenty years. Despite this, they completed the run in an unbelievable six days.

Afterward, the dog Balto got most of the credit and the fame, since he led the final team that arrived in Nome. Yet beforehand, all eyes were on the twelve-year-old Siberian husky Togo, the legendary team leader for the most famous musher in Alaskan history, "King of the Trail" Leonhard Seppala.

Togo had led Seppala's dogsled teams for about seven years, and together they'd covered 55,000 miles of trails, won nearly every sled race they'd entered, and set several long-distance records. The pair were cut from the same cloth: small, scrappy, unusually strong athletes who were determined to go farther and run faster than anyone else.

Siberian huskies, in fact, had been bred by native Russian peoples for the particular rigors of dogsledding. Among their many notable attributes, they could withstand temperatures of minus 80 degrees.

Lead dogs, however, had to display more than toughness, smarts, and determination. They had to handle the pressure of leading, finding the trail, and making independent decisions. In their story about the Nome serum run, *The Cruelest Miles*, Gay Salisbury and Laney Salisbury wrote that lead dogs needed "a sixth sense when it came to danger," but even more, they had to "know when to disobey a bad command, no matter how forceful a driver may be."

A good lead dog was a driver's partner, and the dog understood this. Despite the era's scientific certainty otherwise, mushers believed their dogs exhibited emotions, intelligence, self-awareness, and pride. A driver's hardest and most important work on the trail was caring for his animals: feeding them, massaging their muscles, and tending to their emotional well-being. For the human, mushing was the easy part.

As partners, Togo and Seppala were inseparable, not just in the public mind, but in Seppala's heart. Seppala respected and trusted Togo above all other dogs. Togo had saved his life numerous times in treacherous conditions because, Seppala once said, Togo simply knew what to do.

CROSSING NORTON SOUND

For instance, some years before the Nome serum run, Togo became famous for another remarkable life-saving event that highlighted his extraordinary talents.

Along the Fairbanks-to-Nome trail, no section was more dangerous than over Norton Sound, an inlet off the Bering Sea that Alaskans dubbed "the ice factory." By crossing the sound's hard surface, a forty-two mile shortcut, drivers could save an entire day, but they had to evaluate the weather and winds carefully.

The surface could be a ridged, hummocky obstacle course or scoured flat into a slippery sheen of "glare ice." Barreling gusts of wind could knock dogs over and literally lift an entire team off the ground. It was easy to become disoriented crossing mile after mile of featureless ice. Most of all, floes might crack, break off in chunks, and drift away into the Bering Sea.

On one such crossing of Norton Sound, Seppala and Togo were just a few miles offshore when they heard an ominous crack. Before Seppala could even give the command, Togo turned the team full speed toward land. Then, almost to the shore, Togo abruptly jumped up and backward, landing on the other dogs and crashing the team to a halt.

Six feet ahead, a widening water channel blocked their way. Seppala led the team along the perimeter's edge, searching for a place to escape, but found none. They were on a floe drifting out to sea. Eventually, to conserve their strength, Seppala huddled the dogs and waited, hoping for an onshore wind to push them back.

Hours later, Togo gave a yelp, alerting Seppala to a favorable shift in the wind. Seppala harnessed the team and for the next nine hours hunted for a point to cross onto the shorefast ice.

Eventually, he found a five-foot gap. It was too far to jump the sled, so Seppala tied a long lead to Togo and heaved the dog across water. As Seppala said later, "Togo seemed to understand what he had to do." The dog dug in and strained on the lead, trying to pull the floe to him.

Then the lead broke and slipped into the water. Togo and Seppala faced each other, distraught. As the Salisburys wrote, "Seppala was speechless. He had just been given a death sentence."

At that point, Togo might have done any number of things; he himself was free to reach land safely. What he did, according to Seppala, was dive into the freezing water, snatch the lead in his teeth, and climb back onto the far ice. He then rolled over the line till it was wrapped several times around his shoulders, and he pulled and kept pulling until the floe was near enough for Seppala and the team to leap across.

THE NOME SERUM RUN

On the Nome serum run, Seppala was just as dependent on Togo, if not moreso. Seppala's team ran the longest, the most dangerous, and the most physically challenging leg of the relay—mostly because it included the treacherous crossing of Norton Sound.

To meet up with the relay, Seppala left Nome and for three days traveled 170 miles east. On January 31, still heading east, he and Togo crossed Norton Sound in the morning and soon met up with the westbound relay team carrying the serum. After securing the medicine, and a brief rest, Seppala turned his team around and mushed west toward Nome.

When the team reached Norton Sound for the second time that day, it was dark, and the weather had worsened. The roaring wind from the approaching blizzard was hitting them full in the face. Seppala couldn't see or hear the ice. Prudence demanded avoiding Norton Sound in these conditions and taking the much longer coastal route.

But Seppala's eight-year-old daughter was in Nome, and each day lost meant life or death for someone. Plus, Seppala had Togo.

In blinding, frigid conditions—with the temperature an estimated minus 30 degrees, and the wind chill minus 85 degrees—Togo successfully guided the team back across Norton Sound. When it was done, they had traveled eighty-four miles in a single day, and the team collapsed in the roadhouse at Isaac's Point. After five hours of sleep, the team got up and traveled another fifty arduous miles, up the steepest part of the trail, to reach the next relay team.

All told, Seppala and Togo traveled 91 miles of the serum run—which was twice to four times the distance of any other team, racing for their lives the whole way.

What happened next? After Seppala's leg, the blizzard became a devastating hammer that nearly destroyed the final relay team, driven by Gunnar Kaasen and his lead dog, Balto. Displaying heroic perseverance, Kaasen and Balto survived the storm, made it to Nome with the serum, and saved the town, but that's another story . . .

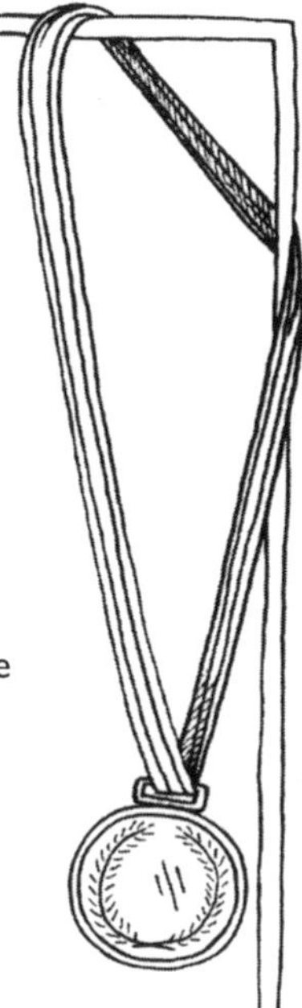

THE IDITAROD

The Nome serum run was the greatest event in Alaskan sled-dog history. It was also the last hurrah of an ancient tradition that dated back centuries and was essential to the settling of interior Alaska.

As technology improved, airplanes soon supplanted sled teams for overland travel, and after commercial snowmobiles arrived in the 1950s, forget it. The day of the Alaskan sled dog was over.

The trails disappeared, the roadhouses fell apart, and the nights grew quieter, absent the ritual sled-dog howl.

However, Alaskans hoping to preserve their sled-dog heritage formulated a variety of races. In 1967, the Iditarod Trail Seppala Memorial Race was a twenty-five-mile contest celebrating Leonhard Seppala (who died that year) and the original US purchase of Alaska.

Building off this, the first Iditarod Trail Sled Dog Race was organized in 1973. The race has been held every year since, on the first Saturday in March, and it runs about 1,150 miles between Anchorage and Nome. The Iditarod's western portion approximates the original serum-run trail route.

About sixty-five mushers, each leading teams of sixteen dogs, compete annually. In the 1970s, winners took nearly three weeks to finish, but today the first team crosses the finish line in eight to ten days.

As for Togo, he died in 1929. His body was preserved and is today displayed in the Iditarod Trail Headquarters in Wasilla. Thus, in body and in spirit, Togo continues to preside over the race he helped inspire.

CHIPS, DOG 11-A . . . TAKES ITALIAN PRISONERS

NAME: *Chips*

SPECIES: *Mixed-breed German shepherd, collie, and husky*

DATE: *1942 to 1945*

LOCATION: *Africa, Sicily, Italy, and France*

SITUATION: *World War II*

WHO WAS SAVED: *American soldiers*

LEGACY: *WWII's most-celebrated combat dog, famous for having his military medals revoked*

Napoleon Bonaparte knew the worth of military dogs. In 1798, he successfully used dogs as sentries in Alexandria, Egypt, and he once recommended in a letter that another French general do the same. Many nations, like France (see page 257), have long histories of using trained dogs in their armed forces, but not America.

The US military did not develop a formal war-dog program until WWII. When they did, the first animal to show how useful and heroic canines could be was Chips, who became that conflict's most-decorated war dog.

THE K-9 CORPS

The US military had long understood that dogs are morale boosters. Stubby, the WWI hero (see page 272), was just one high-profile example of the hundreds of dogs who had been adopted over the years as mascots across every branch of service. As important as these animals were for providing comfort and lifting spirits, however, they had no formal role and were often officially discouraged.

Largely pushed by the volunteer organization Dogs for Defense, the military established the K-9 Corps in March 1942. Taking Napoleon's advice about 150 years late, they first trained dogs for sentry duty, but the program's scope expanded to include search-and-rescue work, scout patrols, and messenger missions. The military also experimented with bomb-detection and parachuting dogs, but training methods were haphazard and these efforts were scrapped. Their day had not yet come.

Each branch was encouraged to develop dogs for their own needs. In particular, the Marines were very successful using Doberman pinschers, dubbed "Devil Dogs," as scouts and messengers in the South Pacific.

Especially initially, the suitability and appropriateness of using dogs in combat was often questioned within the US military. One Marine trainer, Captain Jackson Boyd, succinctly characterized the program's purpose:

"The dogs are not to be considered as a new weapon; they have not replaced anyone or anything. They have simply added to security by their keen perception, and their use should be limited to situations where that increased perception is of service."

CHIPS TAKES THE POINT

Chips, whose military number was 11-A, was a mutt: part German shepherd, collie, and husky. He was among the first dogs trained, solely for sentry duty, and he was attached to the 30th Infantry, Third Infantry Division, along with three other dogs: Watch, Pal, and Mena.

In October 1942, the dogs joined their division as part of a North African invasion fleet, landing in Vichy-held French Morocco. Working as sentries, the dogs successfully deterred nighttime sorties by the enemy, and no soldiers were killed while on duty with the dogs. However, Mena could not handle the gunfire and thunderous explosions of battle, and she soon became too scared and confused to work.

In fact, the aural cacophony of war overwhelmed many animals, and preparing dogs for this would become essential to later training.

In July 1943, Chips joined Patton's Seventh Army during its amphibious landing in Sicily, where his greatest heroics occurred. Not long after landing, in the predawn light, Chips and his handler, Private John Rowell, were working inland from the beach. Though Chips was not trained as a scout, he was working the point anyway, for handlers often improvised during battles.

Suddenly, machine gun fire erupted from a camouflaged pillbox. Chips instantly broke from Rowell's grasp and ran full-tilt at the hidden bunker, covering the three-hundred-yard distance in a flash. The machine-gun fire abruptly stopped, and within moments, an Italian soldier stumbled out, flailing in terror at the slashing and biting dog. Three more soldiers then emerged, arms raised in surrender. Rowell called off Chips and took the four Italians prisoner.

Chips suffered a minor scalp wound and powder burns, indicating the Italians had tried to shoot Chips with a firearm, but the four men were no match for a single dog. After treatment, Chips went back to work that same night. While on duty, he alerted as ten Italian soldiers walked down a road, and once again, Rowell took all the men prisoner without firing a shot.

In September 1943, Chips continued with the Seventh Army into Italy and saw action in two more campaigns, often working as a tank guard dog. In one incident, Chips alerted on an ambush, and then as fighting erupted, he ran back to base with a phone cable attached to his collar, allowing the platoon to call for needed backup.

CELEBRITY AND CONTROVERSY

As the press got wind of Chips's heroic exploits, his celebrity grew quickly. General Eisenhower even made a point of greeting Chips personally while in Italy—though when Eisenhower tried to pet the dog, Chips gave him a warning nip.

This gaffe aside, Chips was an exemplar of what a war dog could be. As such, in October 1943, the military waived the regulation that prohibited giving medals to animals and awarded Chips both a Silver Star and a Purple Heart.

For some, this went too far. The national commander of the Military Order of the Purple Heart, William Thomas, wrote to President Roosevelt and the War Department in protest, saying this demeaned all those who'd received the award. He wrote: "It decries the high and lofty purpose for which the medal was created."

As the feel-good story threatened to turn into a political black-eye, the military reversed course. They took the medals back and restored the prohibition against giving military decorations to "other than persons."

This prohibition is still in effect today, though it's an attitude that is not shared by most soldiers. As Michael Lemish observed in his book *War Dogs:* "No one who ever worked with a dog felt it demeaning to have a medal bestowed upon the animal."

In Italy, Private Rowell and several other soldiers created their own medals for Chips, and they honored him in a private ceremony out of the public eye.

THE TRAUMA OF WAR

In December 1943, after more than a year of war, Chips began to show signs of battle fatigue. He was becoming skittish, and so he was sent for a few months to the rear for quiet sentry duty, away from the gunfire and exploding artillery.

In August 1944, Chips returned to the front lines and joined troops in southern France for a succession of campaigns. But after awhile, Chips again displayed evidence of stress, and perhaps of a bad diet, and he was reassigned to POW sentry duty.

WWII officially ended in September 1945, and Chips returned to the United States a month later, in October. After a few months, he was then discharged back into the care of his previous owners, who had originally donated him to the army.

Unfortunately, Chips never fully recovered from the trauma of three years in active combat. His kidneys were failing, and after only a few short months of civilian life, he died on April 12, 1946.

The US used thousands of dogs in WWII, and most exhibited exceptional valor and resilience, but none became as famous as Chips.

CLEVER HANS: THE FAMOUS HORSE WHO DIDN'T ADD UP

When it comes to animal intelligence, perhaps the most famous cautionary tale in all of science is that of Clever Hans, a German horse at the turn of the twentieth century who became legendary for his ability to understand both German and mathematics. Clever Hans is a fun story that sheds light on how our assumptions can often guide our conclusions, and it's worth telling.

Besides, there is an unwritten law that you must mention Clever Hans in any book on ethology. Whip this out in science class for guaranteed extra credit.

A HORSE IS A HORSE, OF COURSE

In late-nineteenth-century Germany, a former math teacher, Herr Wilhelm von Osten, claimed that he had taught his draft horse, Hans, how to read, spell, and add. Before increasingly large crowds, Herr von Osten would ask Hans to spell a word, or show him an addition problem, or present him with a number story, like: "If the eighth day of the month comes on a Tuesday, what is the date of the following Friday?"

Hans would then paw or tap the ground until he had reached the correct number. Almost without fail, Hans would stop on the right answer, and his fame soon spread worldwide. The public became enthralled with the horse's unique and amazing intelligence, even as the scientific community grumbled that it must be a trick. No horse could do what Hans was said to do.

So in 1904, a commission investigated Herr von Osten and his marvelous animal. Yet despite their best efforts, they could find no chicanery, no hoax of any kind. Much to their chagrin, they had to admit that Clever Hans was the real deal.

THE ANSWER IS IN THE QUESTIONER

Still, one of the psychologists on the commission, Oskar Pfungst, remained unconvinced. Though Herr von Osten seemed genuine—he truly believed in Hans's abilities—Pfungst continued testing the horse.

To eliminate any possible coaching, Pfungst questioned Hans himself, alone, and he had strangers question Hans. But no matter who asked the questions, Clever Hans gave the right answers nearly 100 percent of the time.

However, Pfungst noticed something interesting: If Hans was shown a word to read or a math problem to solve, he never looked at the paper, but, Pfungst wrote, "he would always make the most strenuous efforts to see the questioner."

Further, if the questioner didn't know the answer, or if the person stood out of the horse's line of sight, Clever Hans almost never got the answer right. In these situations, the horse's accuracy plummeted to less than 10 percent.

Based on this, Pfungst determined that the horse couldn't understand language or do math at all. The only thing Hans was "reading" was body language.

SMART, BUT NOT WHAT YOU THINK

Pfungst unmasked the mystery of Clever Hans's "genius," and ever since scientists have used this story to illustrate the dangers of anthropomorphism and observational bias, as well as the inadequacy of anecdotes. Researchers need to guard carefully against seeing more in an animal's behavior than is there. Or seeing only what they want to see. Animal studies must rigorously avoid situations where animals perform in ways to please observers without truly understanding what a test is asking of them.

Clever Hans mimicked intelligence he did not have, but he wasn't trying to fool anyone. On the contrary, Clever Hans knew exactly what his questioners wanted—for him to tap until they thought he should stop. Invariably, Clever Hans performed best with people who believed in him and wanted him to succeed. However, the horse was so good at reading people that he knew when someone felt he should stop despite the person's best efforts not to show it. Face-to-face, Clever Hans could not be fooled.

This, in itself, is rather remarkable. And today, many scientists now "defend" Clever Hans: In the kerfuffle over Hans's supposed mathematical abilities, his real talents were overlooked. That is, how did Clever Hans figure out the "game" Herr von Osten was playing? Why did he decide to play along with anyone and everyone? And how sensitive must horses be to read human thoughts and emotions from the tiniest physical cues?

These, then, are the "other" lessons of Clever Hans. First, as dog expert Elizabeth Marshall Thomas wryly notes, that "he proved himself to be a better observer than the most prominent scientists of his day."

But also, as anthropologist Pat Shipman writes, "the Clever Hans phenomenon is not a story about a failure to teach an animal language but rather a success story about achieving a fairly sophisticated level of communication across species boundaries."

This intuitive communication and openness to humans is what natural horsemanship trainers like Ray Hunt depend on, and it probably helps explain why horses sometimes provide such powerful therapeutic benefits. Maybe horses can't read, and they'll never talk like TV's fictional Mr. Ed, but they possess gifts that are still worth marveling at.

SOURCES
AND
FURTHER READING

Many resources contributed to the stories and ideas in this book. General works, and those that contributed overall, are gathered and listed in the Introduction for easy reference. Sources for specific stories are listed separately by story title and section, and sources are arranged alphabetically. Book page numbers usually refer to specific quotes.

INTRODUCTION

Balcombe, Jonathan, *Second Nature: The Inner Lives of Animals* (New York: Palgrave Macmillan, 2010).

Bekoff, Marc, *The Emotional Lives of Animals* (Novato, CA: New World Library, 2007).

———, *Why Dogs Hump and Bees Get Depressed* (Novato, CA: New World Library, 2013), 117 (for Cambridge Declaration).

Bekoff, Marc, and Jessica Pierce, *Wild Justice* (Chicago and London: University of Chicago Press, 2009).

Charleson, Susannah, *The Possibility Dogs* (New York: Houghton Mifflin Harcourt, 2013).

de Waal, Frans, *Our Inner Ape: A Leading Primatologist Explains Why We Are Who We Are* (New York: Riverhead Books, 2005), 181.

———, *The Bonobo and the Atheist: In Search of Humanism Among the Primates* (New York: Norton, 2013).

Hauser, Marc D., *Wild Minds: What Animals Really Think* (New York: Henry Holt & Co., 2000), 7, 109.

Keltner, Dacher, *Born to Be Good: The Science of a Meaningful Life* by (New York: W. W. Norton, 2009).

Linden, Eugene, *The Parrot's Lament and Other True Tales of Animal Intrigue, Intelligence, and Ingenuity* (New York: Dutton, 1999).

———, *The Octopus and the Orangutan* (New York: Dutton, 2002).

Masson, Jeffrey Moussaieff, and Susan McCarthy, *When Elephants Weep: The Emotional Lives of Animals* (New York: Delacourt Press, 1995).

Olmert, Meg Daley, *Made for Each Other: The Biology of the Human-Animal Bond* (Cambridge, MA: Da Capo Press, 2009).

Pacelle, Wayne, *The Bond: Our Kinship with Animals, Our Call to Defend Them* (New York: William Morrow, 2011).

Page, George, *Inside the Animal Mind: A Groundbreaking Exploration of Animal Intelligence* (New York: Doubleday, 1999).

Reiss, Diana, *The Dolphin in the Mirror* (New York: Mariner Books, 2011), 7.

Shipman, Pat, *The Animal Connection: A New Perspective on What Makes Us Human* (New York: W. W. Norton, 2011).

Thomas, Elizabeth Marshall, *The Social Lives of Dogs* (New York: Simon & Schuster, 2000).

von Kreisler, Kristin, *Beauty in the Beasts* (New York: Jeremy P. Tarcher/Putnam, 2001).

PART 1: DOMESTIC COMPANIONS

☆ LuLu the Pot-Bellied Pig . . . Stops Traffic p.29

Beaver County Times, "Pig to Receive Heroism Award," January 28, 1999, http://news.google.com/newspapers?nid=2002&dat=19990128&id=-G4yAAAAIBAJ&sjid=DrYFAAAAIBAJ&pg=5328,6265947.

Bekoff, Marc, telephone conversation with author, February 26, 2014.

Big Wave Productions, "The Pig That Called for Help," episode 5 of *Hero Animals*, producer/director Adam Mallins, aired in 2009 by *National Geographic*, http://www.bigwavetv.com/productions/hero-animals-the-pig-that-called-for-help.

Farran, Christopher, *Animals to the Rescue!: True Stories of Animal Heroes* (New York: Avon Books/HarperCollins, 2000), 20-23.

Fuoco, Michael, "Oinking for Help," *Pittsburgh Post-Gazette*, October 10, 1998, http://old.post-gazette.com/regionstate/19981010pig2.asp.

———, "LuLu the Heroic Pig Now Known Worldwide," *Pittsburgh Post-Gazette*, April 9, 2002, http://old.post-gazette.com/neigh_west/20020409lulu0409p1.asp.

h2g2, "LuLu the Pig," December 30, 2005, http://h2g2.com/approved_entry/A5849049.

Lash, Cindi, "That'll Do, Lulu. That'll Do," *Pittsburgh Post-Gazette*, February 7, 2003, http://old.post-gazette.com/localnews/firstlight/20030207firstlightfl2p2.asp.

von Kreisler, *Beauty in the Beasts*, 26-27.

For "Love Me, Love My Pig":

Derschowitz, Jessica, "George Clooney: Why Pigs Make Good Pets," *CBS News*, February 9, 2012, http://www.cbsnews.com/news/george-clooney-why-pigs-make-good-pets/.

Fuoco, "LuLu the Heroic Pig."

The Independent, "George and Max: A Love Story Made in Hollywood," December 6, 2006, http://www.independent.co.uk/news/world/americas/george-and-max-a-love-story-made-in-hollywood-427257.html.

☆ Dory the Rabbit . . . Leaps into Action p.34

BBC News, "Rabbit Saves Diabetic from Coma," January 29, 2004, http://news.bbc.co.uk/2/hi/uk_news/england/cambridgeshire/3441337.stm.

———, "Giant Bunny Saves Owner in a Coma," January 30, 2004, http://news.bbc.co.uk/cbbcnews/hi/animals/newsid_3444000/3444111.stm.

———, "Life-Saving Rabbit Wins Top Award," March 5, 2004, http://news.bbc.co.uk/2/hi/uk_news/england/cambridgeshire/3535655.stm.

For "Rabbits to the Rescue, Again":

Wulff, Jennifer, "Superpets!" *People 66,* no. 10 (September 4, 2006), http://www.people.com/people/archive/article/0,,20060178,00.html.

☆ Mkombozi the Dog . . . Rescues an Abandoned Baby p.38

BBC News, Kenyan Baby Girl "Rescued by Dog," May 9, 2005, http://news.bbc.co.uk/2/hi/africa/4530423.stm.

Dog Heirs, "Mkombozi the Stray Saved the Life of a Newborn Baby, blog post by Tamara, February 13, 2012, http://www.dogheirs.com/tamara/posts/533-mkombozi-the-stray-dog-saved-the-life-of-a-newborn-baby.

"Mkombozi—The Heroic Dog," The Nairobi Stories, A Big Brother Production, uploaded to YouTube April 19, 2011, http://www.youtube.com/watch?v=Q3i9a18Gcqc

Ngowi, Rodrique, "Stray Dog Rescues Abandoned Baby," *Associated Press*, May 10, 2005, http://seattletimes.com/html/nationworld/2002269200_dogbaby10.html.

News24, "Doggie Story 'Fishy'," May 11, 2005, http://www.news24.com/Africa/News/Doggie-story-fishy-20050511.

For "Canine Rescuers":

CNN, "Dog Protected Abandoned Newborn, Doctors Say," August 23, 2008, http://edition.cnn.com/2008/WORLD/americas/08/22/argentina.dog.tale/index.html.

Huffington Post, "Jade, Hero German Shepherd, Saves Newborn Baby Abandoned in Birmingham Park in England," December 9, 2013, http://www.huffingtonpost.com/2013/11/03/german-shepherd-baby_n_4208441.html.

Schweimler, Daniel, "Argentine Dog Saves Abandoned Baby," *BBC News,* August 23, 2008, http://news.bbc.co.uk/2/hi/americas/7577275.stm.

Sieczkowski, Cavan, "Dog Saves Newborn Baby Tossed in Thailand Garbage Dump," *Huffington Post,* June 6, 2013, http://www.huffingtonpost.com/2013/06/06/dog-saves-newborn-baby-thailand_n_3396929.html.

Vinter, Phil, "Abandoned Newborn Baby Girl Rescued by Hero Dog After Sniffing Her Out Under a Bridge in Ghana," *Daily Mail,* June 9, 2012, http://www.dailymail.co.uk/news/article-2156885/Abandoned-newborn-baby-girl-rescued-hero-dog-sniffing-bridge-Ghana.html.

For "Maternal Instincts":

Olmert, Made for Each Other, 25.

Bekoff, *Why Dogs Hump*, 7-8.

☆ Frisky the Dog . . . Kisses His Owner p.43

Dakss, Brian, "Old Dog Saves Owner from Katrina," *CBS News*, September 9, 2005, http://www.cbsnews.com/news/old-dog-saves-owner-from-katrina/.

National Geographic, "The Dog That Gave First Aid," episode 6 of *Hero Animals*, producer/directer Adam Mallins, Big Wave Productions (2009), http://www.bigwavetv.com/productions/hero-animals-the-dog-that-gave-first-aid/.

Markle, Sandra, *Animal Heroes: True Rescue Stories* (Minneapolis: Millbrook Press, 2009), 25-31.

Wulff, "Superpets!"

☆ Honey the Cocker Spaniel . . . Meets the Neighbors p.45

ABC News, "Man Saves Dog, Dog Saves Man," November 2, 2005, http://abcnews.go.com/GMA/story?id=1273192.

Bosch, Michael, "Honey to the Rescue!" *Guideposts* (August 2006), http://www.guideposts.org/inspiration/inspirational-stories/pet-stories/honey-to-the-rescue.

"Hero Pup," *People* 64, no. 21 (November 21, 2005), http://www.people.com/people/archive/article/0,,20144994,00.html.

Whitaker, Tad, "Hero, Victim Reunited," *Marin Independent Journal,* November 4, 2005, http://www.marinij.com/marin/ci_3182923.

For "Buddy, We Need to Get Help!":
Celizic, Mike, "Hero Dog Brings Help to Burning Home," *Today,* April 23, 2010, http://www.today.com/id/36733102/ns/today-today_pets/t/hero-dog-brings-help-burning-home/#.UpObjRxLash.

D'Oro, Rachel, "Reward for a Valiant Dog: Engraved Bowl," Associated Press, April 23, 2010, http://www.adn.com/2010/04/23/1247550/mat-su-dog-honored-for-leading.html.

Halpin, James, "Troopers Say Hero Dog Buddy Led Them to Rural Mat-Su Fire," *Anchorage Daily News*, April 22, 2010, http://www.adn.com/2010/04/22/1246098/hero-dog-leads-trooper-to-caswell.html.

Holt, Lester, "Hero Dog 'Communicated' with Trooper," *Today Show,* April 24, 2010, http://www.nbcnews.com/id/36754385/ns/us_news-wonderful_world/t/alaska-dog-honored-leading-troopers-fire/#.Ugj_jBy22Ok.

☆ **Shana the Half-Breed Wolf . . . Digs a Tunnel of Love p.51**
Couch, Debra, "Shana—an Exceptionally Caring and Capable Soul," Shining World Hero Awards, http://godsdirectcontact.us/sm21/enews/htm/181/aw_52.htm.

Dog Heirs, "Incredible Rescue of Elderly Couple by Heroic Wolf Dog," posted by Martha, January 26, 2012, http://www.dogheirs.com/larne/posts/445-incredible-rescue-of-elderly-couple-by-heroic-wolf-dog.

Fox News, "Half-Breed Wolf Dog Hero Rescues Elderly Owners from Snowstorm," December 6, 2006, http://www.foxnews.com/story/2006/12/06/half-breed-wolf-dog-hero-rescues-elderly-owners-from-snowstorm/.

MacLeod, Joe, interview with Eve Fertig, conducted at International Wildlife Rehabilitation Conference, Niagra Falls, NY, October 13, 1996, http://theiwrc.org/interviews/fertig.html.

Plants, Ron, "Dog Saves Elderly Couple from Sudden Snow Storm," *KARE 11,* December 5, 2006, http://www.kare11.com/news/news_article.aspx.

☆ **Toby the Golden Retriever . . . Performs the Heimlich Maneuver p.55**
Associated Press, "Life-Saving Dog, Cat Honored for Heroic Acts," November 2, 2007, http://www.nbcnews.com/id/21595558/ns/health-pet_health/t/life-saving-dog-cat-honored-heroic-acts/.

BBC News, "Dog Saves US Owner with Heimlich," March 28, 2007, http://news.bbc.co.uk/2/hi/americas/6503991.stm.

Goss, Scott, "Wonder Dog Is All Golden: Woman Claims Pet Pooch Gave Her the Heimlich," *Cecil Daily*, Mary 27, 2007, http://www.cecildaily.com/news/article_6c8cd5fe-10dd-5890-b043-811a7de9ed82.html.

———, "Heroic Hound's Tale Makes for Dog-gone Good Story," Cecil Daily, March 28, 2007, http://www.cecildaily.com/news/article_adfaef31-aa1f-5769-94d0-5f104288e3c4.html.

Linden, *The Parrot's Lament,* 124.

For "Will People Ever Learn to Chew":

Corcoran, Kieran, "This puppy learns fast! Trainee guide dog saves choking woman's life by knocking a chocolate out of her mouth with paws," *Daily Mail,* January 13, 2014, http://www.dailymail.co.uk/news/article-2538620/Trainee-guide-dog-saves-choking-womans-life-knocking-chocolate-mouth-paws.html.

Traynor, Luke, "Dog Saves Woman's Life with Heimlich Manoeuvre after She Began Choking on a Chocolate," *The Mirror,* January 14, 2014, http://www.mirror.co.uk/news/uk-news/dog-saves-womans-life-heimlich-3019293.

For "Mirrors Inside, Mirrors Outside":

Bekoff, *Emotional Lives of Animals,* 128-31.

Bekoff, Marc, telephone conversation with author, February 26, 2014.

Blakeslee, Sandra, "Cells That Read Minds," *New York Times,* January 10, 2006, http://www.nytimes.com/2006/01/10/science/10mirr.html.

de Waal, *Our Inner Ape*, 177, 184-86.

Omert, *Made for Each Other,* 5.

☆ Khan the Doberman Pinscher . . . Tosses the Toddler p.60

The Courier-Mail, "Doberman Saves Toddler," October 30, 2007, http://www.adelaidenow.com.au/news/national/doberman-saves-toddler/story-e6fre-a8c-1111114765415.

Daily Mail, "Family Dog Saves Toddler from Deadly Snake," November 1, 2007, http://www.dailymail.co.uk/news/article-490953/Family-dog-saves-toddler-deadly-snake.html.

For "All Indiana Jones Needs Is a Dog":

ABC7News Denver, "Tiny Chihuahua Steps Between Rattlesnake, Toddler," July 23, 2007, http://www.thedenverchannel.com/news/tiny-chihuahua-steps-between-rattlesnake-toddler.

Leary, Alex, "Just Call Him National Hero Dog," *St. Petersburg Times*, May 6, 2004, http://www.unchainyourdog.org/news/040506Hero_Dog.htm.

Recede, Kay, "Dog Saves Hueco Tanks Girl from Rattlesnake Bite," *KTSM News,* August 9, 2013, http://www.ktsm.com/news/dog-saves-hueco-tanks-girl-rattlesnake-bite.

Smeaton, Paul, "Pup Saves Tots from Snake," *Queensland Times*, January 18, 2012, http://www.qt.com.au/news/pup-saves-tots-from-snake/1240900/.

Stienstra, Tom, "Hero Dog Saves Marin Hiker from Rattlesnake," *San Francisco Chronicle*, June 18, 2013, http://blog.sfgate.com/stienstra/2013/06/18/hero-dog-saves-marin-hiker-from-rattlesnake/.

☆ Willie the Quaker Parrot . . . Learns a New Word p.64

Associated Press, "Hero Parrot 'Willie' Saves Choking Girl," March 24, 2009, http://www.huffingtonpost.com/2009/03/24/hero-parrot-willie-saves-_n_178586.html.

Good Morning America, "Parrot Helps Save Choking Toddler," ABC News, March 18, 2009, http://abcnews.go.com/GMA/video?id=6236050.

Powell, Joanna, "3 Amazing Pet Hero Tales," *Reader's Digest Canada* (April 2010), http://www.readersdigest.ca/pets/fun-facts/3-amazing-pet-hero-tales.

The Telegraph, "Parrot Saved Toddler's Life with Warning," March 25, 2009, http://www.telegraph.co.uk/news/worldnews/northamerica/usa/5048970/Parrot-saved-todlers-life-with-warning.html.

Tilley, Karlyn, "Parrot Saved Girl's Life with Warning," *CBS4 Denver*, November 14, 2008, http://www.flickr.com/groups/featherpants/discuss/72157608887587426/.

For "Bird Brains":

Pepperberg, Irene M., *Alex & Me* (New York: Harper Collins, 2008), 178-79, 207, 221.

☆ Inky the Cat . . . Knocks on the Door p.68

Ross, Kathryn, "Wellsville Cat Featured in USA Today for Saving Owner," *Wellsville Daily Reporter,* December 23, 2010, http://www.wellsvilledaily.com/x934178835/Wellsville-cat-featured-in-USA-Today-for-saving-owner.

Sledge, Gary, "America's Hero Pets," *Reader's Digest* (August 2011), http://www.rd.com/slideshows/americas-hero-pets/.

Wellsville SPCA, Pets & News "Inky: Our Hero Cat," http://spcaallegany.org/post_find_GET.php?article_id=5.

For "Cats Raise a Ruckus":

Associated Press, "Life-Saving Dog, Cat Honored for Heroic Acts," November 2,

2007, http://www.nbcnews.com/id/21595558/ns/health-pet_health/t/life-saving-dog-cat-honored-heroic-acts/.

Chronicle News Service, "Cat's Screeching Saves Family from Fire," January 25, 2008, http://blog.mlive.com/chronicle/2008/01/cats_screeching_saves_family_f.html.

Dodd, Johnny, "Schnautzie the Cat Saved Her Owners from Deadly Gas," *People*, April 21, 2010, http://www.peoplepets.com/people/pets/article/0,,20494160,00.html.

☆ Angel the Golden Retriever . . . Wrestles a Cougar p.72

CBC News, "Boy Calls Dog Who Fought Off Cougar His 'Guardian,'" January 3, 2010, http://www.cbc.ca/news/canada/british-columbia/boy-calls-dog-who-fought-off-cougar-his-guardian-1.874080.

———, "Mountie to Name Son after Boy Who Escaped Cougar," January 6, 2010, http://www.cbc.ca/news/canada/british-columbia/mountie-to-name-son-after-boy-who-escaped-cougar-1.874077.

Celizic, Mike, "Hero Dog Saves Boy, 11, from Cougar Attack," *Today*, January 5, 2010, http://www.today.com/id/34701355/ns/today-today_news/t/hero-dog-saves-boy-cougar-attack/.

Daily Mail, "Pictured: The Golden Retriever Called 'Angel' Who Took on a Mountain Lion and Saved His 11-year-old Owner," http://www.austinforman.net/cougar-attack/pictured-the-golden-retriever-called-angel-who-took-on-a-mountain-lion-and-saved-his-11-year-old-owner/.

Dodd, Johnny, "Angel to the Rescue," *People* 73, no. 5 (February 8, 2010), http://www.people.com/people/archive/article/0,,20342876,00.html.

Robinson, Cheryl, "Family's 'Angel' Dog Saves Boy From Cougar Attack," *CNN*, January 5, 2010, http://www.cnn.com/2010/WORLD/americas/01/04/boy.cougar.attack/index.html

For more information:
Austin Forman Fan Site, http://www.austinforman.net.

☆ "Free-of-Charge Mutts" . . . Fend Off a Suicide Bomber p.76

Bekoff, Marc, telephone conversation with author, February 26, 2014.

Bishop, Jeff, "Soldier, Rufus, Target Adjust to Home Life," *Newnan Times-Herald*, Georgia, August 8, 2010, http://www.times-herald.com/local/Soldier-Rufus-Target-adjust-to-home-life-1234018.

Cook, Chelsea, "Injured Soldier Reunited with K-9 Hero," *Atlanta Journal Constitution*, July 29, 2010, http://www.ajc.com/news/news/local/injured-soldier-reunited-with-k-9-hero/nQh2H/.

Fagen, Cynthia R., "Hero to Be Reunited with Soldier He Saved," *New York Post*, July 27, 2010, http://nypost.com/2010/07/27/hero-to-be-reunited-with-soldier-he-saved/.w

Glor, Jeff, "Heroic Afghan Dog Reunited with U.S. Soldier," *CBS News*, July 29, 2010, http://www.cbsnews.com/8301-18563_162-6726122.html.

Nordland, Rod, "5 U.S. Soldiers Injured in Afghan Suicide Attack," *New York Times*, February 12, 2010, http://www.nytimes.com/2010/02/13/world/asia/13khost.html.

Oprah Winfrey Show, "Ultimate Amazing Animals: The Ape Who Has Conversations with Humans," October 4, 2010, http://www.oprah.com/oprahshow/Rufus-and-Target-Save-US-Soldiers.

Sledge, "America's Hero Pets."

☆ Stormy the Quarter Horse . . . Drop-Kicks a Feral Boar p.81

Barriere, Sharlee, "Stormy Saves the Day," *KATC.com*, November 25, 2010, http://www.katc.com/news/stormy-saves-the-day/.

Reynolds, Tamara, *Reader's Digest TV*, video uploaded on YouTube on February 12, 2012, http://www.youtube.com/watch?v=dwX0dYEUyJo.

Sledge, "America's Hero Pets."

For "Equine Guardians":

Powell, "3 Amazing Pet Hero Tales."

The Scotsman, "Horse Rides to Rescue as Owner Attacked in Field by Raging Cow," August 14, 2007, http://www.scotsman.com/news/scottish-news/top-stories/horse-rides-to-rescue-as-owner-attacked-in-field-by-raging-cow-1-913741.

☆ Kabang the Aspin . . . Stops a Motorcycle p.85

Alipala, Julie S., "Pet Dog Saves 2 Girls, But Loses Her Face," *Inquirer Mindanao* (Philippines), February 18, 2012, http://newsinfo.inquirer.net/147865/pet-dog-saves-2-girls-but-loses-her-face.

———, "Hero Dog Draws Sympathy, Visitors with Gifts," *Inquirer Mindanao*, February 22, 2012, http://newsinfo.inquirer.net/150329/hero-dog-draws-sympathy-visitors-with-gifts.

———, "'Kabang' Ended Poor Family's Dog-Eating Days," *Inquirer Mindanao*, February 24, 2012, http://newsinfo.inquirer.net/151165/heroic-dog-changed-master's-life.

———, "Kabang's Master Seeks Help to Keep Hero Dog's Life Comfortably in

Zamboanga City," *Inquirer Mindanao*, June 9, 2013, http://newsinfo.inquirer.net/423371/kabangs-master-seeks-help-to-keep-hero-dogs-life-comfortable-in-zamboanga-city.

———, "Kagang's Owner Given House and Lot by Zamboanga City Government," *Inquirer Mindanao*, June 11, 2013, http://newsinfo.inquirer.net/424541/kabangs-owner-given-house-and-lot-by-zamboanga-city-government.

Daily News, "Kabang: Dog that Lost Half Her Face Returns Home to Hero's Welcome in Very Own Motorcade and Award from Mayor," June 10, 2013, http://www.nydailynews.com/news/world/hero-dog-kabang-returns-home-article-1.1368165.

Fimrite, Peter, "Kabang the Hero Dog Heals, Heads Home," *San Francisco Chronicle*, June 4, 2013, http://www.sfgate.com/news/article/Kabang-the-hero-dog-heals-heads-home-4573197.php.

Fong, Tillie, "Kabang, the Snoutless Dog, Goes Home to the Philippines," *Sacramento Bee,* June 4, 2013, http://www.sacbee.com/2013/06/03/5467973/kabang-the-snoutless-dog-goes.html.

For more information:
Care for Kabang, http://www.careforkabang.com.

Kabang the Hero Dog, https://www.facebook.com/KabangThePhilippineHeroDog.

☆ Pudding the Maine Coon . . . Plays Doctor p.91

Bekoff, Marc, telephone conversation with author, February 26, 2014.

Coffey, Laura T., "Cat Named Pudding Rescues Owner Hours after His Adoption," *Today Show*, February 23, 2012, http://www.today.com/id/46504285/ns/today-today_news/t/cat-named-pudding-rescues-owner-hours-after-his-adoption/.

Hernandez, Samantha, "Kitty Earns His Keep," *Green Bay Press-Gazette*, February 17, 2012, http://www.greenbaypressgazette.com/article/20120217/ADV01/120217059/Kitty-earns-his-keep.

Sledge, Gary, "Hero Pets: Pudding the Cat's Life-Saving Sense," *Reader's Digest* (November 2012), http://www.rd.com/advice/pets/hero-pets-puddings-good-sense/.

☆ Lilly the Pit Bull . . . Confronts a Freight Train p.95

Ortiz, Erik, "Hero Pit Bull Pulls Owner from Train tracks in Life-Saving Rescue," *New York Daily News*, May 9, 2012, http://www.nydailynews.com/news/national/hero-pit-bull-pulls-owner-train-tracks-life-saving-rescue-article-1.1075467.

Caraganis, Katina, "Pet Pit Bull Drags Unconscious Owner Off Shirley Tracks with Train Bearing Down," *Sentinel & Enterprise*, May 9, 2012, http://www.sentinelandenterprise.com/topstory/ci_20581749/pet-pit-bull-drags-unconscious-owner-off-shirley.

Loncich, Julie, "Pit Bull Saves Owner from Freight Train," *NECN.com*, May 8, 2012, http://www.necn.com/05/08/12/Pit-bull-saves-owner-from-freight-train/landing_newengland.html.

WCVB.com, "'Hero' Pit Bull Heads Home to Recover," May 12, 2012, http://www.wcvb.com/news/local/metro/-Hero-pit-bull-heads-home-to-recover/-/11971628/13208710/-/9at8de/-/index.html.

For more information:
Lilly the Hero Pit Bull, http://lillytheheropitbull.com.

For "Into the Fire":
KOCO.com, "Pit Bull Hailed Hero, Saves Oklahoma Family from Fire," February 13, 2013, http://www.koco.com/news/oklahomanews/okc/Pit-bull-hailed-hero-saves-Oklahoma-family-from-fire/-/11777584/18540240/-/1o6orx/-/index.html.

☆ Czarue the Stray . . . Keeps a Lost Girl Warm p.99

Blake, Matt, "'Hero' dog saves girl, 3, from icy death by cuddling up to her throughout the night after she went missing in a Polish forest," *Daily Mail*, March 4, 2013, http://www.dailymail.co.uk/news/article-2287814/Hero-dog-saves-girl-3-icy-death-cuddling-night-went-missing-Polish-forest.html.

BBC News, "Dog 'Saved Life' of Missing Polish Girl," March 2, 2013, http://www.bbc.co.uk/news/world-europe-21643100.

For "A Doggie Blanket":
Gilchrist, Inga, "Goat Saves Farmer's Life," *Herald Sun*, October 30, 2002, http://tech.groups.yahoo.com/group/MDGA/message/2545.

Green, Aimee, Mark Larabee, and Katy Muldoon, "Everything Goes Right in Mount Hood Search: The Three Climbers and Their Dog Are Brought to Safety," *The Oregonian,* February 20, 2007, http://blog.oregonlive.com/clackamascounty/2008/02/two_earlier_rescue_attempts_tw.html#eight.

Markle, *Animal Heroes,* 32-39.

Phippin, Weston, and Brittany Williams, "Lost Ariz. Tot Safe on Cold Night," *Arizona Republic,* February 20, 2010, http://www.azcentral.com/arizonarepublic/news/articles/20100220childfound0220.html.

Proudman, Dan, "When a Dog Helped Save Its Owner," *Newcastle Herald*, April 16, 2013, http://www.theherald.com.au/story/1436402/when-a-dog-helped-save-its-owner/.

PART 2: TRAINED TO SERVE, INSPIRED TO HEAL

Part Intro:

Linden, *The Parrot's Lament,* 167.

☆ Fonzie the Dolphin . . . Makes a Boy Laugh p.109

Farran, *Animals to the Rescue!,* 37-41.

BYU TV, "Island Dolphin Care Turning Point," directed by Steve Olpin, October 17, 2012, http://www.youtube.com/watch?v=R43iN_HCt0Y.

O'Brien, Soledad, "Island Dolphin Care," *Today Show* (2002), http://www.youtube.com/watch?v=x-duA8TDe00.

O'Hare, Jeffrey, "Dolphin Discovery," *Exceptional Parent* (March 1998).

Powell, Joanna, "A Boy, a Dolphin, and a Miracle," *Good Housekeeping* 232, no. 4 (April 2001).

Quinones, John, "Joey's Best Friend," *Prime Time Live* (January 30, 1992), http://www.youtube.com/watch?v=d--dilzRssU.

For more information:

Island Dolphin Care, www.islanddolphincare.org.

Deena Hoagland, *Breaths that Count* (self-published, 2012).

☆ Dakota the Golden Retriever . . . Predicts Heart Attacks p.114

Brody, Jane E., "Easing the Way in Therapy with the Aid of an Animal," *New York Times*, March 14, 2011, http://www.nytimes.com/2011/03/15/health/15brody-animals.html.

DART News Release, "DART's Dakota Is Top Dog," November 1, 1999, https://dart.org/news/news.asp?ID=85.

Green, Ranny, "Getting Recognized For It," *Seattle Times*, October 27, 1999, http://landofpuregold.com/heroes3.htm.

Lingenfelter, Mike, *The Angel by My Side* (Carlsbad, CA: Hay House, 2002), 3-4, 15-16, 20, 45, 170.

Markle, *Animal Heroes*, 53-57.

For "Are Animals Psychic?":

Sheldrake, Rupert, *Dogs that Know When Their Owners Are Coming Home* (New York: Crown Publishers, 1999).

☆ **Endal the Labrador Retriever . . . Becomes Endal, the Wonder Dog! p.120**

Able Magazine, "An Unstoppable Partnership" (2007), accessed on Wikipedia, http://en.wikipedia.org/wiki/Endal_(Dog).

BBC News, "Owner Saved by Wonderdog," November 13, 2002, http://news.bbc.co.uk/2/hi/uk_news/england/2459283.stm.

Blystone, Richard, and Mallary Gelb, "Assistance Dogs Are Trained as Partners for the Disabled," *CNN Health*, August 10, 2000, http://edition.cnn.com/2000/HEALTH/08/10/super.dog/.

Daily Mail, "I Thought This Was Bark-lays Bank..." March 1, 2007, http://www.dailymail.co.uk/news/article-439421/I-thought-Bark-lays-bank-.html.

Daily Record, "Movie Tribute to Endal the Wonder Dog," September 3, 2009, http://www.dailyrecord.co.uk/news/real-life/movie-tribute-to-endal-the-wonder-dog-1035676.

Mouland, Bill, "Disabled Officer Bids Farewell to Remarkable Labrador Who Saved His Marriage and His Life," *Daily Mail,* March 16, 2009, http://www.dailymail.co.uk/news/article-1161903/Disabled-officer-bids-farewell-remarkable-labrador-saved-marriage-life.html.

Parton, Allen, "Endal's Legacy Will Live On," *Sussex Express*, March 17, 2009, http://www.sussexexpress.co.uk/news/local/endal-s-legacy-will-live-on-1-1510662.

For more information:

Allen and Sandra Parton, *Endal* (New York: Harper Collins, 2009).

Endal: The Dog of the Millennium, http://www.milleniumdog.freeserve.co.uk.

For "In an Emergency, Dial 911":

NBC News, "'Hero' Cat Apparently Dials 911 to Help Owner," January 2, 2006, http://www.nbcnews.com/id/10663270/ns/us_news-weird_news/t/hero-cat-apparently-dials-help-owner.

Smith, Leef, "A Bite and Bark That Saved a Life," *Washington Post*, June 19, 2006, http://www.washingtonpost.com/wp-dyn/content/article/2006/06/18/AR2006061800857.html.

USA Today, "Dog Calls 911, Saves Owner's Life," September 14, 2008, http://usatoday30.usatoday.com/news/offbeat/2008-09-14-dog-911_N.htm.

WMUR-TV, "Specially Trained Dog Dials 911 to Save Master's Life," March 13, 1996, http://www.cnn.com/US/9603/nineoneone_dog/.

☆ **Roselle the Seeing-Eye Dog . . . Leads the Way Out p.126**

Giannangeli, Marco, "9/11: My Brave Guide Dog Led Us to Safety in Tower Inferno," *Daily Express*, September 11, 2011, http://www.express.co.uk/news/world/270481/9-11-My-brave-guide-dog-led-us-to-safety-in-tower-inferno.

Hingson, Michael, "A Blind Man, His Guide Dog and Lessons Learned on 9/11," *Fox News*, September 6, 2011, http://www.foxnews.com/opinion/2011/09/06/blind-man-his-guide-dog-and-lessons-learned-on-11/.

Hingson, Michael, with Susy Flory, *Thunder Dog* (Nashville, TN: Thomas Nelson, 2011), 10-11, 51, 61, 66-67, 99, 108-110, 116, 122-23.

For more information:

Roselle's Dream Foundation, http://rosellefoundation.org.
Michael Hingson's website, http://michaelhingson.com.

For "Blind Love: Salty & Omar":

McCabe, Marsha, "Partners in Courage," *Standard Times,* April 28, 2002, http://www.southcoasttoday.com/apps/pbcs.dll/article?AID=/20020428/LIFE/304289941.

National Geographic, "9/11: Where Were You?," directed by Allison Argo, produced by Argo Films, August 30, 2011, http://www.orvis.com/news/dogs/Video-The-Incredible-Story-of-Salty-and-Omar/#.Ug0zYBxdZfw.

☆ **Trakr the German Shepherd . . . Finds the Last Survivor p.132**

Bauer, Nona Kilgore, *Dog Heroes of September 11th: A Tribute to America's Search and Rescue Dogs* (Allenhurst, NJ: Kennel Club Books, 2006), 6-17, 22, 89.

BioArts International, "BioArts International Clones 9-11 Hero Dog—Owner to Receive Five Cloned Puppies," press release, June 17, 2009.

Corp Communications, "Legendary German Shepherd Hero 'Trakr' Dies at Age 16," press release, April 30, 2009, http://www.prweb.com/releases/Trakr/Hero_Dog/prweb2373444.htm.

Pilkington, Ed, "Dog Hailed as Hero Cloned by California Company," *The Guardian,* June 18, 2009, http://www.theguardian.com/world/2009/jun/18/trakr-dog-september-11-clone.

Romero, Frances, "Top 10 Heroic Animals," *Time* (March 21, 2011), http://content.time.com/time/specials/packages/article/0,28804,2059858_2059863_2060232,00.html.

Shaer, Matthew, "Survivor, Last Pulled Out," *New York* (August 27, 2011), http://nymag.com/news/9-11/10th-anniversary/last-survivor/.

Woestendiek, John, *Dogs, Inc.* (New York: Avery/Penguin, 2010), 94.

———. "Five Clones of Trakr Meet the Media," ohmidog! blog, June 17, 2009, http://www.ohmidog.com/tag/james-symington/.

For "Appollo & the Dogs of 9/11":

Bauer, *Dog Heroes of September 11th.*

Johnson, Bryan, "Top 10 Rescue Dogs from 9/11," TopTenz blog, September 11, 2012, http://www.toptenz.net/top-10-rescue-dogs-from-911.php.

☆ Rocky the K-9 . . . Catches an Armed Fugitive p.137

ABC7 News Denver, "Police Dog Recovering after Being Shot," August 6, 2002, http://www.thedenverchannel.com/news/police-dog-recovering-after-being-shot.

Buddy the Greyhound blog, "Wounded Police Dog Catches the Crook," All-Ears News, http://www.archer2000.net/buddyhound/buddynews93.html.

Bunch, Joey, "Lakewood Police Mourn Hero Dog," *Denver Post*, August 7, 2008, http://www.denverpost.com/headlines/ci_10130588.

Reuters, "Hero Police Dog Succumbs to Cancer—Morris Animal Foundation Honors 'Rocky,'" August 18, 2008, http://www.reuters.com/article/2008/08/18/idUS186657+18-Aug-2008+PRN20080818.

Rocky Mountain News, "Heroic Police Dog Rocky Succumbs to Cancer," August 7, 2008, http://m.rockymountainnews.com/news/2008/Aug/07/hero-police-dog-rocky-dies/.

Warren, Cat, *What the Dog Knows: The Science and Wonder of Working Dogs* (New York: Simon & Schuster, 2013), 33.

☆ Cheyenne the Pit Bull . . . Keeps a Vet from Suicide p.141

Duell, Mark, "Saved by a Six-month-old Pit Bull: Puppy Comes to Rescue of Traumatised War Veteran Seconds Away from Shooting Himself," *Daily Mail,* July 26, 2011, http://www.dailymail.co.uk/news/article-2019089/Puppy-comes-rescue-traumatised-war-veteran-Dave-Sharpe-seconds-away-shooting-himself.html.

Haynes, Maresha, "Former Airman Saves Dog, Saves Himself," Air Force Wounded Warrior website, November 21, 2011, http://www.woundedwarrior.af.mil/news/story.asp?id=123280790.

Hendrix, Steve, "Racked by PTSD, A Veteran Finds Calm in a Pound Pup Named Cheyenne," *Washington Post,* June 21, 2011, http://www.washingtonpost.com/local/racked-by-ptsd-a-veteran-finds-calm-in-a-pound-pup-named-cheyenne/2011/06/16/AGLiYIeH_story.html.

Reid, Chip, "War Veterans Find Peace of Mind with Pets," *CBS News,* July 26, 2011, http://www.cbsnews.com/news/war-veterans-find-peace-of-mind-with-pets/.

For more information:

Companions for Heroes, www.companionsforheroes.org.

For "PTSD in Dogs":

Bekoff, *Why Dogs Hump*, 164-67.

Dao, James, "After Duty, Dogs Suffer Like Soldiers," *New York Times*, December 1, 2011, http://www.nytimes.com/2011/12/02/us/more-military-dogs-show-signs-of-combat-stress.html?hp.

Goodavage, *Soldier Dogs,* 230-32.

☆ Betsy the Quarter Horse . . . Bows to a Child p.147

Isaacson, Rupert, *The Horse Boy: A Father's Quest to Heal His Son* (New York: Little, Brown & Co., 2009), 18-19, 21, 25-26, 35, 37-38, 46, 48, 53-54, 315, 344, 348-49.

McVeigh, Tracy, "Not Just Horsing Around . . . Psychologists Put Their Faith in Equine Therapies," *The Guardian*, February 25, 2012, http://www.theguardian.com/society/2012/feb/26/horses-therapists-stress-autism-addiction.

Moorhead, Joanna, "Autism: A Healing, Not a Cure," *The Guardian*, January 22, 2010, http://www.theguardian.com/lifeandstyle/2010/jan/23/autism-horse-boy-rupert-isaacson.

For more information:

Equine Therapy, http://www.equine-therapy-programs.com/therapy.html.

Horse Boy Foundation, www.horseboyfoundation.org.

PATH International, http://www.pathintl.org.

For "Thinking in Pictures":

Grandin, Temple, "Thinking the Way Animals Do," *Western Horseman* (November 1997), 140-45, http://www.grandin.com/references/thinking.animals.html.

Grandin, Temple, and Catherine Johnson, *Animals in Translation* (New York: Scribner, 2005).

Hamilton, Christine, "On Horses and Autism," *America's Horse Daily*, March 22, 2011, http://americashorsedaily.com/on-horses-and-autism/#.Us94JhybS6U.

Isaacson, *The Horse Boy,* 59.

☆ Molly the Pony . . . Loses a Leg and Inspires Hope p.154

Clisby, Heather, "Molly's Story," video interview with Kaye Harris, posted on You-

Tube, October 6, 2010, http://www.youtube.com/watch?v=vIDSLI2smI4.

Daily Mail, "Meet Molly, the Three-legged Pony Who Is Giving Hope to New Orleans Three Years after Katrina," June 5, 2008, http://www.dailymail.co.uk/news/article-1024136/Meet-Molly-legged-pony-giving-hope-New-Orleans-years-Katrina.html.

Goodman, Brenda, "After Surviving Hurricane and Being Mauled by Dog, Pony Is Still Standing," *New York Times,* May 15, 2006, http://www.nytimes.com/2006/05/15/us/15pony.html.

Guttner, Ginger, "LSU School of Veterinary Medicine Performed Rare Surgery on Hurricane Survivor Pony," LSU School of Veterinary Medicine press release (Fall 2006), http://www.equine.vetmed.lsu.edu/mollystory.html.

For more information:
Molly's Foundation, http://mollythepony.com.

For "Oxytocin: The Biology of Good Feelings":

Olmert, *Made for Each Other*, xv, xvii.

Shipman, *The Animal Connection*, 271-72.

☆ Chancer the Golden Retriever . . . Calms the Storm p.160

Centers for Disease Control and Prevention, *The Story of Iyal*, film transcript, May 18, 2009, http://www.cdc.gov/ncbddd/fasd/videos/index.html.

Greene, Melissa Fay, "Wonder Dog," *New York Times*, February 2, 2012, http://www.nytimes.com/2012/02/05/magazine/wonder-dog.html.

Oliviero, Helena, "Service Dog a Calming Presence for Entire Family," *Atlanta Journal-Constitution*, November 6, 2009, http://www.ajc.com/news/news/local/service-dog-a-calming-presence-for-entire-family/nQY3h/.

Winokur, Donnie Kanter, "A Dog's Devotion Brings Healing," *Guideposts* (September 2012), http://www.guideposts.org/pet-stories/a-dogs-devotion-brings-healing.

For more information:
The Chancer Chronicles, http://www.thechancerchronicles.com.

For "Theory of Mind":

Balcombe, *Second Nature*, 63, 66-67.

Bekoff, *Why Dogs Hump,* 49-51, 129.

de Waal, *Our Inner Ape*, 179-80.

Linden, *The Parrot's Lament,* 81-82, 92.

☆ Treo the Labrador Retriever . . . Sniffs Out a Bomb p.166

Chesshyre, Robert, "Dogs of War: Sniffer Dogs Lead the Way in Afghanistan," *Daily Telegraph,* January 20, 2011, http://www.telegraph.co.uk/news/worldnews/asia/afghanistan/8269095/Dogs-of-war-sniffer-dogs-lead-the-way-in-Afghanistan.html.

Daily Mail, "Black Labrador Treo 23rd Animal to Receive the Dickin Medal After Serving in Afghanistan," February 24, 2010, http://www.dailymail.co.uk/news/article-1253312/Black-Labrador-Treo-23rd-animal-receive-Dickin-Medal-serving-Afghanistan.html.

Daily Telegraph, "Dog Awarded Medal for Heroism in Afghanistan," February 24, 2010, http://www.telegraph.co.uk/news/newsvideo/7308473/Dog-awarded-medal-for-heroism-in-Afghanistan.html.

Fryer, Jane, "Meet Treo, the Hero Army Dog Who Took on the Taliban," *Daily Mail,* February 25, 2010, http://www.dailymail.co.uk/news/article-1253566/Meet-Treo-hero-army-dog-took-Taliban.html.

Goodavage, *Soldier Dogs,* 11-12, 24.

Ritland, Mike, with Gary Brozek, *Trident K9 Warriors* (New York: St. Martin's Press, 2013), 160, 246.

For more information:
PDSA Dickin Medal: http://www.pdsa.org.uk/about-us/animal-bravery-awards/pdsa-dickin-medal.

For "The Nose Knows, But the Heart Finds":

Goodavage, *Soldier Dogs,* 162.

Tyson, Peter, "Dogs' Dazzling Sense of Smell," *Nova PBS*, October 4, 2012, http://www.pbs.org/wgbh/nova/nature/dogs-sense-of-smell.html.

Warren, *What the Dog Knows*, 50-51, 222-24.

☆ Ricochet the Surfing Dog . . . Rides with the Disabled p.171

Bates, Claire, "Ricochet the Surf Dog Makes a Splash . . . Helping Disabled Youngsters to Conquer the Waves," *Daily Mail*, September 12, 2010, http://www.dailymail.co.uk/health/article-1310437/Meet-Ricochet-sea-dog-makes-splash-helping-disabled-children-surf.html.

Bates, Emily, "Interview: Surf Dog Ricochet Helps People with Disabilities," Surf Channel, October 14, 2013, http://www.thesurfchannel.com/news/20131014/interview-surf-dog-ricochet-helps-people-with-disabilities/.

Carlson, Chris, "Surfing Dog Makes a Big Splash," *Associated Press*, October 15,

2009, http://www.youtube.com/watch?v=LhbOVaISWhA.

Goldman, Laura, "Surf Dog Ricochet Saves Life of Soldier with PTSD—and Will Save Others, Too," I Love Dogs blog, December 10, 2013, http://www.ilovedogs.com/2013/12/surf-dog-ricochet-saves-life-of-soldier-with-ptsd-and-will-save-others-too/#.UrHO5Rzr-Om.

Lloyd, Janice, "True Stories of Heroic Dogs," *USA Today*, January 13, 2010, http://usatoday30.usatoday.com/life/lifestyle/pets/2010-01-13-petheroes13_ST_N.htm.

McCormac, Patty, "Service Dog Hits the Waves to Help," *Union-Tribune San Diego*, October 8, 2009, http://www.utsandiego.com/news/2009/oct/08/service-dog-hits-waves-help/.

For more information:
Surf Dog Ricochet, www.surfdogricochet.com.

For "Definitions: Service and Therapy Animals":

US Department of Justice, Americans with Disability Act, "Service Animals," July 12, 2011, http://www.ada.gov/service_animals_2010.htm.

Pet Partners, "Service Animal Basics," http://www.petpartners.org/Service_Animal_Basics.

Charleson, *The Possibility Dogs*, 5-6, 23-25.

☆ Daisy the Labrador Retriever . . . Detects Breast Cancer p.178

BBC News, "Medical Detection Dogs Train Animals to 'Sniff Out' Breast Cancer," March 14, 2013, http://www.bbc.co.uk/news/uk-england-beds-bucks-herts-21769807.

Ferris, Robert, "These Amazing Dogs Can Smell Cancer," *Houston Chronicle*, August 15, 2013, http://www.chron.com/technology/businessinsider/article/These-Amazing-Dogs-Can-Smell-Cancer-4736338.php.

Five News, "Claire Guest—Cancer & Bio Detection Dogs," March 23, 2010, http://www.youtube.com/watch?v=tR5E_dQderU.

The Independent, "Could Your Dog Save Your Life?," August 26, 2013, http://www.independent.ie/lifestyle/could-your-dog-save-your-life-29527638.html.

Lovgren, Stefan, "Dogs Smell Cancer in Patients' Breath, Study Shows," *National Geographic News,* January 12, 2006, http://news.nationalgeographic.com/news/2006/01/0112_060112_dog_cancer.html.

Ragione, Joanna Della, "The Dogs that Detect Cancer," *Daily Express,* January 1, 2013, http://www.express.co.uk/life-style/health/367975/The-dogs-that-detect-cancer.

Simons, Jake Wallis, "How My Beloved Dog Found My Cancer," *Daily Telegraph*, March 17, 2013, http://www.telegraph.co.uk/lifestyle/pets/9935073/How-my-beloved-dog-found-my-cancer.html.

Stocks, Jenny, "The Dogs that Can Detect Cancer: Meet the Four-legged 'Bio Detectives' Who Are Pioneering a Health Revolution," *Daily Mail*, November 16, 2011, http://www.dailymail.co.uk/health/article-2062000/The-dogs-detect-cancer-Meet-legged-bio-detectives-pioneering-health-revolution.html.

For more information:
In Situ Foundation, www.dogsdetectcancer.org.
Medical Detection Dogs, https://medicaldetectiondogs.org.uk.

☆ Cairo the Belgian Malinois . . . Assists Navy SEAL Team Six p.182

Callahan, Maureen, "Zero Bark Thirty," *New York Post*, April 14, 2013, http://www.nypost.com/p/news/opinion/opedcolumnists/zero_bark_thirty_5Q5vfvWqrin9A4fqb0LBUO.

Goodavage, Maria, "Navy SEAL Book Reveals New Information About Hero Dog in Bin Laden Raid," Soldier Dogs blog, September 4, 2012, http://www.soldierdogs.com/2012/09/04/navy-seal-book-reveals-new-information-about-hero-dog-in-bin-laden-raid/.

Harris, Gardiner, "A Bin Laden Hunter on Four Legs," *New York Times*, May 4, 2011, http://www.nytimes.com/2011/05/05/science/05dog.html.

Ritland, *Trident K9 Warriors,* 28, 50, 101, 222-25.

Schmidle, Nicholas, "Getting Bin Laden," *New Yorker*, August 8, 2011, http://www.newyorker.com/reporting/2011/08/08/110808fa_fact_schmidle.

For "A Piece of Equipment Meets the President":
Schmidle, "Getting Bin Laden."

Box Spread: Interview with the Seeing Eye
Doug Bohl, interview with the author, March 11, 2014, at The Seeing Eye, Morristown, New Jersey; www.seeingeye.org.

PART 3: WILD SAVIORS

☆ Jambo the Gorilla . . . Comforts a Fallen Boy p.195

de Waal, *Our Inner Ape,*, 218.

Farran, *Animals to the Rescue!*, 31-36.

Johnstone-Scott, Richard, *Jambo: A Gorilla's Story* (New York: Mark O'Meara Books, 1995), http://www.shoarns.com/Jambo.html.

Le Lion, Brian, "Jambo, The Gentle Giant, The Incredible Story," http://lelion.co.uk/.

For "Darwin's Story: Protect the Keeper":

Darwin from *Descent of Man* quoted in Masson and McCarthy, *When Elephants Weep*, 59.

☆ Ugandan Vervet Monkeys . . . Adopt a Runaway p.200

BBC1, "The Boy Who Was Raised by Monkeys," directed by James Cutler, *Living Proof*, October 1999, http://everything2.com/title/John+Ssebunya%252C+the+Ugandan+Monkey+Boy.

Candland, Douglas, "Tarzan and His Fellows: 'Fact, Fiction, Legend?,'" ERBzine website (2007), http://www.erbzine.com/mag18/1899.html.

Cutler, James, "John Ssubenya, The Ugandan Monkey Boy," no date, http://www.monkeyland.co.za/index.php?comp=article&op=view&id=140.

Ferguson, Euan, "He Was a Wild Child. Really Wild," *The Guardian*, October 9, 1999, http://www.theguardian.com/world/1999/oct/10/euanferguson.theobserver.

Leung, Wency, "Marina Chapman's Wild Tale of a Feral Childhood Sparks Skepticism," *The Globe and Mail*, May 2, 2013, http://www.theglobeandmail.com/life/relationships/marina-chapmans-wild-tale-of-a-feral-childhood-sparks-skepticism/article11690193/.

Molly and Paul Child Care Foundation, http://www.mollyandpaul.org; see page "John Ssebunya."

National Geographic, Feral Children, written and produced by Vicky Matthews and Heidi Christenson (2007), http://www.youtube.com/watch?v=RyB0JCADPXQ.

Ochota, Mary-Ann, "Raised Wild: The Monkey Boy of Uganda," *Animal Planet* (November 16, 2012), http://animal.discovery.com/tv-shows/raised-wild.

———, "Animal Behaviour," Feral Children website, http://feralchildren.info/animal-behaviour/.

For "Modern-Day Mowglis":

Daily Mail, "Boy Who Was Raised by Dogs," no date, http://www.dailymail.co.uk/news/article-54660/Boy-raised-dogs.html.

Daily Telegraph, "Wolf Boy Is Welcomed Home by Mother After Years in the Wild," April 14, 2002, http://www.telegraph.co.uk/news/worldnews/europe/romania/1390871/Wolf-boy-is-welcomed-home-by-mother-after-years-in-the-wild.html.

Newton, Michael, *Savage Girls and Wild Children* (New York: St. Martin's Press, 2002).

Osborn, Andrew, "Siberian boy, 7, Raised by Dogs after Parents Abandoned Him," *The Independent*, August 4, 2004, http://www.independent.co.uk/news/world/europe/siberian-boy-7-raised-by-dogs-after-parents-abandoned-him-6164250.html.

☆ Binti Jua the Gorilla . . . Consoles an Injured Child p.206

Bekoff, Marc, telephone conversation with author, February 26, 2014.

Boccella, Kathy, "Mother Of The Year A Gorilla Named Binti Jua Gently Scoops Up An Injured Child And Snatches Hearts Around The World In The Process. Predictable Animal Behavior, Says One Expert. Genuine Compassion, Says Another," *Philadelphia Inquirer*, August 26, 1996, http://articles.philly.com/1996-08-26/living/25645011_1_binti-western-lowland-gorilla-tropic-world.

Brookfield Zoo, "Binti's Baby," 2005, https://www.brookfieldzoo.org/pgpages/pagegen.121.aspx.

CBS News Chicago, "15 Years Ago Today: Gorilla Rescues Boy Who Fell In Ape Pit," August 16, 2011, http://chicago.cbslocal.com/2011/08/16/15-years-ago-today-gorilla-rescues-boy-who-fell-in-ape-pit/.

de Waal, *Our Inner Ape*, 3, 174.

Farran, *Animals to the Rescue!*, 68-73.

Markle, *Animal Heroes*, 14-18.

Meyer, Erin, "JoJo the Gorilla Settles in at Brookfield Zoo," *Chicago Tribune,* June 26, 2012, http://articles.chicagotribune.com/2012-06-26/news/chi-jojo-the-gorilla-settles-in-at-brookfield-zoo-20120626_1_gorilla-pit-craig-demitros-lowland.

New York Times, "Gorilla at an Illinois Zoo Rescues a 3-Year-Old Boy," August 17, 1996, http://www.nytimes.com/1996/08/17/us/gorilla-at-an-illinois-zoo-rescues-a-3-year-old-boy.html.

Singer, Stacey, "Zoo's New Top Banana: Binti-Jua's Rescue of Boy Thrills Millions," *Chicago Tribune*, August 18, 1996, http://articles.chicagotribune.com/1996-08-18/news/9608180211_1_binti-jua-western-lowland.

Schreuder, Cindy, "Binti, World's Pen Pal," *Chicago Tribune*, October 20, 1996, http://articles.chicagotribune.com/1996-10-20/news/9610200296_1_binti-gorilla-exhibit-jua.

For video of Binti Jua's rescue: http://www.bing.com/videos/watch/video/from-the-archives-gorilla-protects-boy/1d2gkybtt.

For "A Moral Dilemma":

Bekoff and Pierce, *Wild Justice*, 1-12.

Bloom, Paul, *Just Babies: The Origins of Good and Evil* (New York: Crown, 2013).

de Waal, *Bonobo and the Atheist*, 4.

de Waal, *Our Inner Ape*, 191.

☆ Donna Nook Gray Seals . . . Keep a Woman Afloat p.212

Animal People, "Seals Save Life, Need Help," April 1999, http://www.animalpeople-news.org/99/4/tsg.sealssavelife4.99.htm.

Donna Nook Nature Reserve, http://lincstrust.org.uk/reserves/nr/reserve.php?mapref=15.

London Mirror, "Each Time I Sank, Seals Nudged Me Back Up; Swim Woman Tells How Animals Saved Her," February 3, 1999, http://www.thefreelibrary.com/Each+time+I+sank,+seals+nudged+me+back+up%3B+Swim+Woman+Tells+How...-a060393683.

For "Two Days on a Sea Turtle":

Kreisler, *Beauty in the Beasts*, 66.

Montreal Gazette, "Giant Sea Turtle Saved Woman," June 25, 1974, http://news.google.com/newspapers?nid=1946&dat=19740625&id=OYIuAAAAIBAJ&sjid=h6EFAAAAIBAJ&pg=739,2044567.

☆ Lulu the Kangaroo . . . Saves a Farmer p.217

BBC News, "Life-Saving Kangaroo Wins Award," April 29, 2004, http://news.bbc.co.uk/2/hi/asia-pacific/3667733.stm.

CNN.com, "Lulu the Roo Hops to Bravery Award," April 28, 2004, http://www.cnn.com/2004/WORLD/asiapcf/04/28/australia.luluroo/.

Leung, Chee Chee, "Lulu the Kangaroo Hops to the Rescue," *The Age*, September 23, 2003, http://www.theage.com.au/articles/2003/09/22/1064082926928.html?from=storyrhs.

The Post, "Brave Kangaroo Wins Aussie Valour Award," April 29, 2004, http://www.thepost.co.za/brave-kangaroo-wins-aussie-valour-award-1.211678#.UgPfH-hyAHNo.

Sydney Morning Herald, "Lulu the Roo to the Rescue," September 22, 2003, http://www.smh.com.au/articles/2003/09/22/1064082893102.html.

For "A Kangaroo Blanket":

CCN, "Skippy, the Guardian Angel? Australian Boy Says Kangaroo Saved Him During Night Lost in Bush," August 8, 2013, http://www.cnn.com/2013/08/08/world/asia/kangaroo-saves-lost-boy.

Whalan, Roscoe, "Boy Missing in Bush Says Kangaroo Saved Him," *7News Adelaide*, August 5, 2013, http://au.news.yahoo.com/queensland/a/-/news-home/18367974/boy-missing-in-bush-says-kangaroo-saved-him/.

☆ Bottlenose Dolphins . . . Round Up the Lifeguards p.221

CBC News, "Dolphins Save Swimmers from Shark," November 24, 2004, http://www.cbc.ca/news/world/story/2004/11/24/dolphin_newzealand041124.html.

Markle, *Animal Heroes*, 43-49.

Mercer, Phil, "Dolphins Prevent NZ Shark Attack," *BBC News,* November 23, 2004, http://news.bbc.co.uk/2/hi/4034383.stm.

Shears, Richard, "Dolphins 'Saved Swimmers from Shark'" *Daily Mail*, November 24, 2004, http://www.dailymail.co.uk/travel/article-593037/Dolphins-saved-swimmers-shark.html.

Thomson, Ainsley, "Dolphins Saved Us from Shark, Lifeguards Say," *New Zealand Herald,* November 23, 2004, http://www.eurocbc.org/dolphins_protect_lifeguards_from_shark_nz_23nov2004page1802.html.

☆ Ningnong the Elephant . . . Runs from a Tsunami p.224

Asian Tsunami Heroes blog, "Girl Saved by Her Friend the Elephant Ningnong," January 11, 2005, http://asiantsunamiheros.blogspot.co.uk/2005/01/girl-saved-by-her-friend-elephant.html.

BBC News, "Elephant Dash Saved Tsunami Girl," January 11, 2005, http://news.bbc.co.uk/2/hi/uk_news/england/beds/bucks/herts/4165273.stm.

Meyer, Jeremy, "Did Thai Elephants Sense Pending Tsunami?" *Denver Post,* January 11, 2005, http://www.deseretnews.com/article/600103935/Did-Thai-elephants-sense-pending-tsunami.html.

National Geographic, "Hero Animals: The Elephant That Rescued the Girl," directed by John Maidens, Big Wave Productions, no date, http://www.bigwavetv.com/productions/hero-animals-the-elephant-that-rescued-the-girl/.

PBS Nature, "Can Animals Predict Disaster?," November 2005, http://www.pbs.org/wnet/nature/episodes/can-animals-predict-disaster/introduction/130/.

Wiltshire, Jo, "Basic Instinct," *Daily Mail*, March 27, 2005, http://mackenzieproductions.com/Mail_on_Sunday.html.

For "Follow the Dolphins":

PBS Nature, "Can Animals Predict Disaster? Eyewitness Accounts: Chris Cruz," November 2005, http://www.pbs.org/wnet/nature/episodes/can-animals-predict-disaster/eyewitness-accounts/chris-cruz/136/.

☆ Ethiopian Lions . . . Rescue a Girl from Kidnappers pg.229

Associated Press, "Ethiopian Girl Reportedly Guarded by Lions," June 21, 2005, http://www.nbcnews.com/id/8305836/#.Uctjvhwynx9.

BBC News, "Kidnapped Girl 'Rescued' by Lions," June 22, 2005, http://news.bbc.co.uk/2/hi/africa/4116778.stm.

Kifle, Elias, "Kidnapped Girl in Ethiopia Saved by Lions," *Ethiopian Review*, June 28, 2005, http://www.ethiopianreview.com/content/7523.

☆ Bottlenose Dolphins . . . Stop a Shark Attack pg.232

Celizic, Mike, "Dolphins Save Surfer from Becoming Shark's Bait," *Today*, November 8, 2007, http://www.today.com/id/21689083/ns/today-today_people/t/dolphins-save-surfer-becoming-sharks-bait/#.UcHaaRyAGsg.

Free, Cathy, "Shark! How One Surfer Survived an Attack," *Reader's Digest* (July 2008), http://www.rd.com/true-stories/survival/shark-attack-dolphins-save-surfer-from-shark/.

Sanders, Marcus, "Norcal Shark Attack Update," *Surfline*, August 29, 2007, http://www.surfline.com/surf-news/firsthand-account-of-monterey-bay-surfer-badly-bitten-at-marina-state-beach-norcal-shark-attack-update_10788/.

Surfing, "Exclusive Interview with Monterey Shark Attack Victim Todd Endris," September 2, 2007, http://www.surfingmagazine.com/news/great-white-shark-attack-monterrey-todd-endris-090207/.

"The Todd Endris Story," produced and directed by Sheila Gale and Dale Edward, uploaded on YouTube, November 16, 2007, http://www.youtube.com/watch?v=LsQeCO7jkFY.

Wetterau, Paul, "The Post-Shark Bite Experience Has Been Almost as Hectic as the Day Todd Endris Got Chomped," *Monterey County Weekly*, November 8, 2007, http://www.montereycountyweekly.com/news/831_tales/article_d17657e9-33db-5449-9fa9-40647871d34d.html.

For "Flipper Is One Tough Dude":

Farran, *Animals to the Rescue!,* 61-63, 89-95.

Jerusalem Weekly, "Three Dolphins Rescue Tourist from Sharks," August 2, 1996, http://www.jweekly.com/article/full/3738/three-dolphins-rescue-tourist-from-sharks/.

☆ Mila the Beluga Whale . . . Lifts a Drowning Diver p.239

Daily Mail, "The Amazing Moment Mila the Beluga Whale Saved a Stricken Diver's Life by Pushing Her to the Surface," July 29, 2009, http://www.dailymail.co.uk/

news/article-1202941/Pictured-The-moment-Mila-brave-Beluga-whale-saved-stricken-divers-life-pushing-surface.html.

The Telegraph, "Beluga Whale 'Saves' Diver," July 29, 2009, http://www.telegraph.co.uk/news/newstopics/howaboutthat/5931345/Beluga-whale-saves-diver.html.

The Mirror, "Amazing Rescue: Drowning Diver Saved by Beluga Whale," July 29, 2009, http://www.mirror.co.uk/news/weird-news/amazing-rescue-drowning-diver-saved-409479.

For "Lifeguards of the Sea":

Anda, Redempto, "Dolphins Save Puerto Princesa Fisherman," *Philippine Daily Inquirer*, December 16, 2008, http://www.inquirer.net/specialreports/theenvironmentreport/view.php?db=1&article=20081216-178325.

Daily Record (Scotland), "Dolphin Saves Boy's Life," August 30, 2000, http://www.eurocbc.org/page158.html.

Farran, *Animals to the Rescue!,* 13-19.

IOL News, "Elian Says Dolphins Saved His Life," March 27, 2000, http://www.iol.co.za/news/world/elian-says-dolphins-saved-his-life-1.33676#.UgqWbxzLpeQ.

Leonard, Tom, "Dick Van Dyke: Pod of Porpoises Saved Me from Death After I Fell Asleep on My Surboard," *Daily Mail,* November 12, 2010, http://www.dailymail.co.uk/tvshowbiz/article-1328806/Dick-Van-Dyke-Pod-porpoises-saved-I-fell-asleep-surfboard.html.

For "Definitions: Domestic Versus Tame":

Olmert, *Made for Each Other*, 235-37.

Shipman, *The Animal Connection*, 192-93.

Box spread: Evolving Together: How Animals Made Us Human

Derr, Mark, *How the Dog Became the Dog* (New York & London: Overlook Duckworth, 2011), 39.

Shipman, *The Animal Connection*, 64, 210, 276, 279.

PART 4: LEGENDS AND FOLKTALES

☆ Mediterranean Dolphins . . . Give a Greek Poet a Ride p.249

Bulfinch, Thomas, "Arion - Ibycus - Simonides - Sappho," in *Bulfinch's Mythology: The Age of Fable or Stories of Gods and Heroes* (1855), http://www.mythome.org/bfchxxv.html.

Catton, Chris, "Dolphins in Ancient Mythology," in *Dolphins* (New York: St. Martin's Press, 1995), http://www.pbs.org/wgbh/pages/frontline/shows/whales/man/myth.html.

Morford, Mark, Robert Lenardon, and Michael Sham, *Classical Mythology*, 9th ed. (New York: Oxford University Press, 2010), http://global.oup.com/us/companion.websites/9780195397703/student/archives/herodotus.

Reiss, *Dolphin in the Mirror,* 28.

☆ Gelert the Wolfhound . . . Saves the Baby p.254

BBC, Wales History, "Gelert," http://www.bbc.co.uk/wales/history/sites/themes/society/myths_gelert.shtml.

Beddgelert Tourism Association, "Gelert, " http://www.beddgelerttourism.com/gelert/.

Ben Johnson, "The Legend of Brave Gelert," Historic UK, http://www.historic-uk.com/HistoryUK/HistoryofWales/The-legend-of-brave-Gelert/.

☆ Moustache the Poodle . . . Joins the French Revolution p.257

Kistler, John, *Animals in the Military* (Santa Barbara, CA: ABC-CLIO, 2011).

New York Times, "The Use of Dogs in War," April 7, 1889.

Poodle History Project, "Army Dogs," http://www.poodlehistory.org/PARMY.HTM.

Wikipedia, "Moustache_(dog)," http://en.wikipedia.org/wiki/Moustache_(dog).

For "Napoleon's Tears":

Lemish, Michael G., *War Dogs: A History of Loyalty and Heroism* (Washington, DC: Brassey's, 1996), 4-5.

Goodavage, *Soldier Dogs*, 224.

☆ Barry der Menschenretter . . . Saves Travelers in the Swiss Alps p.262

Blumberg, Jess, "A Brief History of the St. Bernard Rescue Dog," *Smithsonian* (January 1, 2008), http://www.smithsonianmag.com/history-archaeology/st-bernard-200801.html.

Brackman, Jane, "Barry, St. Bernard Hospice mountain rescue dog," Doctor Barkman blog, posted October 11, 2012, http://doctorbarkman.blogspot.com/2012/10/barry-st-bernard-hospice-mountain.html.

Fondation Barry du Grand Saint Bernard, "History," http://www.fondation-barry.ch/en/history.

Natural History Museum in Bern, "Saint Bernard Dog," various pages, no date, http://www.nmbe.ch/research/vertebrates/research/kynologie/swiss-dog-breeds/saint-bernard-dog.

☆ Pelorus Jack . . . Guides Ships Through Rocky Straits p.267

Alpers, Antony Francis George, "Pelorus Jack," in *An Encyclopaedia of New Zealand* (Christchurch, NZ: Caxton Press, 1966), http://www.teara.govt.nz/en/1966/pelorus-jack.

Cowan, James, "Pelorus Jack: The White Dolphin of New Zealand with Maori Legends," (Christchurch, NZ: Whitcombe & Tombs Ltd, 1911).

Hutching, Gerard, "Dolphins—Humans and dolphins," in *Te Ara—the Encyclopedia of New Zealand*, entry by updated July 9, 2013, http://www.TeAra.govt.nz/en/photograph/4696/the-story-of-pelorus-jack.

Joy Stephens, "Pelorus Jack: A World Famous Dolphin," The Prow.org, 2012, http://www.theprow.org.nz/events/pelorus-jack/#.UrkMHBztlwc.

☆ Sergeant Stubby . . . Sniffs Out Gas in WWI p.272

Connecticut Military Department, Connecticut Military History, "Stubby the Military Dog," no date, http://www.ct.gov/mil/cwp/view.asp?a=1351&q=257892.

Goodavage, *Soldier Dogs*, 15.

Smithsonian National Museum of American History, "Stubby," no date, http://amhistory.si.edu/militaryhistory/collection/object.asp?ID=15.

Zimmerman, Dwight Jon, "Sgt. Stubby, American War Dog," Defense Media Network, July 27, 2010, http://www.defensemedianetwork.com/stories/sgt-stubby-american-war-dog/.

For "The Mercy Dogs of WWI":

Lemish, *War Dogs,* 11-17.

Warren, *What the Dog Knows,* 189-90.

☆ Wolves in India . . . Raise Two Girls in Their Den p.277

Maclean, Charles, *Wolf Children* (London: Allen Lane, 1977), 55, 60-61, 64-67, 82, 302.

Newton, Michael, *Savage Girls and Wild Boys: A History of Feral Children* (New York: St. Martin's Press, 2002), 182-89, 235.

Singh, J.A.L., and Robert Zingg, *Wolf-Children and Feral Man* (New York: Harper & Row, 1942), 5.

Wikipedia, "Amala and Kamala," http://en.wikipedia.org/wiki/Kamala_and_Amala.

For "The Feral Child: Real and Romanticized":

Siderius, Edmund, "Wild Through the Ages: Kamala, Amala, and the Focus of Folklore," The Starry Messenger blog, August 7, 2011, http://edmundsiderius.wordpress.com/2011/08/07/wild-through-the-ages-kamala-amala-and-the-focus-of-folklore/.

☆ Togo the Siberian Husky . . . Goes the Extra Mile p.284

Clifford, Stephanie, "Spirit of a Racer in a Dog's Blood," *New York Times,* February 12, 2012, http://www.nytimes.com/2012/02/13/sports/spirit-of-a-racer-in-a-siberian-huskys-blood.html.

Houdek, Jennifer, and Tricia Brown, "Togo and Balto, Dog Heroes," LitSite Alaska, University of Alaska at Anchorage, no date, http://www.litsite.org/index.cfm?section=Digital-Archives&page=Land-Sea-Air&cat=Dog-Mushing&viewpost=2&contentid=2561.

Salisbury, Gay, and Laney Salisbury, *The Cruelest Miles: The Heroic Story of Dogs and Men in a Race Against an Epidemic* (New York: W. W. Norton, 2003).

For "The Iditarod":

Iditarod race website, http://iditarod.com.

☆ Chips, Dog 11-A . . . Takes Italian Prisoners p.290

Goodavage, *Soldier Dogs,* 276-77.

Kate Kelly, "Chips, First Dog Sent Overseas in World War II," America Comes Alive!, July 25, 2011, http://americacomesalive.com/2011/07/25/chips-first-dog-sent-overseas-in-world-war-ii/.

History Channel, "This Day in History: March 13, 1942: U.S. Army Launches K-9 Corps," no date, http://www.history.com/this-day-in-history/us-army-launches-k-9-corps.

Lemish, *War Dogs,* 36-40, 62, 73-83.

Box Spread: Clever Hans

Shipman, *The Animal Connection*, 178-79.

Olmert, *Made for Each Other,* 88-90.

Page, *Inside the Animal Mind*, 21-22, 199.

Thomas, *The Social Lives of Dogs*, 17.

Warren, *What the Dog Knows*, 146-47.

INDEX